D1085062

Transcendentalism
and the *Western Messenger*

THE

WESTERN MESSENGER;

DEVOTED TO

RELIGION AND LITERATURE.

N$^{o.}$ I.

CINCINNATI:

PUBLISHED BY T. H. SHREVE, & CO., S. W. CORNER OF

FIFTH AND WALNUT STREETS.

1835.

Front wrapper, *Western Messenger,* volume 1, number 1, June 1835. *Courtesy of the Pennsylvania State University Libraries.*

Transcendentalism and the *Western Messenger*

A History of the Magazine and Its Contributors,
1835–1841

Robert D. Habich

Rutherford • Madison • Teaneck
Fairleigh Dickinson University Press
London and Toronto: Associated University Presses

© 1985 by Associated University Presses, Inc.

Associated University Presses
440 Forsgate Drive
Cranbury, NJ 08512

Associated University Presses
25 Sicilian Avenue
London WC1A 2QH, England

Associated University Presses
2133 Royal Windsor Drive
Unit 1
Mississauga, Ontario
Canada L5J 1K5

Library of Congress Cataloging in Publication Data

Habich, Robert D., 1951–
  Transcendentalism and the Western messenger.

  Bibliography: p.
  Includes index.
  1. Western messenger (Louisville, Ky.) 2. Unitari-
anism—Periodicals. 3. Unitarianism—United States—
History—19th century. 4. Transcendentalism (New
England) 5. Ohio River Valley—Church history.
I. Title.
BX9801.W43H33   1985   288'.05   83-49358
ISBN 0-8386-3204-1

Printed in the United States of America

For Laurie and Sara

Contents

Preface

By the summer of 1841, the Reverend James Freeman Clarke was already a six-year veteran of the intellectual struggle between New England's conservative Unitarians and the radical thinkers who had come to be known as Transcendentalists. Thus he probably felt both amused and surprised when a Unitarian colleague from Pennsylvania, congratulating him on the formation of the Church of the Disciples in Boston, warned him to avoid the "wild and crude notions lately put forth" by Ralph Waldo Emerson, Theodore Parker, and others of the "*new Illuminati.*" But his correspondent's peevish swipe at the Transcendentalists ended on a more sobering note, a reminder that Clarke's last project—the now defunct literary and religious journal he had edited from 1836 to 1839—had, according to some, fallen prey to the same "glaring errors" now threatening the church in Boston: "Had the Western Messenger continued to be conducted upon its original principles, and kept clear of these wild German speculations, it would have been prosperous & useful. For want of this it has expired."[1]

The term *German speculations* covered a broad assortment of liberal ideas in art and theology, but most readers would have agreed that the magazine had departed significantly from its "original principles." Founded in 1835 by a group of young New England ministers settled in the Ohio Valley, the *Western Messenger; Devoted to Religion and Literature,* under the "special superintendence" of Ephraim Peabody in Cincinnati, was intended to "explain and defend the misunderstood and denounced principles of Unitarianism."[2] From the outset, though, its denominational loyalty was difficult to sustain. The first number included an attack on the misplaced "orthodoxism" of Eastern Unitarians, and by the end of the year the journal's announced policy had softened noticeably: "we have *affinities* with what is good in every denomination."[3]

Clarke assumed the editorship with the number for April 1836, moved the journal to Louisville, and announced that the *Messenger* would henceforth serve as a forum in which contributors would "speak of all in a religious spirit" (1:659). For the next three years Clarke made good his promise, throwing open the magazine's pages to spirited examinations of the key social, literary, and theological issues of the day, most notably the wave of "new views" on Man, God, and Nature that steadily eroded the shores of conservative thought. By the time William Henry Channing took charge of the magazine in 1839, the *Messenger* had so departed from its sectarian beginnings that its new editor could declare, "How arbitrary to demand a conformity to our small scale of sound doctrine" (7:1). The magazine founded to "set forth and defend Unitarian views" in the West closed its final number in April 1841 with an apparent renunciation of both the letter and the spirit of its original principles: "The better minds every where are disgusted with Sectarianism, with Controversies, with Orthodoxy, with Dogmatism" (1:[1]; 8:572).

Although its orientation seemed to have shifted radically, its level of quality remained high, for the *Messenger* combined a stimulating range of topics with an impressive list of contributors.[4] Among the American literary figures to fill its pages were Emerson (who offered original poetry), Hawthorne (whose work appeared in reprint), Oliver Wendell Holmes, William Cullen Bryant, and the mystic poet Jones Very, as well as a dozen or more minor writers showcased in the columns on Western poets, and the editors themselves, who supplied verse, translations, sketches, and reviews. In the *Messenger* Margaret Fuller first tried her hand at literary criticism, and in its pages too are some of the earliest and most discerning American reviews of Wordsworth, Coleridge, Shelley, Carlyle, Goethe, and Schiller—even some original poetry by Keats, whose brother George attended Clarke's church in Louisville.

In its examination of social and economic problems the magazine was no less vigorous. The distinguished Kentucky historian Mann Butler provided detailed accounts of Western life and history; other contributors gave essays and sketches on prison conditions, public drunkenness, and the evils of frontier brothels and gambling houses; still others debated, often with considerable heat, the issues of slavery and abolition. When Orestes Brownson published his anticapitalist essay "The Laboring Classes" in 1840, the editors of the *Messenger* came to his defense, as they did for Thomas Carlyle when his explosive *Chartism* reached America. Finally, the magazine gave a full airing to the contemporary religious climate. On the one hand, it exposed the Calvinist West to the liberal views of such Unitarian leaders as Dr. Channing, Nathaniel L. Frothingham, and Convers Francis; on the other, it exposed its readers East and West to nascent Transcendentalism, with defenses and reprints of Emerson, Parker, Bronson Alcott, George Ripley, and other seekers after "German speculations." American culture in the 1830s and 1840s was both volatile and eclectic, and the *Western Messenger* reflects the efforts of its editors and contributors to come to terms with the complexity of their age.

To be sure, there was an inevitable amount of "filling up"— Peabody once complained that the publishers demanded "about 5 verses" to pad out a short page[5]—but on the whole the *Messenger* compares favorably with the best periodicals of the day. In his old age Clarke modestly recalled the magazine as "a rather respectable effort for the young people who wrote in it." More recent scholars have been far less reserved in their praise. "No other periodical that has appeared in the Ohio Valley is richer than it in original and suggestive contributions," writes one literary historian of the region. "The most important magazine published in the [trans-Allegheny] West," says Frank Luther Mott in his survey of American magazines. And Clarence Gohdes compares the *Messenger* favorably with the more famous Boston *Dial* as "a vehicle for the expression of the philosophical vagaries inherent in Romantic individualism." The consensus, in short, is that the *Messenger* is "in many respects a remarkable journal."[6]

But the *Messenger* demands more than encomiums. What we know about the magazine too often comes from piecemeal examinations that consider it one "respect" at a time.[7] But we have not known much, for instance, about the activities and viewpoints of its editors and major contributors, for our understanding is often marred by the genteel circumspection of nineteenth-century biographers. We have known still less about the facts of the magazine's publication: its financial circumstances, the number of its subscribers, the ways in which it was received. Indeed, we have not even known with any certainty who wrote most of the essays, reviews, and poems that appeared in its pages, since many of the *Messenger*'s contributions are anonymous, pseudonymous, or merely initialed. If we cannot reconstruct the entire jigsaw of the *Messenger,* we can at least make better use of those pieces we have—and the picture is surprisingly complete.

Setting the record straight is probably its own justification. The history of the *Messenger* provides ample evidence, however, that the conjunction of biography, bibliography, and intellectual history can not only augment our knowledge of the magazine but change our view of its important cultural context. Small facts can have large implications. As an example we may take the case of William Henry Channing, the journal's last editor. Channing's departure from Cincinnati in 1841 has been attributed to his "frustration and disillusionment" with "pragmatic, loutish, unreflective" Westerners—thus proving that "Transcendentalism's errand into the wilderness had failed." That view in turn confirms O. B. Frothingham's contention that "New England furnished the only plot of ground on the planet" where the new views could flourish.[8]

The image of a beleaguered idealist casting Transcendental pearls before swine has an unmistakable charm to it. But it is difficult to reconcile with the facts. Channing claimed to be quite happy with his Cincinnati congregation. "*I would not exchange my situation with that of any minister* [of?] *our denomination,*" he wrote one of his parishioners only a few months before leaving the West. "I feel in Cincinnati what I could not feel in any earlier parish—*Free. . . .*"[9] Instead, as I show in some detail in chapter 4, Channing left Cincinnati for a variety of reasons, some personal, some professional. His private letters make poignantly clear how painful he found the long separation from his wife, Julia, who preferred Episcopalianism in New York to radical Unitarianism on the frontier. The *Messenger*'s defenses of Orestes Brownson brought Channing the angry criticism of subscribers and sank him even further into debt. And his growing despair over the persistence of dogmatic sectarianism, the narrow-mindedness that frustrated both his marriage and his experience with the *Messenger,* plunged him into what he would years later recall as "the shadow-regions of Sceptical Unbelief."[10] To dismiss Channing's marital, editorial, and spiritual difficulties as a failure of Transcendentalism is at once to magnify the importance of a domestic quarrel and to minimize the complexity of the historical and intellectual forces at work.

The danger of hasty generalization so evident in the case of Channing's departure is writ large over the entire history of the *Western Messenger.* Clarke's Pennsylvania correspondent stands first in a long line of critics and scholars who have pronounced the magazine the first periodical of American Transcendentalism—this despite the fact that the definition of the term *Transcendentalism* is among the most slippery in our literary and intellectual history.[11] Even those considered part of the movement were hard pressed to agree on what the term meant, or indeed whether it meant anything at all. Margaret Fuller hoped that it suggested nothing more than "an active mind frequently busy with large topics" and "the friendship of such men as Mr Emerson, Mr Ripley, or Mr Alcott." Distinctions between the Reason and the Understanding, Clarke worried, were merely "a new form of words" that ought to be "left in the schools with the desks & globes." Brownson insisted in 1840 that members of the new school "agree in little except in their common opposition to the old school."[12]

We have always been skeptical of such vagaries, and rightly so; it is difficult to put much stock in characterizations of the movement like the one Emerson offered in his later years: "only here and there two or three men or women who read and wrote, each alone, with unusual vivacity."[13] But if we need not accept the denials of the Transcendentalists themselves, neither should we ignore them, for they chasten those who would define the group and its complex achievements too rigidly. Even the best attempts are bedeviled by circularity or historical reductiveness. How easy it is to decide, for instance, that a

Transcendental periodical is one "conducted or controlled by people who were known in their day as transcendentalists."[14] Seductive, too, is the dramatic rhetoric of the "Transcendental controversy" following Emerson's Divinity School Address in 1838. Between Emerson's famous dismissal of Unitarianism's "pale negations" and Andrews Norton's condemnation of Transcendentalism as "the latest form of infidelity" lay overlapping assumptions and goals that complicate our understanding of the parochial quarrel within liberal Christianity. When Clarke recorded in his journal for 1838 a "very fine debate—between new & old schools" in Boston, he numbered among the radical crew Chandler Robbins, Artemas B. Muzzey, and James Walker—middle-of-the-road Unitarian ministers who would have been appalled to find themselves siding with infidelity.[15] To characterize the Transcendental controversy as a "modern witch-hunt" is to confuse polemics with substance.[16] The error is as durable as it is wrongheaded.

Attempts to see the Transcendentalists plain have been furthered by a generation of religious and literary scholars whose reassessment of Unitarian historiography has done much to counterbalance our view of nineteenth-century Unitarians as conservative reactionaries.[17] William R. Hutchison's exploration of the achievements of those Transcendentalists who remained in the ministry, Conrad Wright's examination of the complex "supernatural rationalism" of the more moderate Unitarians, and Daniel Walker Howe's work on the moral philosophy taught at Harvard all suggest how fully the two streams of thought merged, as well as where they diverged. The result is a new sensitivity to the continuity, not just the antagonism, between Unitarianism and Transcendentalism, a sensitivity shown by Lawrence Buell in his recent study of Transcendental aesthetics: "Altogether, the Transcendentalist movement was more an evolution than a revolt from Unitarianism, although there were also basic philosophical differences that should not be glossed over. Transcendentalism was in almost every way a logical end result of the momentum of the Unitarian movement. . . ."[18] The patient recovery of the Unitarian past shows that if we are to appreciate how Transcendentalism differed from the liberal tradition that nurtured it, we must also understand how it was similar.

This is not to say that we should ignore the obvious distinctions that place the Transcendental movement at the heart of the American Renaissance, or even that we should be reticent about using the word *Transcendental.* Certainly we should not be. Indeed, it is almost impossible to talk about the period without using the term, and there is ample historical justification for doing so: it had wide currency in the 1830s and 40s, among both the sympathetic and the hostile; it refers to specific manifestations of our literary history, such as the Transcendental Club in Boston; and at any rate it has been so long used that any attempts to avoid it now would be foolish. But our definition must always be recognized for what it is—a convenient working hypothesis subject to confirmation and revision according to the available evidence.

The history of the *Western Messenger* and its contributors can help provide that evidence. In the magazine, and in the activities and viewpoints of those who conducted it, lies a contemporary, seriatim definition of the nascent Transcendentalist movement in America, one composed and revised by the participants themselves. In the *Messenger* we have a detailed record of what some members of the group said to and about each other, as well as the responses they drew from subscribers and other interested readers. Published monthly, the magazine responded quickly to the shifting currents of contemporary thought. Pledged to be "ultra" in nothing (4:431), it offered positions for discussion, not manifestos. A forum for lively discussion of religion, literature, politics, and social reform, the *Western Messenger* is the best sustained index we have to the most critical years in the history of American Transcendentalism, those spanning Emerson's first lecture series and the founding of Brook Farm and the *Dial.*

My goals in this book are to reconstruct the history of the *Western Messenger,* both internal (its major positions and the responses they drew) and external (subscription, publication, and financial information, as well as the activities of its editors and contributors), and to see what that history can tell us about

American literary and religious life during the 1830s and 40s, especially the intersection of Unitarianism and Transcendentalism. Chapter 1 outlines the polemical circumstances of those two groups in 1835 and contrasts their vision of the possibilities of the frontier with the realities of Western life. Chapters 2, 3, and 4 trace the three "phases" in the magazine's development of a progressively more radical point of view. Chapter 5 is an attempt to account for the *Messenger*'s demise, to explain the significance of that failure, and to assess the magazine's achievement.

My major assumption, that even the most apparently disparate facts of our literary and cultural past have value in and of themselves, seems to me so obviously true that I cannot conceive of a need to justify it. Two other assumptions, however, are best clarified at the outset. The first is that a periodical, the product of various hands, can evince a pattern of development and discernible point of view while still remaining responsive to new ideas, alternative opinions. Less problematic for single-topic journals like Garrison's *Liberator,* for instance, the contradiction is potentially troublesome for a study of the *Messenger,* whose contributors cast much wider nets into the sea of ideas and in certain respects stood far apart on the shore. In his "Introductory Remarks" to the opening number, in fact, William Greenleaf Eliot warns readers against assuming a coherence in the magazine's pages: the editors cannot collaborate closely, he says, and "any person therefore [who] looks for unity or perfect consistency in our magazine . . . will be disappointed" (1:3).

Eliot's warning, and with it the general problem, can be dismissed for several reasons, the most obvious being that neither Eliot nor anyone else could predict at the start the degree of consistency the magazine might later achieve. Indeed, he follows his caveat with something of a disclaimer: "we are not the less likely on this account, to arrive at truth, or to preserve in their purity the principles which we advocate" (1:3). Impatient with the artificial constraints imposed by creeds and "isms," the *Messenger* writers refused to march in lockstep with each other, preferring instead the sincere, individual search for truth; but they would have had little patience with what we today are apt to call "relativism." Tolerant of any path, they were confident—as Eliot suggests—that all earnest seekers would arrive at the same place. A close reading of the *Messenger* reveals unmistakable development in emphasis, interest, and point of view—not a "perfect consistency," of course, but not a foolish one, either.

My second assumption is that the fortunes of the magazine influenced significantly the career decisions of its editors, not vice versa. I hope to prove that point throughout this book, but it is worth mentioning here that the opposite assumption seems to have been held by almost everyone who has examined the subject before me. Their arguments are amply summarized by Elizabeth R. McKinsey, who has recently written that each editor " 'found himself' in the West, but found that he did not belong there and returned to the fold in the East."[19] That explanation is true as far as it goes. But to explain the demise of the *Messenger* it simply does not go far enough. For Clarke, Channing, and the others were men of ideas, and the magazine, insofar as it made public the cast of their minds, was for them an extension of self. Admittedly they may each have suffered an identity crisis, but not because they were rejected personally. They were not. A more likely source of their dislocation lies in the rejection of their ideas; had they felt intellectually "at home" in the West it is quite reasonable to assume that they would have stayed there. In short, though the *Messenger* ceased publication *when* its editors left the frontier, it does not necessarily follow that it ceased solely *because* they did so. On the contrary, the evidence suggests that the editors left the West because their magazine, and with it their ideas, no longer excited the imaginations of their readers, and because by 1841 they saw in the East the opportunities for intellectual, literary, and spiritual growth that had drawn them to the Ohio Valley in the first place. Those ideas, and the history of their publication and reception in the pages of the *Western Messenger*, have much to tell us about the development of the intellectual and aesthetic predispositions known as Transcendentalism, if we are content to interpret the facts as we find them, not as we wish them to be.

Acknowledgments

Most of the surviving information about the *Western Messenger* exists in the unpublished papers of its editors and major contributors. For permission to use and quote from such manuscripts in their collections, I wish to thank the Massachusetts Historical Society, the Houghton Library of Harvard University, the Andover-Harvard Theological Library, the Cincinnati Historical Society, the American Heritage Center of the University of Wyoming, the Washington University (St. Louis) Archives, and the Fred Lewis Pattee Library of the Pennsylvania State University. In addition, the staffs of the following institutions have been generous with their information and services: the Chicago Historical Society, the Crawford County (Pennsylvania) Historical Society, the Filson Club, the Kentucky Historical Society, the Louisiana State Museum, the New England Historic Genealogical Society, the New-York Historical Society, the Northumberland (Pennsylvania) Historical Society, the Unitarian Universalist Association, the Sterling Library of Yale University, and the interlibrary loan and microforms divisions of the Fred Lewis Pattee Library. I am grateful for financial support from the Pennsylvania State University College of Liberal Arts Research Fund, administered by Dean Thomas Magner.

I am indebted, too, to a number of scholars and archivists who have answered questions and offered advice. Larry A. Carlson, Gary Collison, Francis B. Dedmond, Joel Myerson, and Leonard Neufeldt shared their expert knowledge of the major Transcendentalists. Of the many librarians who helped in the preparation of this book, Peter Drummey, Mary Jane Neely, and Alan Seaburg deserve particular thanks for their industry and patience. Ira V. Brown, Harrison T. Meserole,

19

and Robert A. Secor of the Pennsylvania State University read an earlier draft of this study. To Robert N. Hudspeth I owe a special debt of gratitude, both for his judicious criticism and for the opportunity to serve for three years as research assistant on his splendid edition of the letters of Margaret Fuller. This book could not have been completed without his advice, his example, and his sustaining friendship.

No written thanks can suffice for the dedicatees of this book, my wife and daughter—two patient hostages of the nineteenth century who helped me, each in her own way, to keep my work in its proper perspective.

Abbreviations and Short Titles

Blackburn, "JFC" Blackburn, Charles E. "James Freeman Clarke: An Interpretation of the Western Years (1833–1840)." Ph.D. dissertation, Yale University, 1952.

DivCat *General Catalogue of the Divinity School of Harvard University 1901*. Cambridge, Mass.: Published by the University, 1901.

HarCat *Quinquennial Catalogue of the Officers and Graduates of Harvard University 1636–1910*. Cambridge, Mass.: Published by the University, 1910.

Heralds *Heralds of a Liberal Faith*. Edited by Samuel A. Eliot. 3 vols. Boston: American Unitarian Association, 1910.

JFCAuto *James Freeman Clarke: Autobiography, Diary, and Correspondence*. Edited by Edward E. Hale. Boston: Houghton, Mifflin, 1891.

J34–36 Clarke, James Freeman. Journal September 1834–29 March 1836. Perry-Clarke Collection, MHi.

J36–39 Clarke, James Freeman. Journal 10 May 1836–3 March 1839. Perry-Clarke Collection, MHi.

J39–40 Clarke, James Freeman. "Journal 1839–40." MH bMS Am 1569.3 (10).

Letters of JFC *The Letters of James Freeman Clarke to Margaret Fuller*. Edited by John Wesley Thomas. Hamburg: Cram, de Gruyter, 1957.

MemJHP *The Memoir and Writings of James Handasyd Perkins*. Edited by William H. Channing. 2 vols. Cincinnati: Trueman & Spofford, 1851.

MemWHC	Frothingham, Octavius Brooks. *Memoir of William Henry Channing.* Boston: Houghton, Mifflin, 1886.
MH	Houghton Library, Harvard University
MH–AH	Andover-Harvard Theological Library, Harvard University
MHi	Massachusetts Historical Society
Miller, "CPC"	Miller, Frederick DeWolfe. "Christopher Pearse Cranch: New England Transcendentalist." Ph.D. dissertation, University of Virginia, 1942.
MoSW	Washington University Archives
NEHGR	*New England Historical and Genealogical Register*
OCHP	Cincinnati Historical Society
PSt	Fred Lewis Pattee Library, The Pennsylvania State University
SubBook	"Subscribers to the Western Messenger," Perry-Clarke Collection, MHi.
Tiffany, *HJH*	Tiffany, Nina Moore, and Tiffany, Francis. *Harm Jan Huidekoper.* Cambridge, Mass.: Riverside, 1904.
WM	*The Western Messenger; Devoted to Religion and Literature*
WyU	American Heritage Center, University of Wyoming

Transcendentalism
and the *Western Messenger*

1

The Ohio Valley in 1835
New England Hopes, Western Realities

Some eight hundred miles separate Massachusetts Bay from the Ohio Valley heartland, a distance requiring in 1835 a wearying, ten-day journey by sailing ship, railroad, stagecoach, and steamboat that deposited the westward traveler in Cincinnati or, sixty miles downriver, in Louisville. In bad weather the trip was likely to be worse: rain-soaked passengers might be asked to pry wagon wheels from a bog of spring mud, and ice frequently locked steamers a week or more in midriver. For the young Unitarians who took this westward route to spread the liberal gospel, the geographical distance between Boston and the Ohio frontier, which they were of course powerless to change, no doubt proved a fitting introduction to the immensity of their task. It was the cultural separation of East and West that they were determined to reduce.

On the surface, certainly, the frontier cities provided an immediate and striking contrast to New England. Dusty, flat, and practically treeless, Louisville in 1835 was in the midst of ungainly adolescence, an active town of nearly twenty thousand—triple the population of only eight years before. Situated at the head of uninterrupted steamboat navigation of the Ohio River, it prided itself on industries—breweries, tanneries, sawmills, iron and brass foundries—that did a $29 million annual business by mid-decade. Its squat brick buildings included fourteen churches, five banks, and a single theater, "little better than a barn" until some civic-minded citizens remodeled it in 1828. For diversion there were private "conversational clubs" and public lectures at the Mechanics Institute on Tuesday evenings;

for excitement, the everpresent waterfront brawls and an occasional duel in the streets. As cities go, James Clarke remembered years later, Louisville was "one of the dirtiest."[1]

Half a day upriver sat Cincinnati, already known as the "Queen City" by the mid-1830s. Like Louisville, it had grown from a frontier settlement to a manufacturing center of 31,000 in 1835, doubling its size in only a decade. Its factories supplied the West with goods from boots and furniture to riverboats and steam engines, but the industry that gave the city its character was porkpacking. The editors of the *Cincinnati Mirror* proclaimed their city "the greatest place for hogs in the world," and the Englishwoman Frances Trollope, a resident from 1828 to 1830, recalled with disgust the sight of pigs being herded to the slaughterhouses through the center of town: "If I determined upon a walk up Main-street, the chances were five hundred to one against my reaching the shady side without my brushing by a snout fresh dripping from the kennel."[2]

If the cities of the Ohio Valley appeared crude and unfamiliar to the sons of Boston who emigrated there, the religious climate was even more foreign. By the 1830s Unitarianism had attracted some of the best minds in New England and become the accepted faith of the educated, the prosperous, and the socially elite. Following the appointment of Henry Ware, Sr., to the Hollis Professorship of Divinity at Harvard in 1805, Unitarian usurpation of Congregationalist pulpits proceeded steadily; Lyman Beecher, the staunch defender of old-guard Calvinism, found to his dismay that by 1826 "all the literary men of Massachusetts were Unitarian; all the trustees and professors of Harvard College were Unitarian; all the elite of wealth and fashion crowded Unitarian churches."[3] Within a generation, the liberal rebels in the Congregational church had established as the intellectual donnée of New England their belief in the benevolence of God, the humanity of Jesus, and the ethical possibilities of mankind.[4]

In the West, on the other hand, the Unitarian presence was scarcely discernible. Thanks to the efforts of the ubiquitous circuit-riders, Methodism claimed the greatest number of adherents, twice as many as its nearest rival by 1840 (or about forty thousand in Ohio alone); a Presbyterian minister on a preaching tour of the Valley complained that "I travelled from settlement to settlement on my errand of good, but in every hovel I entered, I learned that the Methodist missionary had been there before me." Next in numbers, and with their educated ministry first in intellectual influence, were the Presbyterians, who had joined with the Congregationalists in the 1801 Plan of Union to secure the West for Calvinism. In the urban areas especially, Roman Catholicism exerted considerable influence, as did Baptist farmer-preachers in the rural regions.[5]

Early Unitarian attempts to infiltrate the religious life of the Ohio Valley had met with stiff and successful resistance. The old charge of infidelity, with which liberals were saddled during the early days of the Unitarian controversy, begat among the Western orthodox a general fear of New England heresy. Even among the united "Presbygationists," the "full-fledged" Calvinists regarded their Eastern brethren with suspicion.[6] Thus, when avowed Unitarians tried to transplant their liberalism on the frontier, the result was usually holy war. In Kentucky, for example, the trustees of Transylvania University called the Unitarian Horace Holley to the presidency in 1816. The progressive Holley enlarged the faculty, established schools of law and medicine, and expanded the curriculum in his attempt to turn a sectarian academy into a liberal arts college free from denominational control. But the Presbyterians, determined to preserve their school from Unitarian "ungodliness," fought the reforms at every turn, and Holley's resignation in 1827, after a decade of bitter struggle, effectively ended "the possibility of the domination of liberal religious opinion in the state."[7] In Meadville, at the western edge of Pennsylvania, the wealthy Harm Jan Huidekoper founded a small Unitarian society in the early 1820s and began importing young Harvard ministers to tutor his children and preach the faith. The Erie Presbytery reacted by threatening to excommunicate any of its members who attended a Unitarian service. Huidekoper, incensed, accused the church elders in print of a "spirit of intolerant bigotry," touching off a year-long war in the press. By 1828 the Unitarians were forbidden to conduct evening services in the local Presbyterian church building—a common practice in towns where meeting places were scarce—and after the liberals entered the church one Thanksgiving night through an un-locked window, the sexton began hiding the candles in the foot-stoves to thwart the infidels. Undaunted, Huidekoper moved the services into the local courthouse and continued his work, converting an Episcopalian here, a Presbyterian there.[8] But Ephraim Peabody, writing his mother from Meadville in 1830, painted a bleak picture of Unitarian prospects in the Ohio Valley.

> There are a considerable number of men who are more Unitarians than anything else, but they do not come to our meeting. Unitarianism here is deadly to one's political influence. . . . No Unitarian can be in this country and not be in earnest in his employment when he looks about him and sees the minds and hearts of a whole land crushed down under the blind, brutalizing, palsying doctrines of Calvin.[9]

Given the crudity of life, the strength of Calvinism and (just as disturbing) of Methodist "enthusiasm," and the persistent antipathy of the more established sects, it seems a wonder that a single Unitarian forsook the comforts of New England to spread literary culture and rational religion beyond the Al-leghenies. As Holley and Huidekoper could testify, the West could be an inhospitable place. By mid-decade, however, a group of determined apostles of New England liberalism had stepped off stagecoaches and riverboats into a land at once alien yet promising, and for a variety of reasons, personal, cul-tural, and religious, they stayed. Among them were the four men who in 1835 founded the *Western Messenger*.

Ephraim Peabody (1807–56) arrived first, in late May 1830, a recent graduate of Harvard's Divinity School lured West to tutor the Huidekoper children at Meadville. Finding only "seven or eight Unitarian families or parts of families," he set about converting the natives. To correct misrepresentations of Unitarian doctrine—"men are warned against our places of worship and our books," he complained, and "our arguments are carefully evaded"—he began publishing the *Unitarian Essay-ist* (1831–32), a monthly pamphlet of twelve pages.[10] At "Pomona," the Huidekoper estate, Peabody found life idyllic and his host a stimulating conversationalist. But his future in Meadville was limited; within a year he accepted a call to the fledgling First Congregational Church of Cincinnati (Unitarian in belief, though not in name), was ordained there on 20 May 1832, and left the *Essayist* in Huidekoper's hands.[11]

Unlike Peabody, with his sense of mission, James Handasyd Perkins (1810–49) seemed destined to wander. Forsaking Harvard for a career in business, he entered at age 18 the Boston countinghouse of his wealthy uncle Thomas Handasyd Perkins, who later endowed the Institute for the Blind that bears his name. A moody young man given to poetry, James Perkins discovered Coleridge sometime during his twentieth year and, after a period of depression, speculation, and travel, left Boston for Cincinnati in February 1832. There he boarded at the home of the lawyer Timothy Walker, his former teacher at the progressive Round Hill School, Northampton; under Walker's tutelage he was admitted to the bar in May 1834, but he quickly became disillusioned with his legal duties and gave up his practice after a year. Next he tried journalism, editing the Cincinnati *Evening Chronicle,* which merged with the weekly *Mirror* in April 1835.[12]

James Freeman Clarke (1810–88), the third to arrive, brought with him a rich heritage of liberal dissent. His maternal grandfather, Dr. James Freeman, had established at King's Chapel in 1785 the first openly Unitarian society in Boston and was, with Dr. William Ellery Channing, a patron saint of the movement. Harvard educated, young James enrolled in the Divinity School class of 1833 and appeared assured of a pulpit in the Bay area. But by his senior year his confidence in the sufficiency of historical religion—the Unitarian faith in Scripture as the source of all knowledge and ethics—had been badly shaken. From his reading of Coleridge, Carlyle, and the German Romantics he came to accept intuition as an equally valid mode of perception, following Coleridge's distinction between the Reason and the Understanding. From his friendships with Emerson, George Ripley, Frederic Henry Hedge, and especially Margaret Fuller, he came to admire the power of the questioning, creative mind. And from the lukewarm, if not yet hostile, reception of Clarke's budding transcendentalism among Boston's Unitarian establishment, he came to wonder whether he might not fare better in the open West. At the least, he wrote in his diary, "the good effects of a year spent there on a young man educated here would be great. Constant action—this alone as fixing his character would be admirable. Opportunities of studying human character in a very different state of society from ours."[13]

So Clarke, eager to test his powers, landed at Louisville on 4 August 1833 to replace the ailing missionary George Chapman. Feeling both homesick and challenged, sometimes despairing that his beliefs were "looked upon as pure Infidelity by all Christians," he persevered, convinced that "struggling with difficulties is the element of all worth—to give it up is to be ruined." But he never lost sight of the storm clouds gathering over Boston as the "new views" of Emerson and others encountered the chilly resistance of the Unitarian clergy, and he longed to enter the fray on the side of the Transcendentalists, contributing his "habits of Western recklessness." By 1835 he confided to his sister Sarah his decision to remain in Louisville "till I am called to go elsewhere as plainly as I was to come to this spot."[14] In the meantime, adopting from Goethe the motto "Do thy nearest duty," Clarke kept busy, preaching Eastern liberalism in the West and, in turn, recommending the West to his friends in New England.

One seemed an especially promising prospect. William Greenleaf Eliot (1811–87), entering his last year at Harvard's Divinity School, wrote in October 1833 to ask Clarke's opinion of Western opportunities for "us Young, Unit[ari]an preachers"; Clarke encouraged him to emigrate, appealing to the younger man's strong desire for evangelistic work: "If Unitarianism is to thrive in the West it must be planted *now,* while the cites are young & grow with their growth."[15] Eliot, like Clarke, was afire with a newly discovered love of German philosophy, especially the ethical idealism of Fichte, and like Clarke he was eager to test his ability to improve men by stirring in them the virtuous promptings of the heart.[16] On 17 August 1834 he was ordained as an evangelist at Dr. Channing's Federal Street Church, with the visiting Clarke delivering the ordination address, and at the end of November he arrived in

St. Louis. At first he preached in a schoolhouse to large audiences who had come to hear the blasphemous rantings of an atheist. After the disappointed curious drifted away, however, Eliot found that his congregation numbered little more than two dozen.[17] A month after his arrival he reported his progress and reception.

> There is far less prejudice against us than I expected to find, or rather I should say the prejudices are less stubborn than they generally are where our name has only been heard as a bugbear. Very many of the sternest Presbyterians, and the strictest Episcopalians and Methodists, have been to hear me, and if they are on the one hand disappointed in not finding very much to condemn, they are generally candid enough to acknowledge us to be better than they thought. This is all we can ask.

None of the local ministers had yet acknowledged him; but, he added bravely, "on one occasion our Society was recognized as a Christian [one]."[18] On 26 January 1835 he formally organized his tiny congregation and began soliciting funds to build a church.

New Englanders all, well educated, energetic, and given to a love of the written word, Peabody, Perkins, Clarke, and Eliot brought with them to the Ohio Valley—and ultimately to the *Western Messenger*—an impressive background. As individuals they contributed special talents: the publishing experience of Peabody and Perkins, Clarke's wide reading and Eastern friendships, Eliot's evangelical zeal and gift for organization. Most important, each confronted the strangeness of his new home with an abiding faith in its possibilities.

In part their optimism derived from an excitement about the West deeply ingrained in the national consciousness, an idealized vision of the open frontier that animated the American imagination and assumed, it has been argued, mythic proportions in the nineteenth century. The novels of Cooper, the paintings of George Caleb Bingham, the elections of Jackson and later of Harrison (with his "log cabin and hard cider" campaign), the popular currency of manifest destiny—all remind us how variously and pervasively the American West intruded upon the cultural life of the time: the vast territory beyond the Alleghenies was many things to many people.

For Peabody, Clarke, and the others, however, the real significance of the West lay not in what it was but in what it might become. All around them they saw a culture in flux, in the process of self-definition, and if they were sometimes disheartened by the dirt, the vulgarity, the absence of Boston's amenities, they were at the same time exhilarated by the opportunity to assist at the birth of a new society. In the 1830s, Peabody recalled, "the institutions of Cincinnati and of the West were in a forming state. The chaos was gradually shaping itself into a world. Schools, churches, customs of business, benevolent institutions, were assuming a determinate form. It was the time when foundations were laid for coming generations."[19] Clarke too recognized the formlessness of his surroundings. "All here is incongruous, shifting, amorphous," he wrote Margaret Fuller. "No spirit of order broods over this Chaos." And like Peabody he viewed the scene with enthusiasm. "Everything which liberalizes your mind, which enables you to despise the form in comparison with the spirit . . . is preparation for the West," was his reply to Eliot's inquiries. "Everything here is free, open, active. . . . You feel your life, you feel full of energy, your soul grows and expands with every pulse throb." To his friend William Henry Channing, who would become the *Messenger*'s final editor, he reported grandly, "Everything grows here."[20]

This is not to say that the young Unitarians were blind to the faults of the West. Perkins spoke for the others when he condemned its rampant commercialism and "the individual moral torpor which it brings about" (2:93). And Clarke, at least, understood that his freedom to speak about Goethe or Emerson showed that most of his listeners had not the faintest idea what he was talking about. Yet the net effect of such shortcomings was stimulating, not discouraging. In the "amorphous" West Clarke saw the opportunity for "a bold and self-possessed mind to step in, and lay the foundations of a new and strong edifice of thought." When Peabody found the Western people wandering in the "total darkness" of Calvinism, he resolved "to preach rather more violently against those doctrines than good sense warrants." To Eliot, a few dozen parishioners were justification enough for a new church; the sight of a money-grubbing "mass bent upon gain" spurred Perkins to work for "Spiritual and Religious Education" (2:92, 97). In chaos lay the seeds of a new order; in ignorance, the potential for education. To each man the West offered something that New England no longer could, the chance to shape a young, unsettled society without the "drag" of two centuries of tradition and false opinion. Their mission was to form a culture, not to reform it. The story of the *Western Messenger* reflects the growing recognition that its founders' optimism was misplaced. But in 1835 they felt confident that the prospects of the West were, in Clarke's words, "as full of hope now as ever."[21]

That hope was confirmed by recent developments in the religious life of the Ohio Valley, a situation "chaotic" in the extreme. For the first three decades of the century the entire country had been beset by bitter sectarianism, "a fury of division, and subdivision," Frances Trollope sniffed, "that has the melancholy effect of exposing *all* religious ceremonies to contempt."[22] Beyond the Alleghenies religious fragmentation had reached critical proportions. The camp meetings at Cane Ridge, Kentucky, in August 1801—where thousands of pioneers, whipped into frenzy by preachers on stumps and wagons, fell into spasms of religious ecstasy—touched off the decade of evangelical ferment known as the Great Revival, and no church was immune from the danger that a particularly charismatic orator would sweep into town, convert part of its congregation, and move into the next village like a hurricane, leaving established views in rubble.[23] What is more, the older denominations experienced division from within: sometimes over local and niggling issues, as in the dispute over Watts's hymnal that divided the Transylvania Presbytery, but sometimes over fundamental points of doctrine or polity. Thus after the turn of the century the Presbyterians found themselves increasingly divided into Old and New Schools, the latter more evangelical in its preaching, more basic in its doctrine.[24]

Amid this denominational turmoil, each sect scrambled to protect its turf. Resistance to Holley and Huidekoper probably derived as much from the heightened sensitivity to outside interference as from a particular hatred of Unitarianism. "Bible colleges" grew like mushrooms throughout the West to assure the training of ministers, giving rise to the joke that "a settler could hardly encamp on the prairies, but a college would spring up behind his wagon."[25] Proselytizing became more organized: the Methodists meticulously scheduled camp meetings, and the Presbygationists founded the powerful American Home Missionary Society in 1826. And, of course, there were missionaries, "swarms" of them, wrote the Ohio historian Caleb Atwater in 1838, "all in motion, to build up their various sects. . . . There is scarcely a day in the year but there is preaching of some sort, in every town of any size in the state." In Cincinnati Mrs. Trollope heard Presbyterians, Baptists, and Methodists "of more denominations than I can remember; whose innumerable shades of varying belief, it would require much time to explain, and more to comprehend."[26] The Ohio Valley had become in three decades a crazy quilt of denominationalism, hosting Episcopalians, Lutherans, Roman Catholics, Quakers, Shakers, Mennonites, and Moravians, as well as a rapidly growing cluster of German Pietists called the Zoar Society and some twenty thousand Mormons under the leadership of Joseph Smith. Competing sects collided everywhere, hurling charges of infidelity.[27] And if theological hair-splitting failed to excite an audience, appeals to nativism often would. In his *Plea for the West* (1835), ostensibly an argument for supporting Cincinnati's Lane Theological Seminary, Lyman Beecher zeroed in on the "Catholic menace" and elevated sectarianism to a national imperative. The political power of hordes of Western Catholics, Beecher warned, made the choice between "superstition, or evangelical light" a matter of democratic survival.[28]

Beecher's *Plea* and the anti-Catholic sentiments it aroused reveal how heated the sectarian warfare had grown by 1835. But there were indications that people were growing tired of polemics. Many no doubt shared Mrs. Trollope's impatience with the "innumerable shades of varying belief" hawked by preachers sometimes more zealous than pious. Sectarianism had turned the West into a battleground for Christian soldiers, leading Caleb Atwater to sigh, "fewer of them, and those well qualified for their missions, would be a vast improvement."[29]

Sectarianism became known by its excesses—the name-calling, the apocalyptic rhetoric, the frantic competition for adherents. This furious, divisive action bred an equally intense reaction, the measure of which is the growth in the 1830s of a religious movement at once positive, accessible, and strongly antisectarian, calling itself the Christian Connexion.

The "Christians" (or "Disciples" or "Reformers," as they were variously named) grew from and with the revivalistic activity of the early 1800s, and it is useful to see the movement as it saw itself, three separate splinter groups born of a common impulse to restore primitive Christianity and opposed to all sects that had "departed from the *simplicity that is in Christ*, and from the spirit of *love* and *union*."[30] In New England the laymen Abner Jones and Elias Smith led a group split from the Vermont Baptists. In Kentucky the movement crystallized around Barton W. Stone, one of the organizers of the Cane Ridge meetings. From western Pennsylvania into Ohio it spread under the charismatic leadership of Alexander Campbell, whose distrust of historical accretions to biblical truth led him to break with the Western Baptists in 1827.

Though the Disciples adamantly insisted upon congregational autonomy, they shared a basic creed. Strict literalists, they accepted the Bible as a "book of facts" that "reveal[s] God and man, and contain[s] within the reasons of all piety and righteousness." Scripture taught God's absolute sovereignty and boundless, unconditional love for a fallen world. Man is "carnally minded," but he "possesses rational faculties, capable of knowing and enjoying God." Thus, men are moral agents, responsible for their own salvation. God has provided in the Gospel "the means of enlightening, quickening, regenerating, and sanctifying the soul"; all man needs are faith in Christ and "humility of mind" to come within "understanding distance" of the Diety and effect his own regeneration.[31]

This easily understood doctrine had immense popular appeal in a region weary of theological complexities. By eliminating the Calvinist doctrine of double predestination—the imputation of sin combined with the inscrutable randomness of divine election—it provided a religious analogue to the economic and social democracy on which the West prided itself. By stressing virtue of character rather than speculative belief, it justified ethical behavior in a land given to lawlessness. Though not optimistic about man's temporal state, the Disciples shared with Unitarians an Arminian spirit, having, as Conrad Wright aptly puts it, "heightened confidence in the capacity of human beings to *do* the will of God." And finally, the Disciples appealed to the growing antidenominationalism of the West. Their goal was Christian union, and they considered human creeds nothing less than satanic. Said Campbell:

> It behooves all men, then, who wish to be approved by the Lord at his coming, to be up and doing to purge and cleanse the Christian profession from every root and branch of sectarianism, and to endeavor to destroy those destructive sects . . . that have filled the profession with hypocrites, the world with infidels.[32]

Such calls to arms, of course, aroused the more orthodox sects exceedingly. "Stonites" and "Campbellites" (they loathed both names as unscriptural) became anathema in the Ohio Valley. A member of the American Home Missionary Society in 1840 offered typical criticism: "In my opinion Campbellism is the great curse of the West—more destructive and more injurious to the cause of religion than avowed Infidelity itself."[33] Yet the movement could not be stopped. Stone and his followers expanded rapidly throughout Kentucky, and by 1832 they had swept into southeastern Ohio, pulling all but two Presbyterian churches into their orbit. Campbell's group put Baptists on the defensive in western Pennsylvania and Kentucky, and Campbell himself debated all comers, from the free-thinking Robert Dale Owen (whose community at New Harmony Campbell called a "focus of enlightened atheism") to the Catholic Bishop of Cincinnati, Robert Purcell.[34] In 1832 the two groups merged, some eight thousand Stonites and five thousand Campbellites taking the name Disciples of Christ. Precise membership is difficult to determine, but by all estimates the Disciples grew phenomenally in the 1830s and 1840s. In 1850 they claimed about 118,000 members, most in the border states and the Ohio River basin; by 1860 they numbered over 192,000.[35]

Western Unitarians saw in the rise of the Christian Connexion a confirmation of their view of the chaos of the frontier: sectarian turmoil had given birth to a popular faith in God's benevolence, man's ethical and rational capabilities, and the moral leadership of Jesus. The Christian system bore many similarities to Unitarianism, and where one succeeded, the other might also. The masses receptive to the modified Arminianism of Stone and Campbell constituted a potential audience for preachers like Clarke, Peabody, and Eliot, and the young New Englanders knew it. To the General Secretary of the American Unitarian Association Clarke wrote excitedly in 1835, asking support for the Western effort: "Only consider the situation of this region—the unsettled state of opinions—few of the Campbellites can be considered as settled firmly in their opinions—so it is also with the Christian Baptists of this state— Unitarianism can have access to them, and is needed."[36] In the chaotic darkness of the Ohio Valley, the Disciples had kindled a fire, and the Unitarian missionaries there were eager to fan the flames.

While the Christian movement was consolidating the latent antisectarian sentiments of the West, liberal Unitarians in the East were developing a missionary movement of their own. The growing relationship between the two has, however, been either neglected or minimized. In his history of Unitarianism, for instance, George Willis Cooke correctly estimates the West's potential.

> From 1830 to 1850 the Unitarians were confronted by the greatest opportunity which has ever opened to them for missionary activities. The vast region of the middle west was in a formative state, the people were everywhere receptive to liberal influences, other churches had not yet been firmly established, and there was an urgent demand for leadership of a progressive and rational kind.

Yet, he maintains, Eastern liberals largely ignored the opportunity. Elizabeth R. McKinsey takes a similar view, claiming that "Boston Unitarianism hardly noticed the western offshoot at first," that Eastern interest was only "gradually aroused," and that fear of revivalist enthusiasm and the strength of Roman Catholicism finally "alarmed Boston liberals into active con-

cern."[37] Religious historians often date the beginning of
Unitarian evangelism in the West at 1844, when the Meadville
Theological School opened its doors.[38]

Nothing, in fact, could be farther from the truth: Eastern
Unitarians had been closely monitoring the religious situation
beyond the Alleghenies since the mid-1820s. At the founding
of the American Unitarian Association (AUA) in 1825, Henry
Ware, Jr., proposed as its "chief and ultimate object . . . the
promotion of pure and undefiled religion by disseminating the
knowledge of it where adequate means of religious instruction
are not enjoyed"—the goal adopted almost verbatim in the
group's constitution.[39] Unitarians generally were reluctant to
think of themselves as a sect; most preferred less restrictive
designations, such as "rational Christians," to the name
Unitarian, and many, especially those still smarting from the
controversy with the orthodox Congregationalists, were hesi-
tant to support any organized denominational movement for
fear of replacing one dogma with another. Yet the founders of
the AUA, mostly younger men who graduated from Harvard's
Divinity School after 1817, sought a means to represent
thoughts and sentiments that had become known as distinctly
Unitarian and to spread those thoughts and sentiments beyond
New England.[40] That they considered their doctrine "pure and
undefiled religion" rather than a dogmatic "ism" makes their
intent no less missionary.[41] For them, Unitarianism *was*
undefiled religion. The AUA's purpose, as its constitution
states, was "to diffuse the knowledge and promote the interests
of pure Christianity throughout our country."

From the beginning, the AUA set its sights on the West. In
1826, declaring itself interested in the "existence of a body of
Christians in the Western States, who for years have been
Unitarians, have encountered persecution on accouont of their
faith, and have lived in ignorance of others east of the mountains," the Executive Committee dispatched an agent to "make
himself familiar with the religious conditions of the Middle and
Western States." Moses G. Thomas traveled over four thousand
miles from April to September 1826, touring Ohio, Kentucky,
Pennsylvania, and nine other states, as far west as St. Louis; his
report, read in May 1827 at the second annual convocation, was
heartening. Beyond the mountains, it was true, lay a thicket of

hostile sects and revivalistic enthusiasts. But there were real hopes for Unitarianism in Pittsburgh, Louisville, St. Louis, Lexington, and especially, Thomas said, Cincinnati, "by far the most favorable place for the establishment of a Unitarian church of any I have visited."[42]

"Animating prospects," the committee agreed, especially Thomas's report of the progress of the "fraternity" known as the Christian Connexion. Only two months earlier, Boston's *Christian Examiner*, an organ for the Unitarian viewpoint, had printed with approval a detailed statement of the Connexion's beliefs and polity that showed its many affinities to Unitarianism. Both groups agreed on the mercy and sovereignty of God, the reality of Christ's resurrection, the "absolute necessity of holiness of heart and rectitude of life." Both stressed "virtue of the character" above "speculative belief," considered the Scriptures "the only rule of faith and practice," and encouraged men to "search the divine records" and exercise "private judgment" to ascertain their truths. In fact, the Christians declared themselves "strictly Unitarian" in their sentiments, though more evangelical in their preaching.[43] If such a kindred movement could flourish on the frontier, the prospects for Unitarianism there were animating indeed.

When Clarke wrote to the AUA in June 1835, then, he did so fully aware of its ten-year enthusiasm for Western missions. His request for aid, moreover, could not have come at a more opportune time, for in 1835 the evangelistic energies of Eastern Unitarians were running higher than ever before. Their theological dispute with the orthodox at a low ebb, and the Transcendentalist threat still in embryo, Boston's liberals experienced a lull between two storms that left them free for missionary work.[44] Charles Briggs, newly installed as the AUA's General Secretary, brought to the post a zealous commitment to Unitarian expansion, and his enthusiasm was symptomatic of a mounting sense of urgency among the Eastern clergy that year.[45] Before the Ministerial Conference in Berry Street on 27 May, Henry Ware, Jr., spoke warmly of the need to evangelize "that important world in the Western valleys."

Our denomination has its share of that work to perform. We may not dare withhold ourselves from it. A portion of our means, as many as can be spared of our ministers, must be sent out to help in blessing that glorious young giant. Now is the time.[46]

At the AUA's annual meeting, George W. Hosmer (about to leave for a tour of the South and West) argued that "the public mind has left its ancient moorings of religious faith and practice, and is drifting, God only knows whither"; in this "solemn crisis," he prophesied, Unitarianism could moderate between sectarian "bigotry and exclusiveness" and atheistic "liberty without law." William Eliot, in town to solicit funds for his St. Louis church, put the Western situation in stark terms: "either we must have a little help, a kind hand extended during the first stages of our endeavors, or we must fail altogether."[47] The following spring the association claimed for itself in 1835 "much more of the *missionary character* than it has had in any previous year." Significantly, Eastern clergy now saw the West as the Western missionaries did, a culture drifting without a moral rudder. In a report at the 1836 meeting, J. W. Thompson termed the "religious institutions" of the area "a perfect chaos. They need a formative hand, a hand that is skilful to combine materials which have hitherto been in a state of separation."[48] Clearly, the members of the AUA neither ignored nor misunderstood their Western missionaries; on the contrary, they were well informed and highly enthusiastic.

It is easy to overlook this enthusiasm, to see only the rough edges of Western culture, and to conclude that fundamental and irreconcilable disjunctions made Unitarian hopes for the Ohio Valley "an expectation certain to be disappointed." Because the missionaries themselves often felt lonely or inadequate, and because the Unitarians never fully realized their expectations outside of New England, historians have assumed that "the distance between Boston and Louisville was simply too immense." Needless to say, under that assumption the Western missionaries appear either hopelessly misinformed or extremely quixotic.[49]

They were neither—for in 1835 all signs pointed to a favorable reception for their liberal gospel in the Ohio Valley. Clarke and the others believed the chaotic religious life of the West to be on the brink of coming to order, needing only a "formative hand" to shape it properly. They saw in the sudden rise of the Christian Connexion concrete evidence that the Western people, free in spirit and unbound by tradition, were ready for a nonsectarian doctrine of piety, spiritual growth, and rational inquiry. And they found their Eastern brethren in a state of evangelical fervor that promised both financial support and an all-important sense of shared goals. Worth mentioning, too, is the fact that distance from New England, physical and cultural, had its advantages. Even in 1835, a year before Emerson's *Nature,* Boston's Unitarian establishment showed a limited tolerance for the mystical "infidelity" soon to be known as Transcendentalism.[50] For young men like Clarke, Eliot, and Perkins, flirting with German Idealism as a way to enliven their "corpse-cold" denomination, it was safer to muse and speculate out of earshot of New England's orthodox clergy. In the West, Clarke wrote Margaret Fuller in April, you could be "as transcendental as you please."[51] Given these positive signs, it is not surprising that Eastern liberals in the Ohio Valley worked with new vigor in 1835. Indeed, it would be more surprising if they had not.

Paradoxically, the challenge faced by the Western Unitarians in 1835 was not to survive in a closed culture—that is, in a culture secure in its opposition to them—but to thrive in an open one. "We are free to speak here whatever we think," Clarke declared. "Public opinion is not an intolerant despotism, for there is no such thing as Public Opinion." Yet he recognized the extent to which public tolerance rested upon public ignorance; the first permitted Unitarianism a toehold in the West, but the second could prevent it from advancing.

> I need like others [Clarke continued] a basis of received opinions to stand upon, and act upon, and this is not to be found. We want some place to start from, something to argue from, but there are no axioms in mental or moral philosophy given us here. We can address nothing but tastes and feelings. We may sing a pleasant song, and they will come to hear for they are a tasteful race, and they sympathize with any strong emotion, for they have large hearts, but their heads are in a sad situation truly.[52]

Confident that free and rational discussion would yield the truth, and confident that Westerners would embrace the truth once they understood it, the Unitarians set out to educate, not to indoctrinate. As they soon discovered, though, preaching alone reached only a small fraction of the potential audience. What they needed was a more efficient way to disseminate "opinions to stand upon, and act upon." What they needed was a magazine.

It was almost inevitable that the Unitarians' missionary energies would be channeled into print. Clarke, Peabody, and Perkins were experienced authors by mid-decade, and the latter two knew the publishing business firsthand. Harvard training in rhetoric and the practical demands of sermon-writing made organized, forceful writing a familiar, if not always effortless, activity for ministers. As New Englanders they were heirs to two centuries of literary endeavor. And as Unitarians they knew the efficacy of the written word for spreading the faith. In Boston the weekly *Christian Register* and the bimonthly *Christian Examiner* were in Unitarian hands, as was the most influential literary journal of the century, the *North American Review;* and since 1826 the AUA had invested more money and effort in distributing tracts than in any other enterprise, printing an average of 65,000 annually. For Unitarians—indeed, for most denominations—the first half of the nineteenth century was, as Lawrence Buell puts it, "the golden age of the religious magazine."[53]

A more particular influence upon the founding of the *Western Messenger,* beyond the general tendencies of liberalism to seek literary expression, was the proposal in early 1835 of a new journal by New England's Transcendentalists. On 20 February—coincidentally the same day that Clarke sent a prospectus of his Western magazine to Margaret Fuller—Frederic Henry Hedge wrote her that he and George Ripley were also planning a periodical, one "of an entirely different character from any now existing." This "journal of spiritual philosophy," Hedge hoped, would "introduce new elements of thought" and "give a new impulse to the mental action of our country." Hedge planned to enlist the aid of Clarke, Fuller, Emerson, Charles Follen, W. H. Furness, and James Marsh—"all the Germano-philosophico-literary talent in the country"—as well as Thomas Carlyle.[54] For weeks the plan simmered, though the exact character of the magazine remained hazy. Emerson wrote Carlyle about the projected "work on the First Philosophy in Boston" with the tentative titles the *Transcendentalist* or the *Spiritual Enquirer;* Bronson Alcott recorded in his journal some names connected with the plan: "Hedge, Emerson, Peabody, Clarke, Ripley." By April, however, the proposed journal was in trouble. Hedge accepted a pastorate in Bangor, Maine, and suggested Carlyle as editor, an offer that Emerson quickly relayed. But Carlyle, who hailed the magazine as "an interesting symptom" and wished it well, wanted no part in editing it. Nor, apparently, did anyone else. The project fell through before a single issue appeared.[55]

The conjunction of this aborted effort with the founding of the *Western Messenger* is highly suggestive, especially since Clarke and Peabody appear connected with both; but to consider the *Messenger* a direct result of the activity in Boston would be to ignore both chronology and geography. Clarke seems not to have known of the proposed *Transcendentalist*—or his proposed connection with it—until early March, well after the *Messenger*'s prospectus had been circulated.[56] The Peabody of Alcott's list is almost certainly Elizabeth Palmer Peabody, Alcott's assistant at the Temple School and later publisher of the *Dial,* not Ephraim, who was temperamentally, personally, and philosophically less daring than the others. The *Messenger* and the *Transcendentalist* were conceived independently, in different places, by different people, at about the same time.

Less directly, however, the failed attempt to launch a Transcendental periodical offered the *Messenger* both the opportunity and the dangers of articulating the radical views of the new school, and the Western magazine, still in the planning stage, took on an added burden almost by default. Clearly, the Transcendental circle in New England considered Clarke a kindred spirit, as he did them; with existing periodicals closed to them, they must have found it comforting that he planned a journal where the "spiritual philosophy" might be treated sympathetically. Whether the Boston group thought the *Messenger* a substitute for their magazine is a matter of speculation, but the fact

that every contemporary Transcendentalist save Thoreau published there indicates that they found it at least partly suitable.
At any rate, Clarke was surely aware of the pool of talent his
journal might tap and the needs it might serve. Moreover, the
language of Hedge's proposal reminds us how important German literature was to American Transcendental thought. In
Goethe and Schiller, and through the commentary of Coleridge
and Carlyle, the New England thinkers discovered a vocabulary
for, as well as a confirmation of, their faith in man's divinity. As
Stanley M. Vogel has remarked, German Idealism, both
philosophical and literary, yielded for the American Transcendentalists "the idea that the good, the true, the beautiful—
all things of which they instinctively approved—were somehow
connected together" and that knowledge of the Ideal lay
neither in Scripture nor in the senses, as most Unitarians believed, but in the innate Reason, a faculty of perception that
"transcends" historical Christianity and physical sensation.[57]
With the failure of the *Transcendentalist,* discussion of German
literature—at least, that literature which most Unitarians considered heretical in its implications—awaited an American out-
let. From the literary circumstances of the East, in short, the
fledgling *Messenger* received two strong and contradictory demands: to advance Unitarianism among those who considered
it blasphemy, and to promote Transcendentalism among those
who considered it infidelity.

From the West came other considerations, not the least of
which was a literary life active enough to support a quality
periodical but competitive enough to destroy a mediocre one.
During the 1830s Cincinnati developed the technical facilities
for large-scale publishing and became the West's chief pro-
ducer of books and magazines. By one count the Midwest had
over two hundred newspapers in 1834 and dozens of magazines (the distinction between the two is often blurred).[58] Many
of these were sectarian organs, ephemeral productions lasting
only a few months, until the initial spark of controversy died.
Periodicals more strictly literary fared about the same. Often
mere collections of miscellanea reprinted from Eastern journals, with occasional contributions by the editor, they suffered
from an unreliable postal system, writers of questionable talent,

and a fickle, sometimes uninterested readership. As John P. Foote complained in the valedictory of his weekly *Cincinnati Literary Gazette* (1824), belles lettres found only sporadic interest among "a people whose highest ambition would seem to be exhausted in acquiring the means of support."[59]

Yet it is misleading to treat the *Messenger* as "a literary journal in the unliterary West,"[60] for Western interest in literature, though not yet widespread, was vigorous and sustained. Better periodicals, such as James Hall's *Western Monthly Magazine* (1833–37) or William D. Gallagher's *Cincinnati Mirror* (1831–36) and *Hesperian* (1838–39), kept readers abreast of developments in British and American letters with reviews of Coleridge, Scott, and Carlyle, and Irving, Cooper, and Bryant. Just as important, they published the poetry and fiction of Otway Curry, Neville Morgan, and dozens of other Western writers, authors now forgotten—perhaps with good reason—but in their time at the forefront of a burgeoning movement to create an indigenous literature. Gallagher, the area's best (and probably its most prolific) poet, issued three volumes of verse and collected the fruits of Western literature in *Selections from the Poetical Literature of the West* (1841); Poe wrote of him, "He has the true spirit, and will rise to a just distinction hereafter."[61] Hall's tales, in the style of Scott but enlivened by local color and dialect, enjoyed nationwide popularity; his combined work in fiction, criticism, and history made him the foremost Western literary man of his day. Writers of discernment and energy, if not of lasting talent, Gallagher, Hall, and the others worked tirelessly to promote the imaginative interpretation of the frontier in verse, novel, and essay.[62]

Supporting the drive for a Western literature were the conversational clubs that sprang up in the urban centers. Cincinnati had the most distinguished gathering, the Semi-Colon Club, which included the city's *literati*—among others Hall, Dr. Daniel Drake, William Greene, Lyman Beecher and his daughters Catherine and Harriet (later Harriet Beecher Stowe)—and, at various times, almost all of the *Messenger*'s editors and major contributors. The club met each winter from 1829 to about 1846 for "evenings of social relaxation, and rational amusement," as one of its members recalled, attracting many of the transplanted New Englanders who by the 1830s had begun to influence the cultural life of the city to an extent far out of proportion to their numbers.[63] In 1839 William Henry Channing described a typical meeting to his wife:

> The plan of it is that its members shall voluntarily contribute original pieces which are read in the early part of the evening, with intervals for conversation & music. . . . [T]he whole is closed with a dance. We had about 30 or 40 at the meeting.[64]

To be sure, the Semi-Colon was a far cry from the Transcendental Club; it is hard to imagine Emerson or Bronson Alcott suggesting a break for punch and a quadrille. But the Semi-Colon, and clubs like it, testified to the potential Western audience for polite literature and refined criticism of the arts.[65] In the West, as in the East, the literary atmosphere promised support for the Unitarian missionaries' venture into print.

Religious historians tend to ignore the literary side of the *Western Messenger,* and literary historians express surprise that a religious magazine contains better poetry and more perceptive reviews than avowedly literary periodicals.[66] In 1835, however, such objections, in the unlikely event that they were raised at all, would have met with surprise, if not bewilderment. For one thing, the Unitarian clergy, including the more radical ones numbered among the Transcendentalists, were also men of letters in the broadest sense of the term. Translators, critics, essayists, and versifiers in particular, they were as a group intensely interested in the use of language and the implications of literary expression. With good reason O. B. Frothingham called the mainstream of Boston liberalism "literary Unitarianism," for its clergy had high regard for belles lettres—not as mere amusement or even as "delightful instruction," but as the primary means of impressing on the heart the truths revealed by Scripture.[67] With such men as principals, the Transcendentalist controversy developed as much for literary as for religious reasons. In fact, as the Emersonian ideal of the poet-priest reminds us, the two were inseparable.

Moreover, the critical sensibility of the time extended the province of "literature" far beyond works of the imagination, defining the term with such broadness that its connection to religion becomes unavoidable. In his "Remarks on National Literature" (1830), Dr. Channing, by virtue of his essays on Milton and Napoleon one of the most influential critics in America, reflects the prevailing view of literary art and its scope:

> We mean the production among a people of important works in philosophy, and in the departments of imagination and taste. We mean the contributions of new truths to the stock of human knowledge. We mean the thoughts of profound and original minds, elaborated by the toil of composition, and fixed and made immortal in books. . . .It will be seen that we include under literature all the writings of superior minds, be the subjects what they may.

Religion and literature, both providing the truth that sets men free, were for Channing complementary partners in human progress. "The expression of a nation's mind in writing"—not only poetry and fiction, but history, science, law, ethics, politics—he places "among the most powerful methods . . . of forming a better race of men."[68] This all-encompassing concept of literature and its uses had especial relevance in the West, where the perceived need for both education and moral guidance was acute; but the definition was so widely held as to be axiomatic.[69] Who could doubt it? asked James Hall in 1833. "The influence of literature upon good morals, is so obvious, that it seems strange that any should indulge the idea of advancing the one without encouraging the other. It is the most powerful lever that can be used for the direction of public opinion."[70]

When the founders of the *Western Messenger* projected a magazine "devoted to religion and literature," then, they did not intend two distinct missions, nor did they worry that one might dilute or supersede the other. On the contrary, they assumed for art and religion a singleness of purpose, an assumption to which their culture gave overwhelming assent. That purpose, and the intent of their magazine, was (in Hall's words) "the direction of public opinion," and never before had the religious and literary circumstances both East and West combined so favorably to ensure its success. In the religious situation they found ample reason for publication: the West was ripe for rational religion, now that the Christian Connexion had broken the hold of sectarianism, and the East stood ready to aid the cause. And the literary climate promised talented writers, controversial and sophisticated subject matter, and an interested audience, as well as the technical facilities to produce and distribute a monthly magazine. Far from being an anomaly—an Eastern, Unitarian, literary periodical in the Calvinist, "unliterary" West—the *Messenger* was thoroughly a product of its age and place.

Implicit in those favorable circumstances, however, were certain accommodations destined to shape the *Messenger* in its maturity. To convert men to principles without promoting the sect that held those principles was a bedeviling problem for Unitarians in general, but especially so for those anxious not to offend potential sympathizers with the antisectarian "Christian" persuasion. Then, too, there was the need to accommodate three different literary interests: the regional flowering in verse and fiction, the strain of German romanticism at the heart of Transcendentalist thought, and the tradition of genteel letters so valued by more conventional Unitarians. Between Unitarian rationalism and Transcendental idealism, moreover, a third accommodation was necessary—one that would require the most delicate balance of all. Paradoxically, the very cultural situation that nurtured the *Messenger* at its birth held within it these three fundamental conflicts, which would six years later bring about the magazine's demise. But its founders confronted such problems confidently, for in 1835 New England hopes and Western realities seemed to favor their undertaking. To James Clarke, an exuberant Peabody sent word of his plans for a new periodical in January. "I feel as I have never before done," he wrote, "very sanguine & ready with your & Elliotts cooperation to commense at once."[71]

2
1835–1836
"The leading western magazine"

Although plans for the *Western Messenger* may have been begun as early as November 1834, when Clarke discussed a "new paper" with Eliot (visiting Louisville en route to St. Louis),[1] the projected journal took definite shape only after Peabody found a suitable publisher in January 1835. When he arrived at arrangements with William Gallagher and Thomas H. Shreve of Cincinnati designed to guard against "the prospect of pecuniary embarrassment," he wrote Clarke of the details.

> The Publishers of the Mirror with both of whom—fine young men—, I am well acquainted say that they will publish for me a work in the magazine form for less than a dollar a page—containing as much as the Western Monthly Mag. on a page—more than in an Examiner or North Am. Rev. page—They will publish 750 copies of each no. containing 84 pages—monthly—for <less than> 800 dollars for the 12 nos that would fill the year. Let the subscription price be 3.00$ & it wd require but 300 paying subscribers to meet all our expences. 400 subscribers would probably be sufficient to support it—taking into account all the non paying subscribers. And it seems to me that we might calculate on so many—in this region & at the East. . . . We might publish a smaller work-day 72 pages at 3 dollars a year—at this would be probably not more than 750 dolls a year cost to us. But it is desirable to have as much matter as possible.

Providing that matter, Peabody felt, could be "easily done." He, Clarke, and Eliot might do most of the writing, at least at first, but they could count on other sources of material: Huidekoper,

Albert Patterson of Buffalo, local writers ("who would now and then write"), and Eastern correspondents. With sufficient subscribers, Peabody hoped to make it "the leading western magazine."

Before mailing this letter, Peabody evidently spoke again with Gallagher and Shreve, for he appended a corrected set of figures: 750 copies monthly, of eighty-four pages each, would cost not $800 but $980, still "less than a dollar a page" but requiring an additional sixty subscribers if the magazine were to break even.[2] Why Peabody decided to order twice as many copies as subscriptions warranted is not clear. He may have intended to distribute the surplus *gratis* or to reserve enough early numbers to supply later subscribers with full sets. At any rate, the discrepancy in expenses points out the shaky business sense that plagued the magazine from the outset.[3]

Clarke warmed to the plan immediately. On 3 February he arrived in Cincinnati to exchange pulpits with Peabody for the month. Together at midweek, the two surely discussed the magazine before Peabody left for Louisville. Now, however, it was Clarke who took the initiative; relieved of the burden of composing new sermons—his old ones would be fresh in Cincinnati—he devoted his energies to promoting the *Western Examiner,* as the journal was tentatively called. In Peabody's absence, he pruned the size of each number to a "work-day" (but cheaper) seventy-two pages, a reduction that would allow 300 paid subscriptions to cover production costs completely, with some money left over for expenses. He approached Gallagher and Shreve about putting together a specimen number in April to attract subscribers, a plan later quashed by Peabody as an "unnecessary risk."[4] And by the middle of the month, Clarke had arranged for a prospectus to be printed. Incorporating some of Peabody's original ideas, it bore the unmistakable impress of Clarke's suggestions.

According to the prospectus, the magazine's proposed objects were religious: "to promote a manly, intelligent, and liberal piety; and faith working by love; to explain and defend the misunderstood and denounced principles of Unitarianism; to be a bond of Union for western Unitarians, and a connecting link with their eastern brethren." In addition, the magazine would "diffuse sound views on literature, education, schools, and benevolent enterprises"—secular concerns closely tied to the overall Unitarian missionary effort in the West. Eliot, Clarke, Patterson, and Peabody were listed as those "conducting" the magazine, although it would be "under the special superintendence" of Peabody at Cincinnati. The price was $3.00 annually for twelve numbers of "72 large medium octavo pages, making at the end of the year, two volumes, of 500 pages each."[5]

That the proposal was written and distributed in haste, before Clarke and Peabody had thought the plan through, is evident from its inconsistencies. "Large medium octavo pages" may simply be a misprint, but it is difficult to excuse the editors' faulty mathematics: 72 pages monthly total 432 pages per semiannual volume, not the 500 promised. The prospectus also offered a "specimen number by the first of April, if subscribers can be obtained"—Clarke's idea, and a practically impossible one, since the magazine was not even advertised until the third week in March. Moreover, with payment not due until "reception of the second number," the first would be, in fact if not in name, a specimen number anyway.

Despite such inaccuracies, the prospectus established one thing clearly. The *Examiner* would serve a Western audience and remedy a deficiency in Western religious life—ignorance of Unitarian views. To those who opposed Unitarianism, and to those curious about its doctrines, the prospectus explained,

> there is no answer. We have no means of reply, explanation, nor defence. Smitten on the one cheek, we must literally turn the other. The ear of the public is open, but the tongue of the press, so far as Unitarians are concerned, is silent. We think the west demands and will support such a work.—We believe there is a spirit here which asks for LIGHT.

Taking as their motto "Brethren, do not be children in understanding" (1 Cor. 14:20), the editors pledged attention "to everything which concerns the social advance of the great West in civilization and happiness."

In Cincinnati, Clarke received printed copies of the prospectus by 19 February and hurried them along to influential friends in the East: John Gorham Palfrey, editor of the *North American Review;* Jason Whitman, the retiring General Secretary of the AUA; Clarke's cousin George T. Davis, a lawyer and editor of the weekly *Franklin Mercury* in Greenfield, Massachusetts; Harvard classmate Samuel May, minister at Leicester and later General Agent for the Massachusetts Anti-Slavery Society. Margaret Fuller, Sarah Clarke, and friends at Salem and Dayton, Ohio, also received copies, as did the other principals, Peabody, Eliot, and Patterson.[6]

Clarke, neither as sanguine as Peabody about filling the magazine's pages nor as confident about paying the bills, attached to each prospectus a personal appeal for written contributions and for help in filling the subscription book. "We mean to make this a first rate affair, and to combine literature and other miscellaneous matters with religious discussions," he told Fuller. "I wish you to help me by writing on topics of religion, morals, literature, art, or anything *you* feel to be worth writing about." And could she not get Henry Hedge to contribute as well, "a letter if nothing more"? To George Davis, Clarke expressed his hopes that the magazine would "be *Western* in its character, and as free from merely conventional restrictions in spirit as may be," nothing less in fact than "the leading Western periodical."[7] These were lofty goals, to be sure, and Clarke relied not only upon his personal friends but also upon the help of the AUA to reach them. "We hope to make it acceptable & useful," he wrote of the magazine to Jason Whitman on 19 February. "But we shall need the assistance of our eastern friends in procuring us subscribers & contributions." According to Clarke's calculations, the magazine would require four hundred subscribers, one hundred of whom would have to come from Massachusetts and fifty more from elsewhere in the East. Equally as important, though, was the imprimatur of influential Unitarians from New England.

> Besides subscribers we need the sanction of *names*. We are young, few, unknown. We need therefore to be able to show letters of approval from those who *are* known. We want Dr. Channing to send an apostolic epistle to the churches scattered abroad. We wish *you* to write us a letter for the first

No. & other letters and articles of intelligence &c. as often as you can make it convenient.[8]

To this, the first of many appeals to the AUA, Clarke signed his name—and Peabody's.

Clarke was moving quickly, too quickly perhaps for Peabody, whose "special superintendence" of the magazine suddenly seemed a rather empty claim. During the exchange period, usually a respite from pastoral duties, Clarke had assumed responsibility for defining the magazine's character, advertising it, and setting deadlines, consulting Peabody after the fact, if at all. By the time Peabody received a copy of the prospectus, filled with Clarke's changes and "published of a sudden & indeed while I was away," it was already on its way East, and three weeks before the specimen number was due to appear the *Examiner* had not yet attracted a single subscriber.[9] Obviously, the April deadline could not be met. Peabody, so optimistic a month earlier, now found the situation distressing. Still haunted by the *Unitarian Essayist,* a failure largely "on account of the state of money matters," he felt "particularly anxious to have enough subscribers to begin with." "Money losing" periodicals, he confessed to Clarke, "involve so much discouragement & being so slightly circulated are of such meagre use that I have no faith in one that does not pay itself."[10] With plans already in motion when he returned to Cincinnati, Peabody joined Clarke in a drive to place the magazine on firm financial ground. He sought the advice of Nathan Guilford and J. A. James, parishioners who ran successful publishing firms in Cincinnati; Guilford recommended a subscription list of 500, James at least 425 to allow for a loss of thirty-three percent "by means of postage non paying subscribers ⋀& expence of collecting ⋁ &c." By mid-March he had written to Huidekoper and to the wealthy Unitarian industrialist Benjamin Bakewell of Pittsburgh, as well as to a number of towns in Ohio, "Portsmouth—Concord—Peterboro &c N.H. & to some other places East."[11] When his supply of prospectuses ran out, he ordered 150 more. Clarke, in the meantime, continued to solicit subscriptions by mail and by personal visits to members of his society in Louisville.[12]

After a few weeks their efforts began to bear fruit. Peabody, confident in January that Cincinnati would yield between 125 and 150 subscribers, had to be satisfied with the 65 gathered in his home city; along with the names Albert Patterson had collected in Buffalo, the list numbered 83 by 14 March. Eliot sent along 12 more names in St. Louis before he left for the East on 1 April; Peabody signed up another dozen or so in Cincinnati. By late March, however, the rate of increase had slowed considerably—at the most, Peabody reported on the 22d, about 110 subscribers had been found, all of them in Buffalo (18), St. Louis (12), and Cincinnati (75–80). From Lexington he had received no names at all; from Clarke, nothing yet.[13]

From New England the response was especially disappointing. To be sure, there was ample notice of the proposed magazine. The *Examiner* was advertised twice in the *Christian Register:* first on 21 March, when the prospectus appeared in full, and second on 4 April, when Jason Whitman recommended the new periodical as a "silent and unobtrusive missionary." Several weeks later the *Christian Examiner* printed a warm announcement that cited "the great need there is of precisely such a work to serve as a point of union and support to the western Unitarians."[14] Privately, though, Eastern friends were only moderately supportive. Palfrey sent his blessings, though he failed to insert a notice of the proposed periodical in the *North American Review;* Davis's *Franklin Mercury* was also mute. Dr. David Osgood of Boston agreed to help fill the subscription book, but he feared that the young editors would find the project "an oppressive burden and would be obliged to throw it off soon." Whitman offered to process subscriptions through the office of the AUA, but he ignored Clarke's request for a letter of endorsement for the first number.[15] Hedge, on his way to a new pulpit at Bangor, contributed nothing; only Margaret Fuller responded to Clarke's plea for written material from the East.

This lukewarm interest must have been a demoralizing blow to Clarke and Peabody, for they had clearly expected Eastern enthusiasm for the West to translate into material and financial support. On 20 May, when subscriptions stood at 270, Peabody noted with undisguised disappointment that "not more than 15" had come from Boston "& 20 from all the rest of New

England. We must have 150 more."[16] Part of the problem lay in the glut of magazines competing for New Englanders' interest and money. On his Eastern tour Eliot found Bostonians "indisposed to subscribe, because they already have so many periodicals" (1:78). Doubtless, too, many potential subscribers were put off by the proposed magazine's Western focus, and Whitman's letter to the *Register* surely did nothing to pique their interest: he described subscriptions as acts of Christian duty, almost as donations to the magazine "which, if not read by yourself, will be read with interest and profit by many who are not blessed with your high literary and religious privileges."

Fortunately, and despite the fact that the magazine was not heavily advertised in the press, the West proved a better source of subscribers, though not without some effort. (Clarke went to Lexington himself to interest readers but came away with only 10, gotten "with great difficulty.") When the first number of the magazine appeared in late June, subscriptions numbered just over 300, most of them from west of the Alleghenies.[17]

Complicating matters further during the planning stage of the magazine were the strains of multiple editorship. In the introduction to the first number Eliot acknowledged the problem.

> The distance at which the Editors live apart, is a disadvantage which will, to some degree, affect this magazine. We are stationed at different points in an immense territory. . . . Of course we can have little personal intercourse together, and absolutely no concert in regard to the articles which we prepare. . . . A book chiefly prepared by several persons, without concerted action, must be, in some degree, desultory. (1:2–3)

The lack of "personal intercourse together" accounted, for instance, for the embarrassing necessity of changing the magazine's name, after Eliot discovered an atheist journal entitled the *Western Examiner* in St. Louis. Peabody wrote Clarke in a panic, fearing that "the name will prevent subscribers" but unable to decide upon a better one. He considered "Spectator," then dismissed it as sounding "orthodox & indefinite"; on the other hand, he was wary of any title that smacked of radicalism: "Jackson People & Universalists choose such names as Morning

Star Rising Sun—Globe—Truth Teller—Herald of Truth &
such bombastic inanities, wh above all things I desire ever espe-
ciallially [*sic*] to abhor & eschew." Finally, Peabody left the decision to Eliot and Clarke.[18] But Eliot was on his way East, and the
relatively simple decision became a protracted one, with the
magazine remaining nameless for several months (Clarke re-
ferred to it as "the Occidental Repository or whatever we may
call our maga" on 30 March, as the "Western Branch" on
14 June) until one of the editors, probably Clarke, chose the
Western Messenger.[19]

For a professional editor, or at least a more decisive one, the
geographical separation may have presented only a minor in-
convenience. Yet as the deadline for the first number drew
nearer, it became increasingly obvious that Peabody regarded
editorial responsibilities as better delegated than confronted.
Beset with bouts of "lung fever" (probably tuberculosis) and by
nature cautious, he turned to Clarke for help. Clarke, however,
proved an unreliable adviser in the spring of 1835. He had—
although Peabody was unaware of it—decided in a fit of
homesickness to return to Boston, temporarily, he wrote his old
professor Palfrey on 24 April, but as soon as a replacement
could be found. For the next two months he weighed the decision, awaiting a substitute who never came, and by 23 June he
changed his mind, assuring AUA Secretary Charles Briggs that
"I have given up the idea of leaving my society ⟨this year⟩." In
the interim, Peabody gathered articles and struggled with the
decisions alone. "I wish you could come up here only for a day.
There a[re] 20 things I want a consultation on wh. cannot be in
a letter, which 2 hours talk wd make it all straight," he wrote
Clarke in June.[20]

With Clarke distracted, Eliot in Boston, and Patterson
isolated in Buffalo, Peabody assembled the inaugural number
of the *Messenger* by himself in May. Fortunately, each of the
coeditors had sent material, if not advice, and Peabody had
some definite ideas about the scope and purpose of the magazine that made the task of choosing articles somewhat less "de-
sultory" than Eliot feared. Short essays would be best, Peabody
believed, "from 5 to 6 or 7 pages but pungent—containing only
one point forcibly put—not a sheaf of arrows—but one arrow,

keenly barbed." Several years earlier, he had envisioned a successor to the ill-fated *Unitarian Essayist,* a more balanced magazine containing "something doctrinal, something practical" in each issue; that is, a mixture of the theological and the ethical. Moreover, he wanted sufficient variety to appeal to the tastes and interests of the magazine's broad audience, as well as "an article from each principal quarter whence subscribers come." And finally, he favored essays designed not only to entertain but to convince: "If we want our magazine to have a stand, the way & the only way is—*To discuss with more ability than any body else the great questions that agitate* [the] *Western mind*—We must not merely[?] be interesting. We must be strong."[21]

With these standards in mind, he chose the material for the first number. The printers began setting type on 20 May, and Peabody soon realized "how much must be written to order & measure." To fill out pages he was forced to tinker with nearly every piece, an exasperating chore. His pleas to Clarke were nothing if not desperate: "Send some things—Poetry—Critical notices any thing—of a half page—or a page—or intelligence of 3 sentences—Things to be put in or not just as is convenient." On 19 June, after "working like a dog," Peabody learned that the printers were completing the final page; four days later, almost five months after his initial agreement with Gallagher and Shreve, the first number of the *Western Messenger* appeared.[22]

Peabody thought the June issue "a good one," and he had every right to, for by his own standards the issue was balanced and well written. Its religious content leaned toward the doctrinal, as had the *Unitarian Essayist.* Huidekoper, in fact, continued the polemics of the earlier magazine with a "letter" addressed to the Presbyterian minister at Meadville on the deity of Jesus, a calm and clear-headed examination of Scripture presenting the Unitarian position that the Bible provided ample evidence against Christ's oneness with God and no evidence for it (1 : 36–43).[23] In his "Notes on Proof Texts" Peabody reinforced Huidekoper's argument with an exegesis of John 1 : 1 to show Christ's "subordination to the Supreme" (1 : 49). And James Perkins provided a long, cogent review of Beecher's *Plea for the West,* agreeing with the need for religious education but piercing to the heart of Beecher's extremist logic: to guard the United States against subversion by the Catholic church, Perkins pointed out, Beecher "substitutes his own, or his creed's infallibility for that of the Pope and the Roman Councils" and thus risks the very identification of church and state he so fears (1 : 17, 4–5). Balancing this doctrinal material with "something practical," Albert Patterson called for more charitable consideration of Unitarian views by Western Calvinists (1 : 30–35).

Subordinate to the *Messenger*'s religious purposes but important as an adjunct to them was attention to Western literature. Peabody was determined "in some way & in some degree to associate the Maga. with Western Literature," as he told Huidekoper. The first number contained a generous selection of Ohio writers, particularly in its "Western Poetry" column, a feature Peabody hoped someday to extend to prose writers as well. No poet himself—he admitted as much to Clarke—Peabody chose mainly to print representative verse by Gallagher, Hall, and others. Other Western writing was examined in reviews of such diverse works as John L. Riddell's *Synopsis of the Flora of the Western States* and the annual *Transactions* of the Western Literary Institute, a professional association of teachers.

Rounding out the first number were articles devoted to miscellaneous Western affairs. These pieces served two purposes, to capitalize on local interests and to provide the "bond of union" among area Unitarians that the prospectus had promised. Here, as elsewhere, the selection and treatment of local events were colored by religious considerations. Clarke, for instance, reported Alexander Campbell's visit to Louisville, during which the leader of the Disciples preached from the Unitarian pulpit, and reprinted parts of Campbell's sermon on Christian union. "I could agree to all he said, with my whole heart," Clarke concluded. "It strikes me that all this ground, is exactly what Unitarians have always taken, plead, and prayed for" (1 : 60). Peabody provided a less passionate summary of the heresy charges leveled against Beecher by the Presbyterian minister at Cincinnati, Joshua L. Wilson,[24] and filled the final pages with miscellaneous "intelligence": a letter from Eliot on Eastern support for his St. Louis church, news of Unitarian societies in the

West, notice of a projected volume of sermons by J. G. Palfrey.

With few exceptions the contents of the first number of the *Messenger* fulfilled Peabody's demands for both variety and a primarily religious focus. To a great degree, moreover, the four interrelated emphases of that inaugural issue—that is, doctrinal and practical theology, Western literature and news—governed the magazine through the end of the year.

The doctrinal essays fell into two groups: attacks on Calvinism and defenses of Unitarianism. Of the first, the series "Presbyterianism and Christianity" was the most comprehensive, an examination of the biblical foundations of Presbyterianism. Beecher's trial and the impending split between Old and New Schools made the series timely, and the Unitarians had something to gain, of course, by exposing weaknesses in Presbyterian doctrine. In successive installments, four in all by year's end, Peabody and Thomas Maylin, a Cincinnati teacher,[25] rejected the doctrines of natural depravity, imputation, and atonement, concluding that Presbyterianism ran counter to the teachings of Christ and the common sense of man: "Is a system true whose tendency is to make men *slaves* of God, and not *children* of God?" (1:442). The series on proof texts assailed Calvinism on another front, the issue of the Trinity; each month either Peabody or Maylin found Trinitarianism an illogical and scripturally unfounded concept. Huidekoper's letters on the diety of Christ (1:108–116, 186–93), Clarke's argument against the Trinitarian "proof" in the seventh chapter of John (1:75–82), and Maylin's against the first chapter of John (1:552–60)—all helped to maintain a combative posture throughout the first eight numbers of the *Messenger.*

And while they chipped away at the theology of the orthodox, the *Messenger*'s writers defended their own misunderstood faith. Emerson's friend and classmate William H. Furness of Philadelphia answered the charge that Unitarians were arrogant deists who denied the holy mysteries. Mystery, he said, lies not in doctrinal contradictions (such as the concept of the Trinity) but in the "hidden and the unknown" relationships of God and man. "The more rational a man is in his religion," argued Furness, "the plainer is it, not that he rejects, but that he recognizes mystery" (1:284–92). Perkins countered charges that

Unitarianism failed to touch the heart (1:347–50) and that Unitarians "in place of principles . . . are content with mere good *works*" (1:491–93). These were, of course, old accusations in New England; but in the West, where liberal religion was still equated with Arminianism and antinomianism, the *Messenger* once again took up the standard of the much-maligned faith.

The second emphasis, practical religion, examined how doctrinal differences affected behavior and everyday life. The spirit of persecution was so prevalent among Christian sects, wrote Eliot, that "we fear some persons are lead [*sic*] to think that their religion itself affords sanction to this barbarous usage." Recent violence against Catholics and the sensational, sometimes lurid, accounts of Papal atrocities in the popular press were the tragic results of such misconceptions (1:81–88).[26] Clarke, who could be vicious when angered, reported that a Presbyterian minister in Louisville had denied the sacrament to two Unitarian women because he considered them infidels, then paralleled the incident to the parable of the Pharisee and the Publican in the eighteenth chapter of Luke, with the minister cast as the self-righteous Pharisee (1:432–34). Against these examples of bigotry and religious "exclusiveness" the *Messenger* advocated a Unitarian ideal of benevolence and tolerance. When Eliot condemned mob violence (1:204–9) and appealed for aid to the poor (1:311–17), he spoke to immediate conditions in both East and West.

The columns on "Western Poetry" best represent the magazine's commitment to local writing. Intended to encourage regional poets, as well as to attract Western subscribers, the series seemed hamstrung from the outset by Peabody's admission that "men among us are yet living, not writing poems" (1:61). Yet nearly a dozen Western poets appeared in the five installments and in separate contributions, including Gallagher, Shreve, and Hall, and the criticism, though often vapid, was discriminating enough at times to prevent the series from sinking into mere puffery. Shreve, one reviewer wrote, "could take a place in the front rank of American bards, were he disposed to apply himself, and pay more attention—a great deal more would be necessary—to the niceties of versification, the harmony of numbers, and the correctness of rhyme" (1:279). The evaluations of F. W. Thomas were more succinct: in his mind "flowers of poesy are sadly choked up with weeds" (1 : 127), and his novel *Clinton Bradshaw* (1835) was "*mere* story" without a "moral aim" (1 : 444). There was in fact less parochialism than one might expect in a magazine eager to hold its Western readers, in large part because the critical dictates of Unitarian aesthetics demanded more than local color and fidelity to detail. Peabody set the tone for the series with his claim that Western poets should not

> write of wilderness or prairie, of log cabins, or scalping knives. They may write of these matters, and still, in senti-ment and in form, in all that gives character and soul to literature, be servile imitators of the hack-writers of the Lon-don press. [The best Western poetry is] written out of West-ern mind, and colored by Western character. We do not suppose that what is written west, will differ much from what is produced east of the Alleghanies. (1 : 126)

Western "intelligence" was relegated after the first number to the *Messenger*'s back pages, material for the editor's "Balaam box," as Clarke called it, "to fill up with."[27] Though the maga-zine remained committed to diffusing "sound views on litera-ture, education, schools, and benevolent enterprises," those views were increasingly incorporated into religious or literary essays, and the editors seemed content to leave news to the newspapers. In the second number appeared the first install-ment of a series of profiles on Western ministers (1 : 130–33), but Peabody worried that the series might "sink us from preachers in peoples estimation into mere theatre going de-scribers of preachers" and the plan was discontinued.[28] In its place were essays on local geography and history: William Clarke's "Western Sketches" (1 : 225–27), for example, and Pea-body's "Early Discovery in the Mississippi Valley" (1 : 434–39).

The persistence of these four emphases through the end of 1835 would be understandable had a single editor been guiding the magazine. In fact, the *Messenger* had been conducted quite haphazardly all the while, and the consistent point of view and policy shows that even with multiple editors the magazine could, as Eliot predicted, "preserve in their purity" the principles to which it was devoted. Exhausted by his work on the first number and reluctant to subject his already weak lungs to another summer of "bad air" in Cincinnati, Peabody headed east on 13 July with his wife and infant son, after collecting the material for the second (August) number. Behind him he left fifteen or twenty articles of his own, along with contributions from Eliot, Huidekoper, Perkins, Fuller, Clarke, and several local writers—enough, he hoped, to fill three issues—and turned the magazine over to a young New England lawyer, Uriah Tracy Howe of Cincinnati. Two weeks later, on 28 July, Clarke too started east for his annual visit, stopping on the way to confer with Howe and Gallagher about the magazine. Thus by the time the August number appeared, about the first of the month, the *Messenger's* two guiding spirits had temporarily abandoned their journal to the care of strangers.[29]

Howe, a classmate of Perkins at the Round Hill School, had neither theological training nor editorial experience, but as a member of the Semi-Colon Club he could rely heavily on friends who had both. On the whole he did a creditable job, seeing the second issue through the press (much of it had been set up and printed before Peabody left) and supervising the third, which was delayed due to a shortage of paper (1:228). Still, Howe found the editing work "entirely foreign to his profession," as Peabody later admitted to Clarke, and he was engaged to be married in September, so he relinquished his editorship that month.[30]

Exactly who took the reins next is not wholly clear. As Charles E. Blackburn has pointed out, internal evidence in the October and November numbers strongly suggests that James Perkins accepted primary responsibility: four of his essays and three poems appear during those months, and he provided the brief "Critical Notices" usually required of the editor at the last minute. Most probably, though, Gallagher and Shreve shared the control over the magazine with Perkins. After the *Cincinnati Mirror* suspended publication on 24 October, due to financial problems, they were free to lend a hand; Peabody later thanked them for "the aid of their pens, and for their friendly oversight of the work" (1:731); and Clarke, in a letter of 5 November, refers to multiple editors for that month's issue.[31]

By the time Clarke and Peabody returned to the Ohio Valley in early November, four numbers had appeared in their absence, with the December issue partially set in type. Because of Gallagher and Shreve's bankruptcy the *Messenger* had a new publisher, James B. Marshall of Cincinnati, and the transfer delayed the issue a week. From Louisville Clarke mailed suggestions about the selection of material, but it was almost certainly Perkins who supervised the remainder of the December number, not Peabody, for the young minister had returned from his Eastern tour too ill to manage more than his pastoral duties. The rigors of travel, the pressure of composing the annual Harvard Phi Beta Kappa poem, and a busy schedule of visiting and preaching had left Peabody weak and dispirited, and the autumn of 1835 brought devastating personal tragedy, the death of his son Samuel and the sudden blindness of his wife. "I am now perfectly well except my lungs," he wrote Huidekoper bravely, just after Christmas. "But they are so easily irritated & fevered & this is followed by such prostration of body & mind, that I cannot bear much bodily fatigue, nor any responsibility or mental excitement."[32] As in the previous May, help was scarce. Eliot was far away in St. Louis, Albert Patterson sick and discouraged in Buffalo (he would soon leave the Unitarian pulpit for the Episcopal church), and Clarke preparing to leave again, this time for a ten-week missionary tour of the South. Until he returned, Perkins agreed to edit the *Messenger*.[33]

Response to the *Messenger*, meanwhile, had been generally favorable, if not overwhelmingly so. Subscriptions were up, from about 300 in June to some 370 in December, and Peabody observed that the second volume "ought to start at the same rate of increase with 450 subscribers—wh. I think it probably will." Just as important, the magazine was enjoying good reviews. The *Cincinnati Mirror*'s reviewer—surely either Shreve or Gallagher—noticed the first number of the *Messenger* as "handsome and well got up," the second as "generally interesting, and occasionally able," the third as "intelligent, dignified, and interesting" and "the best of the three" so far published. Hall's *Western Monthly Magazine* praised the *Messenger*'s "intellectual freedom and good taste" in literary matters but reserved judgment on its "religious doctrines." In Boston the *Christian Regis-*

ter "most cheerfully" encouraged subscribers to the magazine, "as well for its own merits, as for the aid of an undertaking to spread Christian truth among our brethren of the west," citing the "Presbyterianism and Christianity" series as especially valuable. Most telling, perhaps, was the review in the *Christian Examiner* for November 1835, which hailed the *Messenger* as "a fresh breeze from the West" and predicted success for the magazine "[s]hould it continue to support its present character."[34]

In fact, by early 1836 the *Messenger* had indeed developed a character of its own, albeit a character somewhat different from the one planned and advertised nearly a year before. Less a "bond of union" among Western Unitarians—except insofar as it reinforced the doctrinal positions they already accepted—the magazine was clearly directed toward those rational, literate Westerners who, the editors felt, accepted Calvinism only because they had not yet been liberated by Unitarianism. "Presbyterianism is odious to the mass of this community," Clarke had written confidently to Jason Whitman. "The Western people will not bear it—depend upon that."[35] As a consequence, the *Messenger* under Peabody and his surrogates became, by policy and by circumstances, a missionary to the unconverted rather than a newsletter to believers.

As it ministered to the "spirit here which asks for LIGHT," however, the *Messenger* generated an unavoidable amount of heat. Eliot, recognizing the danger early, had tried in the introduction to the first number to clarify the magazine's position. While opposed to "all bigotry, intolerance and exclusiveness," he wrote,

> we hope to avoid as far as possible a sectarian character. We trust in God that our object is not to build up a sect, but to establish the Truth. . . . We care little for the name of Unitarian. We are willing that the word should be blotted out of the theological vocabulary, if whatever of truth is embodied in it, were but generally diffused.

Sectarianism, he concluded, meant "seeking our own praise more than the truth of God" (1:2). But that fine distinction in theory failed to hold up in practice. Peabody believed that the

Messenger's duty was to "go down into the throng & stand in the front & get standing there & be observed"; he considered "bitter doctrinal" articles best suited to the magazine's readers.[36] In its first eight numbers the *Messenger* attacked Calvinist doctrine, censured Calvinist ministers, criticized Calvinist writers, and advocated a system of theology, morality, and aesthetics readily identifiable as Unitarian. Counting these out, to paraphrase Twain, what was left was nonsectarian.

The liberal voice of the *Messenger,* in short, had begun to sound decidedly illiberal, and while the magazine's defenses of Unitarianism earned it high marks in the Boston press, its combative stance bothered Perkins and Clarke more than a little. To the former, a Unitarian by inclination, not by training, the debates on proof texts and doctrine must have seemed so much hair-splitting, a good deal like the endless indulgence in technicalities that had soured his career as a lawyer.[37] By the end of the year he could be silent no longer. Unitarians, Perkins wrote in the February issue, were as narrowminded as any other sect "in proportion to their numbers and advantages"; it was time to "put off this cant, and arrogant, and contradictory title; talk less of Liberal Christianity; the nonsense of the Trinity; and the unmeaning mystery of the Atonement . . . [and] feel more that we are not the elect of the world, the only wise men" (1:524–25). That Perkins published such a biting attack in the *Messenger* indicates, of course, just how tolerant the magazine's spirit could be. But that he needed to publish it at all—especially the stinging allusion to the Puritan "elect"—indicates how intolerant the *Messenger* had become.

The sources of Clarke's dissatisfaction ran deeper. He and Peabody had quarreled over matters of policy from the beginning. At first the questions were niggling ones: the magazine's name, the anonymity of contributors, the use of catchy titles. In each case Peabody backed down, but Clarke in turn saw Peabody's submissiveness itself as hazardous:

> Peabody you are too *cautious*—your organ [of cautiousness, a phrenological term] prevented you from having the name "Branch"—you feared people would laugh—what if they did? So much the better—it prevented your letting the *names* of authors accompany their articles which is a great mistake.

Every body says it would be much more interesting, if we took the responsibility in that way. . . . Your "caution" avoids what is strange & odd—which is the very thing to excite people. . . . You must not be in such good taste, my friend.[38]

It was Peabody's "good taste" that contributed to the first major breach between the two men. Alone among the Boston friends, Margaret Fuller had contributed generously to the *Messenger,* three long review-essays. Without consulting Peabody, Clarke promised to put Fuller's review of the biographies of George Crabbe and Hannah More in the first issue, and her essays on Bulwer-Lytton and on the play *Philip Van Artevelde* in the second. But Peabody, who was unaware of Fuller's authorship, found her opening remarks in the More and Crabbe piece "overwhelming" and published the essay in truncated form, without the introductory notice. "I read it to the Mirror people," he explained to Clarke on 29 June, "& they said it ought not to go in. It is undignified—you may depend on it—& I cannot believe it suits the West." He worried, too, about the other essays, "good articles" but also unsuited to a Western audience: only the one on Bulwer-Lytton would appear in the August number, "if it seems fitting." And of the articles Clarke himself had written for the second issue, Peabody thought "not one of them worthy of you" and singled out a Clarke piece on phrenology as "neither more nor less than a newspaper squib."[39]

Clarke was embarrassed, hurt, and furious, all at the same time. Peabody, after all, had begged him for articles, and the publishers had no business interfering with editorial decisions. "Suppose that thing on Phrenology *was* a squib—it would be read," Clarke answered on 6 July.

> I tell you, my friend, I have an especial eye to making people read. I knew the Van A. article would not be read *generally*—but then to compensate—a very decent fraction of our subscribers would read it with peculiar relish. Keats for instance & at the east many. But publish only one of them if you choose—& that one had better be Bulwer.

The following day Peabody apologized for the peevish tone of his first letter ("written with a weary hand—a tired mind—a

lonely feeling & late at night"), praised Clarke's writing pro-
fusely, and promised to put the *Philip Van Artevelde* review in the
third number.[40]

By November, however, when the two men returned from
the East, Fuller's essay had still not appeared in print, nor had
several articles Clarke had sent from New England. To his
friend Margaret, Clarke offered his apologies; to Peabody he
was indignant.

> I see they only published *one* of the pieces I sent. Probably
> there was good reason for it—yet I do not like to have my
> articles rejected, feeling in some sort responsible for the
> Magazine, I like to be able to do what I can for it *in my own
> way*. Now we all like to have our own way! For instance the
> Van Artevelde piece—they do not choose to publish it I see
> because it does not exactly suit *their taste*. I know that to many
> it would be *caviare*. . . . You see I want to do something for this
> work, but to the extent of 10 or 12 pp. in each number I must
> feel myself *unlimited* & *absolute*. Is this asking too much?

Once again Peabody sent his regrets, explaining that the substitute editors had done their best and that he had "had nothing
to do with putting articles in or out of late." "If your feelings
are hurt," he reminded Clarke, "you shd remember the circumstances."[41]

When Fuller's essay finally appeared, in the December issue
of the *Messenger*, the immediate occasion for argument ended,
but the fundamental disagreements between Peabody and
Clarke remained. Much more than temperamental differences,
though those were marked, their intellectual incompatibility
accounted in great measure for the course of the *Messenger*.
They differed, first of all, on the significance of the term *western*. Peabody quite clearly saw it as a primarily geographical
distinction: "western" articles were those whose subject matter
was located in the West.[42] For Clarke, on the other hand, "Wes-
ternness" was a state of mind and character, "a free and un-
shackled spirit" usually associated with the geographic West but
not always so: in Cincinnati he perceived "some of the Eastern
spirit of caste and exclusiveness."[43]

The difference in definition—Peabody's simplistically literal,
Clarke's extravagantly romantic—had a major effect on the

early stages of the "leading western magazine." There is more than a touch of paternalism in Peabody's decision to restrict the *Messenger* to "an article in every number on general literature & only one," for he considered his local audience neither interested nor refined enough to appreciate more. "We must first ⟨create a 1⟩ get people to read—" he explained to Clarke.

> Then we may make a taste in our readers. We must not stand on a hill afar off & cry "Come here". . . . Hall's Magazine was absolutely dying a natural death from well written articles— on such matters as Machiavelli—English Statesman &c &c. excellent articles they were. But nobody read or cared about them. . . . So strongly am I convinced of this that if Dr Channing were to send an Article on Milton as good as his first, I shd hardly thank him for it. It would chime in with no strong Western feelings.[44]

The demise of the "Western Poetry" column can be similarly explained. Literary historians have generally assumed that the *Messenger*'s commitment to regional literature flagged because it ran out of local talent.[45] But surely this was not the case; numerous collections of Western verse show that there were poets aplenty in the Ohio Valley.[46] What Peabody *did* feel he had exhausted was the supply of Western poetry in which the Unitarian ideal of "moral beauty" took precedence over description. As Western writers strove to capture the frontier in vivid detail, Peabody's aesthetic sensibility rendered him incapable of appreciating poetry "of wilderness or prairie, of log cabins, or scalping knives." Simply put, he wanted local poetry that transcended the local. Since literary value lay in the stimulation of universal moral sentiments, Peabody saw no particular reason to exalt Western verse over Eastern, beyond the practical need to appease readers with familiar names and subjects.

If aesthetically Peabody adhered to conservative Unitarian tastes, philosophically the stamp of his Harvard training was no less profound. Here too he and Clarke had little in common. As Daniel Walker Howe has demonstrated at length, Harvard Unitarians "believed men ought to be controlled by reason and the moral sense, but they recognized that in practice much, if not most, human behavior stemmed from emotional impulses."[47] Sharing this uneasy skepticism about human nature, Peabody had little patience with Clarke's faith in inner principles. In a remarkably frank letter of 7 July 1835, Peabody made clear how thoroughly he embraced the Lockean empiricism that Clarke found so objectionable. Responding to Clarke's warm notice of Bronson Alcott's teaching methods (1:223), Peabody took the occasion to lay bare his misgivings about "all that German philosophy."

> I am surprised you sh<u>d</u> be so lacking in good sense. Don't you know that people never think—& especially never act from convictions of reason—but always against them. . . . People act from the passions & affections—& you cannot make men fear love hate or desire any thing that is not in some way or other palpable to the senses. . . . The greatest objection to Unitarianism is that it asks men to think—It is an objection that has its foundation in human nature. The most useful ministers are those who make their people think least of the reasons of duty.

As much as any other, this question of man's intuitive moral sense—the transcendental "Reason"—was the rock on which conservative and radical Unitarianism split. Clarke's response to Peabody does not survive, if in fact he made one. But it is not difficult to imagine the reaction of the man who later wrote that "something within me revolted at all such attempts to explain soul out of sense, deducing mind from matter, or tracing the origin of ideas to nerves, vibrations, and vibratiuncles."[48]

Their sharp break over accepted Unitarian epistemology points out, finally, Peabody and Clarke's differing conceptions of Unitarianism as a denomination, and, in turn, their disagreement over the *Messenger*'s role as a sectarian organ. For Peabody, to be Unitarian was to be anti-Trinitarian. Like his patron Huidekoper, who viewed the *Messenger* as the "natural successor" to the polemical *Unitarian Essayist*, Peabody found Calvinism—Presbyterianism especially—the "blind, brutalizing, palsying" force with which Unitarianism could not coexist. What a "curious fact," he told Huidekoper, that in the West belief in the "mathematical absurdity" of the Trinity "constitutes the Christian & no Christian."[49] But so it was. Unitarianism could not grow until Trinitarianism had been rooted out. The *Messenger*'s almost obsessive attention to that key Calvinist doctrine was the inevitable result.

While Peabody isolated Trinitarianism as the chief impediment to the spread of liberal religion, Clarke saw the enemy as orthodoxy—whether it lay in the formal creeds used by other sects to determine heresy or in the unwritten yet powerful pressures within his own denomination to encourage doctrinal conformity. In part his reaction was personal: he had gone West in 1833 to escape what he considered the constricting conservatism of Boston's Unitarian establishment regarding the "infidelity" of German idealism. Andrews Norton he found especially offensive, for the former dean of Harvard's Divinity School had roundly attacked both Goethe and his admirers in the press. To Clarke, Norton represented a narrow-mindedness antithetical to the spirit of Unitarianism, and he feared that Norton's view was the prevailing one in New England. "The whole system of logic & philosophy must be reformed," he wrote boldly in May 1833—but he wrote it in his private diary and remained silent. Instead, harboring the grudge against Norton and his kind, Clarke went West. There, at Emerson's urging, he at last vented his anger publicly, not at Professor Norton but at "Nortonism."[50] In the first number of the *Messenger* he published "German Theology and American Folly. Orthodoxism Characterized," an attack on the "diseased love of orthodoxy, and fear of heresy" which, in Boston and elsewhere, "has gained an undue predominance over the love of truth" (1:43–47).

"The love of truth"—that, for Clarke, was the essence of Unitarianism. Unlike Peabody, who revered the denomination as a body of doctrine, Clarke valued it as a method of inquiry, one whose greatest threat came not from other sects but from rigid, self-imposed boundaries to thought. "Church orthodoxy dwells not in the Love of Truth, but in the dread of Error," he believed; "therefore every honest Seeker dislikes Orthodoxy." His own honest seeking had left him in "quagmires of speculation" about Unitarianism, he confessed to Margaret Fuller, yet he was certain about what it was *not*.

People take Unitarianism because they can understand it—because it is not harsh & violent—because it is not ranting, dogmatising, tyrannical. . . . [I]t is nothing but Rational & Liberal Christianity—Christianity set free from the trammels of system.[51]

He refused to fill his church by preaching sectarian theology, for his goal was to make his congregation "Xns. not nominal but real" rather than "speculative Unitarians." Whereas Peabody considered Unitarianism "the faith I believe to make one truly religious," Clarke's hope for the West lay in "Unitarianism, or something equivalent to it" (1:587). The qualification is all-important. As Clarke insisted to William Henry Channing, he was "no Apostle of Unitarianism." Peabody was.[52]

By the end of 1835, both Clarke and Peabody recognized that their differences in temperament, philosophy, and theology were too acute to be ignored. So when Peabody offered him the sole editorship of the *Messenger* on 3 December 1835, Clarke seized the opportunity to restore the objective for which he believed it had been founded—the broad, nonsectarian examination of religion, literature, and society. After his return from the South, he left for Cincinnati on 9 March to transfer the *Messenger* to Louisville.[53] In a letter of that date, published in the May 1836 number, Peabody bade farewell to the subscribers, promising that under Clarke's supervision the "character and purpose of the work will remain as heretofore—a medium through which western Unitarians may communicate with each other, and make known their views to the world around them." To Clarke himself he added a personal valedictory for the magazine: "make it all that I have wished it to be" (1:731).

If Peabody suspected that Clarke had different intentions—as he surely must have—he did not have to wait long before his suspicions were confirmed. In the April 1836 number, the first under his control,[54] Clarke dedicated the magazine to four principles. The first three, understanding, intellectual freedom, and a spirit of love, were unobjectionable enough. But the last principle may have given Peabody pause.

We desire to show . . . that religion can pervade every thing, and ought to do so. In this Magazine, therefore, we treat of many topics, literary, scientific, philosophic, economical—but we would speak of all in a religious spirit. . . . Religion has been hurt by being looked upon as a separate business, a thing apart from practical life. We would have every thing baptized into religion. (1:658–60)

Whether Peabody read this broad statement of purpose as a slap at his own cautiousness, it is impossible to say. Surely, though, he noticed a glaring omission in the new dedication: not a mention of Unitarianism. So broadly had Clarke conceived of the magazine's scope, in fact, that he pledged that it would be intolerant only of "the Pharisaic spirit of bigotry, tyranny, and sectarianism," and he opened its pages "to all who appear to write with a good purpose . . . [and] with clearness, point, and earnestness" (1:730).

This is not to say that the *Messenger* retained none of its denominational character, but only that under Clarke its exposition of Unitarianism continued for different reasons. Huidekoper's historical examinations of the Trinity (2:145–55), John Q. Day's "Scriptural Proof of the Unity of God" (2:227–30), James Walker's discourse on the "Two Natures of Christ" (2:236–40)—all appeared because they appealed to the understanding, not because they were sectarian. Clarke continued his attacks on Presbyterian "exclusiveness" (2:62–70, 208) not because Presbyterianism was doctrinally false but because in practical affairs its emphasis on human creeds encouraged religious intolerance.[55]

Gone, though, were the relentless exegeses of proof texts, the strident quarrels with Calvinist doctrine, the "liberality of stamping others as illiberal," as Perkins wryly put it (1:524). In their place was a renewed emphasis on Christian union. When Louisville's Baptists accused Unitarians of sympathy for Catholics, German infidels, and Campbellites,[56] Clarke had proudly answered that the *Messenger* had "*affinities* with what is good in every denomination" (1:357); he now devoted the magazine to examining those affinities. Convinced that "the elements of western character are working together with, and modifying religious systems," he declared in his introduction to the second volume that "all Christians are on the same road."[57] Perkins, too, dropped his defenses of Unitarianism, claiming the differences between sects merely the "uninfluential, and therefore in our eyes, unimportant points" of theology, not morality (1:548). And Eliot, in his correspondence from his missionary tours, hailed the spread of the nonsectarian Disciples as "very encouraging to us" (1:604) and maintained that the true missionary spirit "does not impel one sect to labor against another, and fill its own cistern by draining a neighboring one, but it sends all sects to the same well" (1:741).

Though the *Messenger*'s new emphasis on Christian union placed it, Clarke believed, in the mainstream of Western opinion, its social criticism showed it to be no panderer to popular ideas. Led by Perkins, the *Messenger* examined the "leveling influences" of Jacksonian democracy, especially its economic aspects, and declared them dangerous to the West's promise of a new moral order. Opposed not to democracy itself but to its excesses, Perkins saw in the rise of agrarianism and political egalitarianism a dangerous distraction from the cultivation of moral character. Believing that "all institutions of every kind" were subordinate to "the full development of each individual" (1:309), he found rule by the masses no better than rule *of* the masses, for under each system "property, in the place of knowledge and goodness, is made too much the graduating scale" (1:594). He objected not to the right to private property—in fact, he defended that right (1:594)—but to the power of propertied classes to rule regardless of their moral fitness.[58] Economic democracy bred "individual moral torpor" (2:93); political democracy led to irreverence for proper authority and a "sense of self-dependence, and . . . of contempt for all that is opposed to self" (2:94). What Perkins proposed was "Christian Republicanism": rule by a moral, rather than merely a natural, aristocracy (1:318–20). The West was destined to be the seat of this "new practical philosophy," but first "men must be taught not to respect mere wealth nor place, but to consider the intellect, education, and character of each individual . . . as giving him a claim to social influence and standing" (1:598). Politically conservative in its premises, Perkins's social criticism was nonetheless radical in its implications.

The *Messenger*'s literary interests also shifted under Clarke's new editorship. Freed from Peabody's reservations about things

German,[59] Clarke began translating De Wette's *Theodore; or, the Skeptic's Progress to Belief,* which appeared monthly beginning in February 1836. Essentially the chronicle of a young man's religious pilgrimage from rational skepticism to intuitive faith, the translation would, Clarke hoped, serve as a corrective to the widespread fear of German infidelity (1:531). For the same reason he included translations and defenses of Goethe (1:457–59, 474–75, 824–27; 2:59–62) and of Schiller's philosophical letters (2:361–68). In September 1836 a second series of translations began, of the German theologian Wilhelm Krug's argument against the atonement of Christ, contributed by Samuel Osgood, a recent graduate of the Divinity School at Harvard come West to take Peabody's place in Cincinnati.[60] British as well as German writers began to appear in the *Messenger,* among them poets almost unknown in the West.[61] Perkins contributed a long review of Wordsworth (whom he valued "not so much because [he was] a great poet, as because a great Christian Philosopher"), excerpting the Intimations ode and other of Wordsworth's "poetry in the highest, divinest sense,— that which speaks of God in us" (1:460–65). Of Tennyson Clarke wrote, in a review of *Poems, Chiefly Lyrical* (1830), "The thoughts are often very trivial, the sentiment wholly insignificant, but the *form* is so exquisite, that we smack our lips" (2:323–25). And through the poet's brother George, a resident of Louisville, the *Messenger* introduced to the world John Keats's previously unpublished "Ode to Apollo" (1:763) and two sections from his journals (1:772–77, 820–23), which Clarke praised both for their stylistic beauty and for their "sincere depth of religious sentiment" (1:773).

Its religious views more tolerant, its social criticism more incisive, its literary interests sophisticated and eclectic, the *Messenger* under Clarke had become what he had always envisioned it to be: "an arena," as he told Jason Whitman early in 1835, "where all honest truth seekers may meet." But as Clarke quickly discovered, to redirect the *Messenger's* policy was one thing, to contend with its financial problems quite another. For he had inherited from Peabody a business history so muddled that after editing only two numbers he was almost ready to abandon the whole affair in frustration. The problems were as old as the magazine itself: subscribers grumbled that their copies were lost or arrived late, that postage costs or subscription rates were too high. "I have hardly met with an individual who has rec. all his nos." Clarke had complained to Peabody back in November. "I think that our Magazine will succeed now if we can manage only the forwarding so that there may be no more mistakes."[62] With the third number the New England subscription lists had been sold to the Boston bookseller James Munroe, who as agent assumed responsibility for collecting payments, on commission (1:228; 2:352–53). But the haphazard supervision of the *Messenger* in the fall of 1835 left Munroe wondering who was in charge in the West. Numbers for the Eastern subscribers were mistakenly sent to him for forwarding at his own expense, and Gallagher, who Munroe assumed still published the magazine, failed to answer his requests for an accurate statement of accounts. Unless the editors straightened out the situation, Sarah Clarke reported to her brother in March 1836, Munroe would refuse to handle the *Messenger* any longer. At the end of May, financial affairs were in a critical state; Clarke personally owed the printers $300 (about half his annual salary) but had received only $50 to pay the debt. "I have written to Munroe, Patterson, & Day to send along subscriptions—But how we are ever to collect from 100 scattered subscribers is to me a marvel," he wrote Peabody in despair.[63] When volume one closed with the July 1836 issue, only 19 of the 100 New England subscribers had paid, leaving Clarke a mere $15 after postage costs and Munroe's commission. In Cincinnati, where some 90 persons had subscribed, 25 discontinued (2:352–53).

Heavily in debt, a "slave to the Press," and (as he confided to Margaret Fuller) frustrated with his congregation's failure to give him "understanding sympathy," Clarke was especially sensitive in the spring of 1836 to the apparent indifference of the *Messenger*'s friends and subscribers. Where was the support of the Eastern Unitarians, the financial aid, manpower, and dedication promised by the AUA? Not a single leader in the denomination had contributed original writing, though several had sent old sermons for publication. After their initial encouragement, the Boston papers fell silent, and when Sarah Clarke sent the *Examiner* an appeal on the *Messenger*'s behalf, James Walker sent it back, saying that he had already noticed the magazine once and couldn't spare the room. Professor Palfrey toured the West and South but swept through Louisville without stopping to preach. Worst of all, the AUA convened in Boston on 24 May, heard eloquent reports on the Western missions by John Thompson, Jason Whitman, and George Hosmer, and resolved, in ringing words, to heed the "solemn call of duty" and carry the liberal gospel "to the door of every log-house and cabin in the remotest wilds of the West."[64] To the beleaguered Clarke it all seemed empty talk: once again, the AUA pledged not a penny to support the *Messenger.*

As he had done just a year before, Clarke took the Eastern liberals to task in the pages of his magazine, accusing them this time not of "orthodoxism" but of indifference bordering on hypocrisy. "The sight of the indifference and apathy of our eastern brethren has at last filled the cup of our endurance too full," he fumed in the June 1836 *Messenger.* Palfrey had slighted him; missionaries scurried home after only a few weeks; fledgling societies struggled without leadership; the AUA had subscribed $18,000 (a misprint for $1800) for a Western agent who had never shown up. This litany of grievances he closed with a brash challenge to the Eastern leaders to live up to their ideals: "it *was* and *is* the duty of the first men in the eastern pulpits—of the Channings, Gannetts, Walkers, Deweys, &c.—to quit their parishes and go and labor in such places as Pittsburgh until the societies are built up" (1:803–4).

It was a bold stroke, sharply worded and almost certain to offend, but Clarke had committed the *Messenger* to uncompromising pursuit of the truth,   regardless of the consequences, and his charges were in the main true. Privately, though, he worried that he sounded "flippant, presumptious [*sic*], unchristian & impolitic." On 13 June, therefore, he sent the AUA's Executive Committee a judiciously worded request for aid to the *Messenger,* $100 now and an equal grant annually. Subscriptions were increasing by ten or twenty each month, he noted, and the magazine exercised "no contemptible influence in the forming of the Western character." But he had touched a nerve with his barbed criticism, a wound slow to heal. Walker, it is true, wrote highly of the *Messenger* in a letter to Samuel Osgood, and on 19 August Dr. Channing finally answered Clarke's year-old request for material, sending a long letter in praise of the Western effort (2 : 156–70). On the whole, though, the Eastern establishment was not eager to forgive. In July Sarah Clarke reported ominously that "the Theological School is thrown into consternation at your audacity,"[65] a reaction later exacerbated by a letter from William Eliot printed in the September issue. While offering an apology to Palfrey ("nothing would induce me wantonly to injure his feelings"), Eliot once more attacked Eastern complacency.

> Even if we are wrong in this particular instance of complaint . . . it is neither "unwise, nor unkind, nor unjust," in us to speak plainly of the general indifference of "all eastern Unitarians," in regard to the welfare of our small societies. . . . It is a crying evil among us. It is this which makes it so hard for us to build up societies—they are formed, do well for a time, and languish for *want of sympathy*—not such sympathy as can be easily expressed at a meeting of the American Unitarian Assocation—but living, active sympathy. (2 : 120–21)

Not only did Clarke find himself and his magazine at odds with Eastern Unitarians, but his commitment to a policy of open discussion led at the same time to a protracted argument over abolition. The *Messenger* under Peabody had effectively ignored that volatile topic. Like many Unitarians, Peabody considered it a higher duty to regenerate the private heart than to reform public institutions.[66] Moreover, the magazine's geographical position made the issue an especially sensitive one: straddling "slave" Kentucky and "free" Ohio, editors treaded gingerly so as not to stir up passions already dangerously inflamed by the 1830s. Though the Ohio Anti-slavery Society claimed 213 auxiliary societies and over 17,000 members, resentment ran high against abolitionist agitators in the state. In Kentucky, where by contemporary accounts the peculiar institution was generally more humane than in the lower South, James G. Birney organized the Kentucky Society for the Gradual Relief of the State from Slavery in 1833 but was

hounded across the border after he tried to establish an eman-
cipationist periodical. When in July 1836 he attempted to publish his *Philanthropist* in Cincinnati, a mob destroyed his press
and scattered the type, then turned their anger on the black
neighborhood, gutting homes and driving blacks out of the
city.[67] So varied and deeply rooted were responses to the slavery
question, from retention of the system to African colonization
to gradual emancipation to immediate abolition, that to advance one opinion was to alienate the holders of all the others.
In 1836 the *Messenger* could ill afford to offend anyone.

Despite the risks, however, Clarke involved the magazine in
the controversy by publishing excerpts from Dr. Channing's
pamphlet *Slavery* in April 1836. His Louisville friends and
parishioners seemed strongly opposed to the system on moral
grounds, though not so rash as to advocate ending it immediately, and Clarke thought the popular attitude "almost
unanimous against the continuance of this system in the
State."[68] "We are not in the habit of using a gag-law," he proclaimed confidently, alluding to the Congressional resolution
pending in Washington, so he printed a long selection from
Channing's argument, along with an approving summation.

> The substance of this book seems to be—Slavery is a wrong
> and evil; but it does not follow, that immediate emancipation
> is right, or that the slave holder is a sinner. . . . The people of
> the North have a right to form and express opinions on this
> subject; but they must do it so as not to endanger the peace
> and tranquility of the South, and must never address the
> slave, but only his master. To all which we say, Amen. (1 : 614–
> 28)

Until emancipation became a reality, Perkins argued the following month, the slave, "however degraded and unworthy *now* to
be free, still has the right–not to liberty, but to that process
which will fit him for liberty"; that is, the right to a moral
education (1 : 707–12).

The *Messenger*'s position on slavery was clear enough: political emancipation later, spiritual freedom now. Clarke recognized that not all would share Perkins's view, but he added,
perhaps anticipating a reaction, "its spirit, we are sure all must

admire" (1:732). Thomas Maylin, the Cincinnati teacher, was quick to disagree. Both Dr. Channing and the *Messenger*'s writers, he argued in August 1836, were too timid in condemning the slaveholder; their views led inescapably to abolition on moral grounds. "If slave-holding *is* a moral wrong and a moral evil," he asked, "and when God has commanded men every where to repent, can any man delay with impunity? can any plea of procrastination prevail?" (2:52–53). But Clarke, as wary as Perkins of the disordering threat of abolitionism, countered that though slavery as a system had evil consequences, to release slaves unprepared would be a grave disservice to both black and white; the slaveholder may in fact be performing "a high act of virtue" by protecting the slave "till the time comes when emancipation is safe and wise." To reinforce his point, he painted a vivid picture of freed slaves whose "childish disregard of the future" renders them incapable of providing for themselves and forces them into stealing (2:53–59). In the October number and again in November Maylin pressed his case for abolition. Freedom, he said, is the slave's "*acknowledged right,*" not a "boon" conferred at the pleasure of the master (2:178–85).

Clarke was in a bind. Believing the *Messenger*'s compromise position to be both morally sound and amenable to the sentiments of the West—where, he remarked, most slaveowners acknowledged the evil of the institution but "do not know how to get rid of it, without inflicting a greater wrong and evil" (2:215)—he found instead that to travel the middle road was to offend both extremes.[69] On the slavery issue, at least, the *Messenger* participated thoroughly in mainstream Unitarian moral philosophy, for its position reflected the dilemma that kept the denomination from concerted antislavery action in the 1830s: the inability to reconcile its moral ideal of human progress with its social ideal of human order. Embarrassed no doubt by the need to contravene his own editorial policy, Clarke called a halt to the discussion after publishing Maylin's second piece, declaring that to continue "would engage us in an endless controversy, and if not unprofitable, certainly not conducive of the objects, for which this periodical was established" (2:178). To Maylin it must have sounded like an admission of defeat, and he contributed a third argument, which Clarke printed in the interest of fairness but prefaced with another "final" dismissal of the topic: "We think most sincerely that no good can come from agitating the public mind on this subject. Such agitation only serves to excite passion, instead of leading to conviction" (2:262).

The slavery question, forestalled by editorial fiat rather than resolved, left Clarke flustered but the *Messenger* apparently unhurt. The dispute with the AUA, however, would require more diplomacy, for without a transfusion of Eastern money the magazine would never live till its third volume. On 5 September 1836 Clarke set off for Boston to soothe bruised feelings, placate disgruntled subscribers, and drum up support for the *Messenger* and the Western effort; in his absence Osgood edited the October and November numbers, contributing much of the original material himself (2:351). In Boston Clarke spoke three times on aid for the West, twice to large audiences at Dr. Channing's Federal Street Church (2:353–55) and judging by the results his appeals were persuasive indeed.[70] Returning to Louisville early in November, he prepared for the *Messenger* an account of his travels that summarized the magazine's financial straits and acknowledged the "manifestations of the sympathy felt in Boston." From private donations, he reported, $412 had been raised (2:354–55). Of that sum, Clarke earmarked at least $300 for the *Messenger*—enough, with the $49 Eliot sent along from the St. Louis subscribers (2:358), to save the magazine from ruin.[71] As Clarke and Osgood prepared the penultimate number of the second volume in late November 1836, they had reason to be optimistic.

And Clarke especially had the right to be proud of the *Messenger*, for though it could not yet claim to be the leading magazine of the West, it was by Clarke's standards the most Western in character: wide-ranging in its interests, progressive in its theology, independent in its pursuit of truth, even to the point of "recklessness" (as Clarke was fond of viewing himself). In the West, he wrote, "a great movement is going on, although outward forms continue unaltered" ("General Preface," p. xi). To that movement he had dedicated the *Messenger*, and if its renewed support from New England were any indication, the magazine was now working changes on both sides of the Alleghenies.[72]

How far-reaching and turbulent those changes would prove to be, Clarke could not yet know, but his sojourn in the East left him no doubt that they were imminent. In addition to his activities there on behalf of the *Messenger,* he had attended in the company of Alcott, Hedge, Brownson, Ripley, and Emerson two "meetings of the Like-Minded" known as the Transcendental Club, meetings born of a common dissatisfaction with the current state of art and religion. Even Dr. Channing, who seldom had a bad word for anyone, conceded that the spirit of mainstream Unitarianism was "utterly dead and frozen."[73] Not for long, Clarke must have realized, could the great movement continue without altering "outward forms," for in the autumn of 1836 his friends among the radicals had committed their views to print: Emerson in *Nature,* Furness in *Remarks on the Four Gospels,* Ripley in *Discourses on the Philosophy of Religion,* Brownson in *New Views of Christianity, Society, and the Church.* After its January 1837 number, which opened discussion on the first two books and promised reviews of the others, the *Western Messenger's* already uneasy accommodation with prevailing opinions would be strained in new and bitter ways. For when commitment to "honest truth seekers" led to praise for Emerson and Furness, the magazine found itself suddenly caught up in the dispute over the historicity of scriptural miracles—the issue, Perry Miller has shown, "upon which there could be no possible accommodation between the new school and the old."[74]

3
1837–1839
"A living mirror of the times"

For the *Western Messenger,* as for American culture in general, the years 1837 to 1839 were a time for reaping as it had sown.[1] In economics, the Panic of 1837 capped years of reckless financial speculation. In religion, another kind of speculation—equally reckless, some contended—shattered the calm of Unitarianism as the denomination felt the full force of the Transcendentalist insurgency. In politics, the popular triumph of Jacksonian democracy yielded to the bitter discord of the Van Buren presidency. In social reform, the nation strained under the increasing agitation of abolitionists, trade unions, agrarians, and associationists. And in literature, Emerson's *American Scholar* and Hawthorne's *Twice-Told Tales* heralded the flowering of a native romantic tradition. Conceived as a "living mirror of the times" (3:853), the *Messenger* entered an age of passionate extremes.

Thanks to Dr. Channing's stirring letter on Western missions (2:156–70) and to the infusion of Eastern support after James Clarke's Boston tour, 1837 began auspiciously for the magazine. "Our subscription list is more than double what it was at the commencement of the publication, and is now on the increase," announced its editors when the second volume closed in January 1837 (2:431).[2] Privately, Clarke even predicted a "small surplus revenue" (which he wisely decided to keep aside to cover future losses), and for the moment there was an abundance of material on hand to fill the *Messenger*'s pages.[3] Heartening, too, were signs of a growing receptivity in the West to liberal religion (3:500–501), as well as some tangible evidence of the AUA's commitment to the Western effort: a six-month tour of the region by its General Secretary, Charles Briggs (3:644–46), the appropriation of $400 for a ministry-at-large in Louisville, and the donation of $100 for thirty-three subscriptions to the *Messenger*.[4] The Midwestern winter presented the only impediment to progress, for after Clarke and Osgood exchanged pulpits in December the frozen Ohio River left them stranded. Alone in Louisville, Osgood edited the January and February numbers, conferring with Clarke by mail (3:503–4).[5]

With the spring came changes in the *Messenger*'s pool of writers. Osgood, discouraged that the congregation at Cincinnati seemed indisposed to offer him a permanent call, decided to return East as soon as the weather broke. Though he remained a faithful contributor to the *Messenger* for several more years, the loss of the energetic young minister was saddening, to Clarke if not to the Cincinnati congregation.[6] Fortunately for both, the AUA funded more missionaries in 1837 than ever before, fourteen in all, and Osgood's place was quickly filled by Benjamin Huntoon, eighteen years Clarke's senior but youthful in his enthusiasm for the West. There, Huntoon told the assembled members of the AUA, "not only the destiny of our *country*, but the destiny of *Unitarianism* is to be decided."[7] In June the evangelist William P. Huntington arrived in western Illinois to aid Charles Farley, minister to a small but active Unitarian society at Alton, across the Mississippi from St. Louis.[8] James Thurston and William Silsbee, the latter an editor (with Theodore Parker) of Boston's short-lived *Scriptural Interpreter*, also came West in the summer, for what was rapidly becoming an obligatory tour for fledgling Unitarian ministers. Besides welcome camaraderie and the latest news from Boston, these newcomers promised both material for the magazine and—something Clarke could no longer provide—a fresh perspective on the West.[9]

None, however, proved so talented and faithful a contributor as Christopher Pearse Cranch, whose love of poetry, painting, and music was at least as strong as his devotion to the pulpit. The quintessential wanderer, Cranch had preached as an itinerant in Rhode Island, Maine, New Hampshire, and Washington, D.C., landing finally at Richmond, Virginia, in the summer of 1836. But Southerners he found narrow and class-conscious; seeking greater freedom, both social and intellectual, he turned to the West. The idea was not new to him: he had, in fact, hoped to supply for Ephraim Peabody in Cincinnati. But now the presence of his friends Osgood and Clarke, his sister's fiancé, William Eliot, and his brother Edward Pope Cranch of Cincinnati, proved an irresistible lure.[10] On 1 December 1836, en route to St. Louis, Cranch visited Clarke in Louisville and left some of his poetry for the *Messenger,* the first of many contributions. By March 1837 he was preaching in Peoria, Illinois.[11]

Cranch's importance to the magazine is difficult to overestimate. He would twice serve as editor in Clarke's absence, and for two years he provided a steady stream of essays and verse. Next to Emerson and Thoreau he ranks as the most talented poet in the Transcendental circle, and his ready wit buoyed Clarke when the burdens of his pastorate became oppressive. Like Clarke and the others, Cranch was enthusiastic about the "vast, limitless prospect" of the West and eager to develop the "powers within me which I have not yet brought into full use." Like them, too, Cranch gravitated toward the man who, by his example as much as his words, seemed destined to lead a generation of sensitive young men and women to a life of the spirit. "The man of genius, the bold deep thinker, and the concise original writer," as Cranch called him (4:184), Emerson had in Cranch a lifelong defender and sympathetic interpreter.[12]

In 1837 it took courage to defend Emerson and his circle, though the lines were as yet imperfectly drawn between liberals and conservatives within Unitarianism. However threatened more conservative New Englanders may have felt in private, their public responses to *Nature,* to Furness's *Remarks on the Four Gospels,* to Brownson's *New Views,* and to Ripley's *Discourses* early in 1837 showed more concern for the misinterpretation of the "new philosophy" than for the supposed heresy of the radicals themselves.[13] Reluctant to acknowledge publicly the division within their ranks, conservatives saved the full force of their indignation for Bronson Alcott and his *Conversations,* the book

Andrews Norton scored as "one-third . . . absurd, one-third blasphemous, and one-third obscene."[14]

Yet the split, if not openly acknowledged, was real nonetheless, and given their backgrounds and sympathies the *Messenger* writers could hardly have ignored it. Emerson's coyly disingenuous remarks in "Historic Notes of Life and Letters in New England" illustrate how rapidly predispositions crystallized into factions.

> I think there prevailed at that time a general belief in Boston that there was some concert of *doctrinaires* to establish certain opinions and inaugurate some movement in literature, philosophy, and religion, of which design the supposed conspirators were quite innocent; for there was no concert, and only here and there two or three men or women who read and wrote, each alone, with unusual vivacity. . . . I suppose all of them were surprised at this rumor of a school or sect, and certainly at the name of Transcendentalism, given nobody knows by whom, or when it was first applied.[15]

The public break came, as Perry Miller has shown, over the question of scriptural miracles. A complex theological issue from which sprang the other differences between the old and new schools, the miracles controversy forced a showdown. Those associated with the conservative wing of the denomination defined the miraculous as the violation of natural order. Since God alone could abridge his laws, scriptural miracles validated Christianity by providing sensory "proof" of the divinity of the Bible. Historical miracles, in other words, gave men sufficient cause to believe. For the new school, on the other hand, natural laws were themselves divine, signs of Spirit; what was apparently miraculous was not nature violated, merely nature imperfectly understood. Knowledge of the Divine was accessible primarily through an inner Reason rather than through the evidence of the senses or of Scripture. Thus miracles—and to the new school all was miraculous, the infusion of the Divine into the world—might confirm faith, but they were not the reason for it. If Christianity were valid, its authenticity was established by its "coincidence with the divine testimony of our spiritual nature."[16]

At the root of this theological argument stood, clearly, a fundamental disagreement over the nature of man, for the miracles controversy illuminated a disturbing inconsistency within liberal doctrine. If, as Dr. Channing had insisted, "man has a kindred nature with God, and may bear most important and ennobling relations to him," then why, asked members of the new school, also insist on the mechanical "tricks" of miracles as foundations of faith? Was mankind imprisoned by the limits of sensory perception despite its "likeness to God"?[17] Or might not men apprehend the Divinity without the intervention of biblical records, of religious institutions, of Christian revelation itself? Simply put, the Transcendentalists challenged Unitarianism to make its epistemology commensurate with its metaphysics—to acknowledge man's unlimited potential to know, unaided. Nearly two centuries after Boston had purged itself of Anne Hutchinson, the antinomian heresy again threatened the church in New England with the prospect of its own irrelevance.[18]

In 1837, however, banishment was out of the question, and the Transcendentalists showed no signs of leaving of their own accord. Unwilling as yet to condemn their colleagues as infidels, but unable to ignore the threat they posed, the more conservative Unitarian ministers sought to diffuse the danger in three ways. They first isolated the disturbance as a movement and named it Transcendentalism, the easier to dismiss it without engaging in personal attacks. Second, they blamed the excesses of the new philosophy on the subversive influences of foreign thinkers, particularly Coleridge, Carlyle, and the German Idealists. "Abstruse in its dogmas, fantastic in its dress, and foreign in its source," charged Francis Bowen, Transcendentalism "comes from Germany, and is one of the first fruits of a diseased admiration of every thing from that source." Finally, the conservatives discredited the new school as arrogant. Said Bowen in his review of *Nature:*

Both the means and the ends, which other philosophers have proposed to themselves, are rejected by the new sect of hierophants. They are among men, but not of men. From the heights of mystical speculation, they look down with a ludicrous self-complacency and pity on the mass of mankind, on the ignorant and the educated, the learners and the teachers, and should any question the grounds on which such feelings rest, they are forthwith branded with the most opprobrious epithets, which the English or the Transcendental language can supply.

Here, at last, was the real threat of Transcendentalism: to assert the independence of the human spirit was to upset the intricate set of man-made checks and balances by which an imperfect world lurched along toward perfection. Animated by the "dread of a disorganizing tendency" (in O. B. Frothingham's words), old school ministers lashed out at what they considered a sin against God and man. "There are mysteries in nature," said Bowen, "which human power cannot penetrate; there are problems which the philosopher cannot solve." To say otherwise, as the Transcendentalists did, was to seek "the forbidden fruit of knowledge in subjects placed beyond the reach of the human faculties." Bowen had little doubt how to deal with such Faustian longings: "Some bounds must be set to the application of views like these."[19]

Personally, Clarke, Cranch, Osgood, and to some degree Eliot had discernible, if ill-defined, "affinities" with the new school by 1837, each feeling dissatisfied with the excessive negations of their denomination and finding in the spiritual philosophy a welcome antidote to Lockean empiricism. Clarke had identified "orthodoxism" among Unitarians two years before, locating it (in a letter to Emerson) as "Nortonism," after the man Theodore Parker later vilified as "a *born Pope*."[20] But the *Messenger*'s role in the Transcendentalist controversy was not solely an expression of its writers' private sympathies, nor was it an attempt to promote Emersonianism, Brownsonism, or any "ism" at all. Just the contrary. When Norton recommended in November 1836 that the new views should be aired only with the approval of "those who are capable of judging their correctness," he was advocating—as far as the *Messenger* writers were concerned—the restraint of sincere, free thought by a human creed.[21] Opposition to such creeds, to all sectarian "exclusiveness," was precisely the principle to which the *Messenger* had been dedicated. "We do not believe in the principle of concealing the faults of our own party," Clarke reminded his readers in September 1837. "If Unitarians are lukewarm and indifferent in their religion, cold, narrow or intolerant in their conduct, we mean to expose them no less than the opposite party" (4:7). Attempts to silence or discredit the new school confirmed for the *Messenger* writers that established Unitarianism was hardening into a creed every bit as tyrannical as the Calvinism whose bigotry they had opposed in print for nearly two years.

The controversy reached the West with remarkable speed. The December 1836 *Messenger* carried long extracts from Furness's *Remarks* (2:341–49), almost simultaneously with the first reviews in Boston, and just before the number went to press Clarke inserted a notice that the book was available from Louisville booksellers (2:359).[22] Eliot, meanwhile, contributed an essay on miracles that strongly suggested his own sympathies with the new school (2:312–18). In the January 1837 number Clarke turned again to Furness's little book. Among other benefits, he said, *Remarks* would stimulate discussion of the miracles controversy. As if to prove that point, Clarke presented his own view of the matter, one that left little doubt which party *he* favored. Miracles, to Clarke, did not violate nature but had a law of their own; more important, they were "not intended to force men to believe in Christianity," since the truths of Jesus were adequately confirmed by their appeal to man's innate moral sense. Clarke concluded—in case anyone had missed his point—with a swipe at his nemesis in the old school: "It is a matter of surprise to us, that so learned a theologian as Mr. Andrews Norton, should have thought this opinion injurious to Christianity, as he has in a lately published letter" (2:371–82).

In that same January number appeared the first of the *Messenger*'s discussions of Emerson. Osgood's review of *Nature*, the first west of the Alleghenies, was primarily a string of generous excerpts; Osgood clearly found Emerson more inspirational than coherent. Especially puzzling was Emerson's crucial section on Idealism, which Osgood feared would cause many readers "to shut the book in disgust." Because "the idealist, who believes matter to be only phenomenal, will conduct [himself] in exactly the same way, as the most thorough going materialist," Osgood was "unable to perceive the bearing of the writer's argument, in proof of Idealism" (2:391). Emerson, though, had not endeavored to prove any such theory, his point being that while Nature "is ideal to me so long as I cannot try the accuracy of my senses," we act in the common affairs of life as if the world were material and its existence absolute.[23] For Emerson the end of Nature, its service to the developing soul, was the key issue—a point that seems to have escaped Osgood entirely.

Yet the importance of Osgood's review is not diminished by its shortage of insight, for in early 1837 Emerson needed apologists less than he needed defenders, and Osgood offered defense. Though mystified, he was quick to admit that "probably the fault lies in ourselves." Worried that Emerson may have "confounded his idiosyncrasies, with universal truth" (2:392), he refused to equate self-reliance with arrogance, and he applauded Emerson for dreaming the right dreams, for seeing "the temporal in the light of the Eternal" (2:393). If Osgood's conventional concerns for right conduct blinded him to the enduring significance of *Nature,* he at least responded perceptively to its importance in the split between new and old schools. Such books, Osgood said boldly, deserved to be encouraged, not suppressed, for they "redeem the souls of men from the thraldom of the senses" (2:386).

Discussion of the radicals continued into the spring, with reviews of Brownson in March (3:529–39) and of Ripley the following month (3:575–83). *New Views,* wrote Clarke, is an eloquent and inspiring prediction of the demise of Protestant "sensualism" and rise of "perfect freedom of opinion and conscience" (3:533). Osgood found Ripley's *Discourses* heartening evidence of "the happy influence of a higher philosophy than generally prevails—a philosophy of Reason and Faith, and not of sensualism and doubt. . . . [T]he mind has a nature of its own, and is not a mere creature of circumstance, a result of mere sensation, the sport of casual impressions" (3:579). In the April number, too, appeared further extracts from Brownson's book (3:618–22), as well as a startling letter from Brownson himself, who argued that even infidelity is preferable to authoritarian (and hence undemocratic) creeds (3:603–4).

None of the radicals, however, received more attention in the *Messenger* than the one most roundly condemned in New England, Bronson Alcott. With their interest in public education and Sunday schools, it is not at all surprising that the *Messenger* writers kept careful watch on Alcott's progress in his Temple School; in fact, the magazine had taken up discussion of it several times in the past.[24] Clarke knew the school well: his sister Sarah and his friends Margaret Fuller and Elizabeth Peabody had served as Alcott's assistants, and Clarke himself had recently tried some conversations "upon Mr. Alcott's plan" with his Sunday School children in Louisville. But recent events lent a particular urgency to the *Messenger*'s remarks, for Alcott's school was faltering badly, and the tide of hostile public opinion (which would soon drive Alcott out of the classroom and into depression) had begun to swell.[25]

In the March 1837 number Clarke inserted a measured defense of the *Conversations*. It was time, he wrote, to recognize that "a merely intellectual education may be positively injurious"; instead of withdrawing their children from the Temple School, "parents should be counted very fortunate who have an opportunity of placing" them there. Clarke hailed Alcott's book as "a running commentary" upon Brownson's, the first providing practical application of the second's theory (3:540–41).

But Clarke's praise, and similar defenses in Boston by Emerson, Elizabeth Peabody, and the editors of the *Christian Register,* could do little to quell the public outrage that greeted Alcott and the *Conversations*. On 15 April Clarke sent off a letter to the *Register* (published on the 29th), which he expanded in the May *Messenger* (3:678–83). Acknowledging that "wise and good" men are understandably suspicious of new theories, Clarke called Alcott a "prophet" whose book had been wrongly condemned "by those who . . . do not yet appreciate its high and extraordinary merits." One by one he sought to allay public fears about Alcott's impiety—fears that animated clergy as well as laymen, since in discussing topics such as Jesus' birth with his young pupils Alcott had infringed upon territory properly reserved for the ministry. Later in the May number Clarke returned to Alcott, this time in a satiric response to the editor of the *Boston Courier,* who had recommended the *Conversations* to the courts. If Alcott were indicted, Clarke suggests, the charges ought rightly to "be in the words of that formerly found against Socrates" (3:715–16).

Emerson, Furness, Ripley, Brownson, Alcott—during the early months of 1837 the *Messenger* missed no opportunity to defend the men identified then, as now, as the chief exponents of Transcendentalism in America. But the Western writers were clearly not slavish followers of a trend, as their notices show. Osgood in particular, though he identified himself at the time with the new school,[26] had reservations not only about its idealism but also about its apparent disregard for the development of ethical conduct.

> They preach as to saints, rather than as to sinners. They state the holy law of God, and enlarge upon the divine capacities of man, but do not take much hold of the sinful heart. . . . We look to the time, when they who entertain the lofty views of the author of this volume [Ripley's *Discourses*], shall preach them with power, not merely to a select and refined few, but to the sinful world. (3:582–83)

Eliot, like Osgood, found Emerson stimulating but airy: " 'Nature' I have read but once," he wrote in November, "and of course only partially understand" (3:358). Neither Perkins nor Cranch, the first absent on business in eastern Ohio, the second adjusting to life in Peoria, had contributed anything yet on the Transcendental controversy. And Huidekoper, who had labored so long to establish a Unitarian presence in Meadville, watched in dismay as the radicals chipped away at the foundations of his denomination.

Thus, while the *Messenger* consistently argued for the Transcendentalists' right to express their views, it is wrong to conclude that it endorsed the views themselves in 1837. Rather, the New England radicals and the Western writers had common adversaries—Norton, Bowen, and the others who seemed opposed to the spirit of Unitarianism by so dogmatically insisting upon the letter of it. As doggedly as it had defended the non-

denominational Christian Connexion in 1835 and 1836, the
Messenger now applauded the efforts of the new school, and for
quite the same reason: both Campbell and Emerson, as well as
Stone and Brownson, sought truth independent of creeds.

Clarke's closing remarks to his second review of Alcott show
how fully the *Messenger*'s position represented a continuity of its
editorial policy.

> Another great fear is of errors of opinion, false views, &c.
> &c. This is the great bugbear with which we, of this maga-
> zine, have to be constantly contending. We have to be always
> saying what we now say again, that the great danger is rather
> that men shall not think at all, than that they shall think
> erroneously.

"If the mind is suffered to act freely on great subjects," Clarke
maintained, "truth must be in the end the gainer by it." Yet he
was enough a man of experience to know the dangers of
marching before that banner.

> These are the principles to which all cheerfully assent in the
> abstract, but unanimously object to in practice. Few have
> faith enough in the power of truth and its adaptation to the
> human mind to allow of free inquiry and examination.
> (3:683)

The *Messenger*'s work on behalf of the Transcendentalists did
not go unappreciated. Ripley praised the reviews of Emerson
and of Furness ("the first worthy notice") and offered Clarke
$200 to reprint his monthly translations of *Theodore* in Ripley's
new series, *Specimens of Foreign Standard Literature.*[27] Brownson's
letter in the April number included a glowing tribute to the
developing West and the young ministers who labored there for
truth and democracy. In the solitude of his Boston study, the
beleaguered Alcott entered a grateful testimony to the *Messenger* in his journal for mid-March.

> The editor of this fresh and free periodical, gave a favorable
> notice of my "*book*" in the No. of the "Messenger" for this
> month. This is the first d[e]cided and hearty praise which the
> book has received. Mr. Clark[e], the editor, has heretofore

taken a generous view of my enterprize, and labours. He is a free and high-minded young man, bent on finding truth where-ever it shall chance to spring up. His field of labour is ample;—and unencumbered by the conventions of older society, his spirit seems to expand in the west. Our young men grow sturdy and free so soon as they leave the enervating influences of this region of shackle & authority.[28]

The extent to which the Transcendentalists found the *Messenger* a sympathetic and articulate organ for progressive views is illustrated by a letter from Ripley to the historian George Bancroft on 20 September 1837.

I do not count it clearly impossible for new life to be breathed into the languid veins of our liberal Christianity; and with such men as Brownson, and the brave, young writers in the *Western Messenger*, I almost hope to see the time, when religion, philosophy, and politics will be united in a holy Trinity, for the redemption and blessedness of our social institutions.[29]

Despite Clarke's editorial promise to make his magazine a "living mirror of the times," when the members of the new school looked at the *Messenger* in 1837, the reflection they saw was their own.

Apparently, mainstream Unitarians saw it too, for the magazine's recent, warm reception in New England had become decidedly chilly by the middle of 1837. Facing the rising anger of the Unitarian community, the *Register* and the *Examiner* could no longer afford to be noncommittal on the Transcendentalist controversy and came down on the side of the conservatives.[30] Since the *Messenger* relied upon the favorable notice of both papers to sustain its subscriptions in New England, the decision did not bode well. "We . . . rejoice to learn that [the *Messenger*] begins the new year under brighter auspices," said the *Register*'s editor on 21 January, but during the coming months he noticed the magazine only once, and then blandly. The *Examiner*'s editor, James Walker, whom Clarke had once considered "the leader in our body,"[31] printed Bowen's fiery review of *Nature* in January; thereafter his paper was closed to the radicals and their Western sympathizers. Accustomed as they were to gauging their New England reception by notices in the official press of the denomination, the *Messenger* writers could not have missed the signals. They were being snubbed.

But in May the *Messenger* suddenly got more attention in the East than its editors wanted, though not, ironically enough, due to its defenses of the Transcendentalists. That month, Clarke inserted a highly complimentary notice of the annual meeting of the AUA, hoping no doubt to get the organization's support for another year. "For several years, we regarded this meeting as rather an occasion of mourning than of congratulation," he wrote bluntly, but "better days have come! The denomination is awake and active, and filled in a great degree, with a strong desire to perform its duty." Then, however, in what was probably the greatest strategic blunder of Clarke's editorship, he contrasted the group's missionary element with those ministers who still believed it "all vanity and vexation" to engage in organized benevolence.

> One of our brethren of strong conservative feelings, took occasion, we believe, to congratulate his congregation that they had succeeded for 20 years, in keeping themselves from doing any thing. "Their strength," he said, "was to sit still." We think, however, that there are not now many among us, who would think it an occasion for special thankfulness to God that their society had been preserved from doing too much in his cause. (3:716–18)

The unnamed butt of Clarke's sarcasm was Nathaniel Langdon Frothingham, a cultivated scholar noted for his piety and devotion to his flock—the very model of the genteel Unitarian preacher.[32]

Though Frothingham himself made no public reply to the insult, Eastern Unitarians quickly rallied to his defense. On 3 June the *Register* printed a response to what it called an "unhandsome and unwarranted allusion to an highly esteemed Brother." The anonymous correspondent accused Clarke of intentionally misreading Frothingham's sermon, and argued further that though the minister had long supported benevolent activities privately, "he is averse from intricating his religious society *as such* in their machinery." Finally, he reminded the readers of the *Register* that the same number of the *Messen-*

ger to ridicule "a most esteemed" minister had defended Bronson Alcott.

Had Clarke quietly accepted the rebuke, the matter would have quietly ended. But he did not. Instead, he defended himself in the July *Messenger,* asserting that, since he had not mentioned Frothingham by name, "the attack, if it be one, has not been made in the Messenger but in the Register." Worse, Clarke protested that the *Register*'s correspondent had misrepresented *him,* then closed with a grand absolution of the *Register*'s editor, Chandler Robbins, for having printed the letter in the first place.

Robbins reprinted this latest installment in the dispute on 15 July, with a note regretting "that there should be cause for any misunderstanding." On the 22d Clarke's opponent responded again with a promise to converse with Clarke soon, at which time "I feel assured that he will see reason to manifest a little penitence." The matter was dropped, but the damage lingered. Frothingham was hurt, Robbins embarrassed, and the graduation exercises at the Divinity School filled with "a good deal of animadversion" about the unseemly exchange, according to Osgood. Even George Ripley was shocked at Clarke's breach of propriety; he feared the young minister had become "too *Western*" and needed some of the Eastern "element of restraint."[33] Coming on the heels of the *Messenger*'s defenses of the Transcendentalists, the attack on Frothingham added to the fund of ill will building in New England toward the brash young minister and his magazine. During his summer tour of the East, Eliot surveyed the damage. Many still found the magazine refreshing and interesting, he reported on 10 August.

> But do not flatter yourself that *all* expressions of opinion are thus favourable. That would be far from the truth. . . . It is thought by some that the "Messenger" goes out of its province when it makes an attack upon those who live East of the mountains, and that we young men ought to be more cautious in speaking of our Elders. This is the sum of what evil I have heard said of you, although it has sometimes been said very bitterly. (4:139)

Eliot encouraged Clarke to persevere, but advised him also to "avoid being personal, or so direct in your remarks as to give

offence to individuals" (4:140)—advice that Clarke would ignore. Not at all surprisingly, the AUA approved no new support
for the *Messenger* at its May meeting, nor does its annual report
indicate that the magazine was ever considered for funding.

Depressed, lonesome, and convinced that he had "come to a
standstill," Clarke took a riverboat north on 7 August 1837 for
a leisurely journey to New England, apparently (and understandably) in no hurry to reach Boston.[34] William Silsbee supervised the opening number of the *Messenger*'s fourth volume in
September, with the help of Edward Jarvis, a Harvard-trained
physician recently settled in Louisville.[35] In mid-September
Cranch relieved Silsbee of the pulpit and found himself
saddled as well with editing the next two numbers, a job he
assumed with his usual good humor. "Not more than half the
requisite matter is furnished," he wrote to his sister from Louisville,

> and most of that is spun from the brains of your humble
> servant C. P. C. Clarke just lets his offspring go to the dick-
> ens. If it had not been that C. P. C. happened to adhere to the
> south bank of the Ohio in his way down stream, and take root
> awhile in these diggings, where had been the flowers & fruits
> that must spring therefrom to fill the Messengers demands? I
> look about now like a hungry lion seeking for prey. . . .
> Nevertheless I give myself no uneasiness. The young ravens
> are fed, and so will the Messenger be in time.[36]

Hungry though the *Messenger* was, it did not suffer from
mere "filling up" in Clarke's absence. Margaret Fuller contributed poetry (Clarke had begged her for "a whole parcel" of
articles), Osgood sent brief reviews and travel essays, Eliot began a series of "Letters on Unitarian Christianity" refuting
Trinitarian proof texts, and Cranch pillaged his commonplace
book for "scraps & ends to publish anonymously." Nor did
Clarke's absence diminish the magazine's independent spirit.
Cranch praised Emerson's *American Scholar* (4:184–88) and
called upon Unitarians East and West to actively pursue social
and religious reform (4:158–64). In perhaps the most strident
criticism of Carlyle yet published in America, James Perkins
declared his essay on the revolutionary Mirabeau not only gro-
tesquely written ("a marked style, to be sure, but pock-

marked") but also morally dangerous, since it immortalized a leader motivated by ambition rather than virtue (4:87–91). John Champion Vaughan, a South Carolinian soon to become Edward Cranch's law partner in Cincinnati, contributed a two-part essay on "The Crisis," in which he castigated Westerners for their greed and moral laxity and blamed the country's economic woes on the triumph of partisan politics over "individual effort and independent mind" (4:47–52, 94–98).[37]

Quite apart from their intrinsic merits, the essays by Cranch, Perkins, and Vaughan marked an important development in the *Messenger*'s editorial stance. Long opposed to religious factionalism, the magazine had now extended its opposition to political factionalism as well. As Cranch, and Clarke before him, had argued for "Christian truth—not Unitarian-*ism*, nor any other *ism*" (4:160), so Vaughan railed against the prevailing "reliance upon names" in politics and social reform (4:94). By the end of 1837 the disparate points of view of the *Messenger*'s contributors had begun to converge on a single theme: opposition to "parties" of every sort, religious, political, philosophical. Under a variety of headings—"bigotry," "exclusiveness," "sectarianism," "factionalism"— the *Messenger* writers raised their collective voice against a single evil, the deadening tendency toward the creeds or "isms" that delimited the search for truth.

It was a noble stand, but one certain to cause problems in an age rife with controversy, for it was interpreted as neutrality or lack of conviction or iconoclasm. The magazine had already run afoul of the Unitarian establishment by refusing to conform to the shape of the denomination; its editorial policies now angered abolitionists, who simply could not fathom why a religious periodical would not come out in favor of their cause. A year earlier Clarke had closed discussion of the subject, but in July 1837—when subscriptions came due for the fourth volume—he received letters from two Cincinnati abolitionists canceling their subscriptions to protest the *Messenger*'s apparent neutrality on the slavery question. "I feel ashamed and mortified," wrote Thomas Maylin,

> that a professed advocate of "broad and generous views of Christianity" . . . should be chargeable with such glaring in-

consistency, as to support a system built upon a flagrant violation of that *Law* of Love [and] vindicate the acknowledged
oppress*or* against the oppress*ed.* (4:65)

Good Christians, agreed the second correspondent, "C. D."
(probably Charles Dana, a subscriber from Cincinnati), "are
guilty of a neglect of duty if they do not speak plainly in opposition" to the peculiar institution (4:65).[38]

In his response, printed in the September *Messenger,* Clarke
reminded his readers that the magazine had never defended
slavery, merely recognized the practical difficulties of immediate emancipation. "Is there no medium," he asked in frustration, "between being a champion of Abolitionism and a
champion of slavery?" (4:67). Clearly there was, but just as
clearly the abolitionists were in no mood to countenance it. Yet
the *Messenger*'s position remained unchanged. Writing in the
November number on the proposed annexation of Texas, Perkins declared antiabolitionism "an argument that . . . with open
brow, may be pleaded before the throne of God" (4:165);
Clarke, reviewing Theodore Dwight Weld's *The Bible Against
Slavery* (1837), cited the biblical precedent of slave-keeping and
censured "abolitionists of the ultra sort" for trying "not to convince, but to bear down by a storm of popular feeling" (4:255).
With nothing to be gained by further discussion, the argument
degenerated into angry sniping. On 26 December a writer in
the *Philanthropist,* the official organ of the Ohio State Anti-
slavery Society, sarcastically asked Clarke to

concede that it is possible the world may grow a little wiser as
it grows older [and] that even abolitionism may have got hold
of a truth, which had escaped the grasp of "Biblical critics
and commentators."[39]

"It has been not the least of our trials," Clarke admitted in his
introduction to the fourth volume, "to risk losing some of our
best friends by what we felt called on to say" (4:7). By the end
of 1837, the *Messenger*'s continuing opposition to dogmatic "exclusiveness" of all kinds had indeed lost the magazine readers
among the conservative Unitarians and radical abolitionists. In
September he issued a bold challenge to the *Messenger*'s

readers: "Let those who disapprove these views, withdraw their patronage from us" (4:8). When he returned from New England early in November, the answer to that challenge had become painfully clear.

Since March 1837, Clarke—publisher as well as editor after he assumed control of the magazine—had ordered a monthly press run of 550 copies; probably the total number of subscribers was slightly less than that.[40] Had all of them paid, and paid promptly, the *Messenger*'s financial health would have remained stable, if not strong; but many still owed for the first three volumes, and rather than accept the loss Clarke continued to carry them on the books, hoping no doubt that regular receipt of the magazine might prod them into paying. Harried by other duties and inept in business, Clarke had little heart for the publisher's chores, though he did not—Cranch's flippant comment notwithstanding—let them "go to the dickens." He found it cheaper, for instance, to have paper routed from Boston through New Orleans rather than overland from the East, and he arranged a discount for bills paid in cash. He convinced a Boston druggist, Joseph M. Smith, to serve as agent for the New England subscriptions and hired a collector to visit delinquent subscribers. Clarke's brother Samuel, an energetic businessman, agreed to the onerous task of untangling the magazine's accounts.[41]

It was all for nothing. On 14 November Samuel sent his brother the dismal news that at least seventeen New England subscribers had discontinued, with many others "absent" when the collector called and still others "uncertain" whether they would continue taking the magazine. On the 25th Samuel reported that only $80 had been received from New England subscribers, not even enough to cover the *Messenger*'s outstanding debts, and the prospects for further collections were bleak: "All interest in the success of the work seems to have died away, except with a few choice spirits. I doubt if you will realize more than $100 from the N. England list this year." Even that modest estimate proved optimistic, for three weeks later when the former agent James Munroe turned over some $54 he had received for old accounts, the *Messenger*'s balance stood, after Clarke paid his bills, at $19.61.[42]

Desperate, Clarke laid his troubles before the *Messenger*'s readers in the December 1837 number. In the last three months, he wrote, "WE HAVE LOST SEVENTY OR EIGHTY SUBSCRIBERS," many of them wealthy, some of them ministers. Without help, the magazine would fold at the completion of the fourth volume (4:284). On 15 December he requested an additional $100 from the AUA. "Hard times and other causes," he explained in a letter to Charles Briggs, had reduced the *Messenger*'s subscription list to about 450, perhaps two-thirds of them in the West and South.[43] The January 1838 issue carried a call for additional subscribers ("old names are falling off, and no new ones coming in") and a reminder to delinquent readers to pay quickly (4:359). A month later, though, Clarke was forced to admit that his pleas had gone unheeded. Of some fifty collection letters he had mailed, only two or three produced results. With several hundred dollars in outstanding subscriptions—Clarke was apparently unsure of the exact amount—and the printers crying to be paid, the *Messenger* could not continue publication unless "a sufficient number of new names are forwarded to us" (4:431–32).

Exactly why did the magazine suffer such a devastating reversal of its good fortunes of a year before? Certainly part of the problem lay in the economic depression of 1837, which hit charitable organizations such as the AUA first and hardest.[44] In August, Eliot had found it so difficult to collect from Boston subscribers that he gave up trying, convinced that "more harm than good would come from any efforts in that direction" (4:285). Of the seventeen subscribers who had recently discontinued, Samuel Clarke reported in November, five had given financial "embarrassment" as their reason. The economic trauma pointed out, moreover, the haphazard bookkeeping that had always plagued the magazine. When Clarke could no longer afford to rely upon his subscribers' good faith and had to hire a collector, he discovered that some readers had changed addresses, others had been getting duplicate copies, and a number insisted that they had never subscribed in the first place.

Still, the *Messenger* seems less a casualty of the economy than a victim of its own editorial policies. The continuing bitterness over abolitionism illustrates the practical consequences of the magazine's independence. "Abolitionists discontinue whenever we utter a word in extenuation of slave-holders," Clarke complained, and "slavery men discontinue when we say any thing in condemnation of the system" (4:431). Nor was slavery the only rub. Some accused the *Messenger* of encouraging the Transcendentalists;[45] others took offense at its remarks about Frothingham and Norton; and still others must have wondered whether the magazine stood for anything at all. Clarke confessed the magazine partial to "whatever is earnest, deep, and original," yet the more he tried to articulate its precise position, the more flaccid and illogical he sounded.

> We are not ultra in any thing. We are not Radical Reformers, or stiff Conservatives. We are not ultra-Unitarians. . . . We are not ultra peace men. . . . We are not ultra in our love of change or novelty. We think the views of Furness, Emerson, Brownson and Ripley may be defective and in some respects one-sided. And we trust we are not even ultra in our moderation. (4:431–32)

To the *Messenger* writers, well schooled in the practical effects of extremism, *any* ideological commitment fettered the mind: to be "ultra" was to limit possibilities. Ironically, though, their steadfast refusal to be "ultra" became itself a form of extremism. Quick and biting in its criticism, the magazine appeared to have little positive to offer beyond airy platitudes. Its writers' reluctance to advocate wholeheartedly any specific body of ideas effectively prevented them from attracting loyal or enthusiastic readers.

Finally, Clarke's imprudent use of the editor's columns to single out individuals for praise or blame cost the magazine measurably. His correspondents often cautioned him that their letters were "off the record," knowing that in moments of editorial desperation he might rifle his mail for last-minute filler.[46] He was clearly not averse to continuing personal quarrels in print, either. In 1836 and 1837, for instance, he and James Hall, the Ohio novelist, carried on an increasingly venomous war in the *Messenger* and the *North American Review* over Hall's recent collections of Western sketches, which Clarke called "a piece of literary fraud" (3:498). In all it was a petty exchange, a reminder of how circumscribed the Western literary world was in the 1830s.[47] But the episode had serious consequences, for Clarke's sharp tongue offended the most tireless booster of native literature in the Ohio Valley, at the very time when the inexperienced editors most needed support and advice.

When the abolitionist newspaperman Elijah Lovejoy met his death at the hands of an Alton mob in November 1837, the *Messenger*'s critical voice again cost it support. The small band of Unitarians in that Illinois town were precisely the type of broadminded Westerners Clarke thought he could count on, but the attack on Lovejoy caused him to reconsider his confidence. In the January 1838 *Messenger* he accused the entire town of complicity in the murder, which he attributed (largely on incomplete and hearsay reports) to a fear of losing a lucrative trade with slave states. "The mass of the people" in Alton, Clarke wrote angrily, shared full responsibility for the crime, since they "encouraged it, and now justify it" (4:360). An appalled Charles Farley demanded a retraction of the remarks,[48] but Clarke's only response was to high-handedly caution Alton against its "spirit of mobism." "It is a mistaken patriotism," he warned, "which would now refuse to listen to tones of rebuke" (4:432). Half of Alton's twelve subscribers chose to listen no longer and immediately discontinued the *Messenger* (4:431).

As Westerners became disenchanted with the *Messenger,* so Clarke grew increasingly disenchanted with them. For one thing, his congregation—who constituted most of Louisville's seventy subscribers—had come to resent his jaunts to New England and the time his editorial work stole from his proper pastoral duties. "Some of them growl at your absence," Osgood had warned him early in 1837, and when Clarke left suddenly for Boston in August the growls grew louder. To Clarke his parishioners' failure to see the magazine as an integral part of his missionary work was disappointing; worse, they responded only half-heartedly to the vitality of his sermons, the intellectual challenges of his prose.[49] Excited in 1835 by the possibilities of the Western people, Clarke now understood that his high expectations would be realized slowly, if at all. The Disciples,

whose antisectarianism once seemed to auger the spiritual freedom of the West, showed disturbing signs of "exclusiveness,"
becoming themselves a distinct sect; Alexander Campbell still
clung insistently to baptism by immersion as the test for true
believers. "To be wholly tolerant seems almost beyond the human power," Clarke lamented in the *Messenger* (4:322).

More and more the East, not the West, seemed the locus of
vital activity in religion and art. Letters from New England
brought tantalizing news of Emerson's lectures and of Brownson's sermons to the working classes. In February 1838 Osgood
predicted a "furious storm between the conservatives & radicals" within Unitarianism.

> There is a deal of life of all kinds, political, literary & moral
> in our city at this present moment. Emerson & Walker by
> their lectures have set the whole city agog to penetrate the
> mysteries of transcendentalism. Ripley is all alive & his book
> just out. There are weekly meetings of a "Progress" Club at
> Jona. Phillips room, where Dr Channing & all the friends of
> humanity regularly congregate & to two of which I have been
> admitted. Then again, ever so many books are just out,
> among others, the Dean's—& in short there was never so
> much excitement on subjects, that do not relate to "bread
> alone," as at present.[50]

By comparison, Clarke's possibilities in Kentucky seemed to
him pale and limited. Expect "no Transcendentalism, nor
Emersonianism" in Louisville, he warned Bronson Alcott when
the controversial teacher considered a move West in April
1838.[51] In his darker moments Clarke complained about the
West's aborted promise as bitterly as he had denounced New
England's constrictions five years earlier. "I stiffen in routine, I
am choked by custom, I lack mental stimulus," he wrote Margaret Fuller in August; "all around me are flat, heavy, worldly,
like Dutch marshes, and my feeble taper expires in this moral
miasma."[52] In the *Messenger*'s apparent failure Clarke surely
found a correlative for his personal despair.

Reports of the magazine's demise, however, proved prema-
ture. Clarke's pleas roused enough of his audience from their
lethargy that the *Messenger* resumed publication, after a
month's hiatus, in April 1838. Possibly stung by guilt, more

likely prodded by Charles Briggs and by Dr. Channing—who, Sarah Clarke reported, was particularly distressed over the magazine's plight—the Executive Committee of the AUA had appropriated $100 in aid on 21 December 1837, even before Clarke's request reached them.[53] Huidekoper sent $30, a Kentucky schoolmaster $20, and the minister at Mobile the names of sixteen new subscribers (4:411–13; 5:67–69). Once again the *Messenger* had staved off financial ruin at the last minute.

The six months that followed were relatively placid, a welcome relief to Clarke after the near collapse of the magazine. Friends East and West contributed material, relieving Clarke of the primary responsibility for filling the *Messenger*'s pages, and giving volume 5 a range of subject matter unequaled before or after. Margaret Fuller reviewed William Ware's popular *Letters from Palmyra* (1837) for the April number (5:24–29), Henry Hedge offered—at last—a previously unpublished sermon (5:82–88), Furness contributed proofsheets from his forthcoming book, *Jesus and his Biographers* (5:413–20), and Clarke's classmate Oliver Wendell Holmes obliged his old friend with an "insignificant little affair" from his commonplace book of poetry (5:78–80).[54] From Osgood came a perceptive essay on the histories of Bancroft, Carlyle, and William Prescott (5:1–6); from Perkins (now returned to Cincinnati, his venture in mining a failure) came poetry, sketches, and essays on public education. Cranch's verse, maturing from commonplace piety to the concrete imagery and studied meditation of pieces like his "To a Humming Bird" (5:372–73), improved the belletristic quality of the magazine. Under less pressure to churn out prose, Clarke temporarily smoothed over the difficulties with his parish, and when he did write he wrote well: on miracles again, on phrenology, on Scott and Shakespeare, on Ripley's new series of foreign translations. Even the reprinted matter that filled open pages lent variety and quality to the magazine— excerpts from Brownson on popular sovereignty and reformers (5:104–9, 313–18), selections from Tennyson and Goethe and George Herbert, and a sketch by a little-known writer from Salem named Nathaniel Hawthorne, in whose work Clarke found "all of Washington Irving's delightful man-

ner, with profounder meaning and a higher strain of sentiment" (5:248–56).

Yet a single article by Clarke in the June number ensured
that the *Messenger* would not long continue its steady course.
Surveying the prospects of the Unitarian church, Clarke called
up the old stereotypes of the sect as cerebral, lethargic, nega-
tive—and agreed with them. "We have been, as a sect," he
admitted, "comparatively cold, and indifferent to the great interests of the Redeemer's kingdom" (5:152). But the "torpor
and apparent death" of Unitarianism he found an encouraging
herald of the "new and more glorious form" the sect would
assume, led by men of vision like Dr. Channing, Furness,
Brownson, and Emerson (5:152–58).

This "Letter on the State of Unitarianism at the East,"
Clarke's fourth "slap at the East" (as he termed it in his diary) in
as many years, crystallized the tensions between the *Messenger*
and the Unitarian establishment. To criticize an irrational fear
of German thought, to chastise the AUA for apathy, even to
insult a revered minister like Frothingham: all these indiscre-
tions could eventually be forgiven. But to pronounce the entire
denomination dead—in a publication twice rescued by the
AUA's generosity, at a time when the sect felt acutely threatened
by the Transcendentalist insurgence within its ranks—this was
unpardonable. Clarke surely realized how inflammatory his remarks were, for he cautiously signed his essay "A Western
Unitarian" and disguised it as a letter to the editor; he could
not, however, have predicted that a month after his "slap"
reached New England, Emerson would also pronounce historical Christianity ready "to totter to its fall, almost all life extinct"
and exhort the seniors at Harvard's Divinity School to "refuse
the good models . . . and dare to love God without mediator or
veil."[55] By the time Emerson's address shattered the fragile tis-
sue of decorum separating the new and old schools, Clarke's
anonymous essay, less eloquent yet more sharply focused on the
Unitarian denomination, had already strained relations to the
breaking point. By a coincidence in time but as a direct result of
its continuing editorial policies, the *Messenger* became inextric-
ably linked with the Emersonian heresy. Conservatives cast the

Divinity School Address as the "latest form of infidelity," but they regarded the *Messenger* as nothing less than the periodical of Transcendentalism. Its continuing criticism of the denomination's leaders and doctrines made it equally as subversive to Unitarianism as Emerson's individualism or Brownson's radical church polity.

Leading the assault for the conservatives was, once again, the redoubtable Andrews Norton, who took the occasion of Emerson's address to expose the fraud of the new school once and for all. In the *Boston Daily Advertiser* for 27 August 1838, Norton assailed the new views on the familiar three charges: as a definable movement within liberalism, as a product of "the crabbed and disgusting obscurity of some of the worst German speculatists," and as a manifestation of "the most extraordinary assumption." What made the situation particularly alarming, Norton said, was the ease with which the Transcendentalists had lately seduced "silly young men" from true faith and embued them with a delusion of self-importance. "The writer of an article for an obscure periodical, or a religious newspaper, assumes a tone as if he were one of the chosen enlighteners of a dark age." Even in "a professedly religious work, called the Western Messenger," Norton fumed, "the atheist Shelley has been quoted and commended."

No greater indictment could be made against the *Messenger,* and the fact that Norton could reach back to February 1837 for evidence of the magazine's pernicious influence indicates how long he had brooded over the *Messenger*'s radical course. Emerson had his supporters in New England; but virtually no one had anything good to say about Shelley.[56] In fact, the *Messenger*'s essay "Shelley and Pollok" (3:474–78), signed "D. L." but written by Osgood, was no blind commendation of the controversial poet, who was coolly received by the radicals in the 1830s.[57] Osgood repeatedly mourned Shelley's "extravagancies of action and opinion," though he suggested that the poet's atheism developed from "opposition to the prevalent ideas of bigots"— much as Unitarians had reacted to the harsh Calvinism of their time (3:474–75).[58] Osgood's point was that Shelley's verse was valuable despite the poet's infidelity, for it showed "much more true Christian feeling" than the relentless fury of such versifiers as the Presbyterian Robert Pollok (3:475). "We had rather be damned with Percy Bysshe Shelly," Osgood concluded, echoing Shelley's preface to *Prometheus Unbound*, "than go to Heaven with John Calvin and Robert Pollok" (3:478). Had Norton read the essay objectively, he would have seen that Osgood's purpose was not to commend atheism but to attack, in quite conventional Unitarian fashion, the "false and abominable" Calvinist doctrine of divine retribution.

But as Osgood used Shelley for his own purposes, so did Norton, who found the poet's name—as he had elsehwere found Goethe's and Carlyle's—a convenient and effective weapon for bludgeoning the magazine whose editor had been nipping at his heels for years. Clarke, not Osgood, replied to Norton's criticism, in the *Advertiser* for 28 September 1838. After quoting Osgood's essay briefly in its own defense, Clarke addressed what he perceived to be the true issue: Norton's intolerance. After years of priming, Clarke was at last ready for the confrontation with Unitarianism's most formidable polemicist, and the young minister was devastating. Did Norton really think that "a man who *says he has faith* must be a believer, and he who says he has *not* faith, cannot be a believer?" asked Clarke. Did Norton object to charity toward sinners? Perhaps he would remember that Jesus' accusers had found him guilty of precisely the same "crime."

> Perhaps they went away and said that a professedly religious teacher had praised Sodom and Gomorrah. No doubt they could excite much prejudice against him in this way; and it is easy now, to excite prejudice against those who venture to find any thing good in Infidels and Atheists.

Norton responded in the *Advertiser* on 3 October with aloof disdain, quoting from "Queen Mab" and *Prometheus Unbound* to show Shelley's "glowing hatred against all that is established or reverenced" and hoping that Clarke would someday "be ashamed of the article and its defense." Clarke's audacious comparison to the Pharisees Norton dismissed with a sniff.

> He compares me to a hardened Jew, who might have uttered a foul calumny; and himself, in praising Shelley, to Jesus

Christ. It is impossible that one should feel provocation from such an attack. I quote it merely to show the tone and temper of modern ultra liberality, overflowing with indulgence toward all who attack the foundations of human happiness.

During the exchange Clarke had carefully omitted any defense of Emerson or the new school, concentrating solely on the injustice to himself and to his magazine. But in October, during the customary break between volumes, he worked almost daily on a detailed response to the charges brought against the Transcendentalists. He also wrote again to Charles Briggs about the *Messenger's* continuing financial instability, encouraging the general secretary to impress upon new missionaries the need for more subscribers. "Let them describe the Messenger as an Independent Magazine," Clarke advised, not a doctrinaire organ of the Eastern church.[59] That was surely a superfluous observation after the exchange with Norton and the accumulated radicalism of the past year. No longer did Clarke bother to ask for the AUA's subsidy; never again did the organization offer it.

On 22 October Clarke left Louisville for his annual journey to New England, careful this time to notify his congregation in advance and to secure Cranch as his replacement in the pulpit and as editor of the December *Messenger.* On his way north Clarke stopped at Cincinnati, there visiting the new minister, his old friend William Henry Channing, who had at last accepted the call to come west. They spent the afternoon discussing Emerson and the turmoil over the Divinity School Address.[60] A month later Clarke was in New England, talking with Emerson, visiting Margaret Fuller at her new home in Providence, debating with old school men, and attending meetings of the Transcendental Club.

For Clarke personally, affiliation with the new school was no longer at issue—nor, after the November 1838 number, could there be much doubt about the *Messenger's* sympathies. Volume 6 opened with an essay on Unitarian reform, in which Clarke defined his denomination's proper goals as progress toward Christian union and complete freedom from "scholastic trammels" (6:5–10). In another piece, on German theology, he once again criticized those Americans—it is difficult not to read Andrews Norton—who "are so afraid of having their small modicum of faith swept away by the Neology of Germany that they conceive the only safe course to be that of Ulysses, and to stop their ears against these sirens" (6:57). He was plowing old ground here, but his words now carried the weight of accumulated experience and the tone of an established polemicist, not a feisty neophyte. Despite Norton's dismissal of the *Messenger* as "an obscure periodical," friends and enemies alike no longer ignored the magazine, for no other periodical so consistently ran afoul of the received wisdom of the church establishment. When in November the *Messenger* at last addressed the Transcendental controversy on its own terms, its position came as no surprise.

"R. W. Emerson, and the New School" and "The New School in Literature and Religion," the response to the conservatives that Clarke had worked on during October, are properly two headings of a single essay. It begins with a calm summary of the controversy over the Divinity School Address, as if the whole matter were no cause for alarm. In fact, said Clarke, it was not, for it showed the strength of the Unitarian denomination. Unlike other sects, he claimed disingenuously, Unitarians argue so thoughtfully that "the bitterness all dies away—for men who seriously set themselves to *thinking* are not apt to get angry." As for Emerson, "we are convinced that if [he] has taught any thing very wrong, it will be found out" (6:39). But *had* Emerson taught heresy? Not to Clarke: Emerson had simply—though "without perhaps sufficient care against misconstruction"— developed the biblical commonplace that "the letter [of Scripture] is a dead weight in the mind, if the spirit does not animate it" (6:40). Surely, Clarke implied, no true Unitarian would argue in favor of mere lip service to the Gospel.

About the rumored new school, Clarke pretended ignorance. If, as the writer in the *Advertiser* had claimed, it consisted of admirers of Carlyle, the French eclectic philosopher Victor Cousin, and the German Friedrich Schleiermacher, how disparate a group would be included (6:43). If, on the other hand, assumption and ignorance characterized the new school, "these traits may be found united even in those, who cherish the deadliest hostility to Transcendentalism." Nor could members of the school be classed by their belief in intuition, since all men would agree that some ideas, causality for instance, "belong to a common sense which is back of all logic" (6 : 44–45). And if bad taste was the hallmark of the school, Clarke asked, who could presume to set standards (6 : 45)? Clearly, Norton's criteria were deficient.

Nevertheless, Clarke concluded, such a school did exist, composed of "thinking men and educated women" of all sects, bound by their desire for "LIFE, soul, energy, originality" in religion and literature. No slavish disciples of Carlyle or Emerson or Brownson or Furness, they respected "genuine, earnest, independent thought," and were thus drawn by "strong sympathies" to each of those thinkers. Not Emerson but Dr. Channing represented the consummation of the new philosophy, for he of all men most sympathized "with every effort of struggling humanity to bring on . . . a happier and better day" (6 : 46–47). The new school, far from being a body of doctrine, was by definition antidoctrinal, characterized by its breadth of inquiry—precisely Clarke's definition for Unitarianism in its purest form.

It was a marvelous response to "Nortonism," rhetorically tight, calculated to disarm rather than defeat, perhaps the most mature piece of prose Clarke ever wrote. The persona of the humble seeker of truth worked particularly well, for with it Clarke could dismiss his critics' definitions yet continue to ask their questions. And his own criteria for the new school effectively isolated the old school from the mainstream of the denomination without forcing him to endorse Emerson or the new school. The salient point, in fact, is that Clarke nowhere endorses "Emersonianism," though he defends Emerson throughout. It was the "genius, life and manliness" of Emerson's thought that inspired, not the ideas themselves. Ironically, to embrace those ideas would be by definition to violate the "impulse to independent thought" characteristic of the Transcendental movement (6 : 47). If there truly were subversion within liberal Christianity, its leaders were the Nortons and the Bowens, Clarke argued, those who would fetter the mind with the chains of orthodoxy.

William Henry Channing sounded the same cry in the December *Messenger*, in a review of the *Christian Examiner* signed "C. G." The *Examiner*'s editors had suggested in November that "the instructors of the [Divinity] School . . . should hereafter guard themselves" against opinions such as Emerson's "within *their own* walls." Channing was shocked. Less than a decade before, he recalled, a leading Unitarian had called the school the only institution in America where "the sentiments of the professors and instructors are not swathed and stiffened and cramped by the tight folds of a human creed" (6:120). Those were the words of F. W. P. Greenwood—now coeditor of the *Examiner*.[61] How far the denomination had come, when the pursuit of truth gave way to censorship and doctrinal conformity, Channing observed pointedly. "This is indeed a 'New View'" (6:118). Like Clarke, Channing thus turned the tables on the conservatives: they, not the new school, had departed from the spirit of Unitarianism. "Lay not the corner stone for a prison of Creed," he warned the Eastern clergy, for the result will be the quick death of liberal thought.

> If this policy, which we sincerely hope, though we "are not well convinced" is but a hasty suggestion, hastily expressed, should actually find entrance into the Unitarian body;—we shall not be surprised to see the day, when the Examiner will become not the mouth-piece for all free hearts, which it *ought* to be, but a mere echo of the opinions of its editors or of a clique;—when the Register will be placed under the guardianship of advisers, who may prescribe what it is prudent and politic to publish; when the Executive committee of the Unitarian Association will be an inquisitorial board to take an oversight of all churches and clergymen, all people and pastors, and exterminate "heresy" not indeed by dungeon and faggot, but by a seasonable word spoken in secret. (6:119–20)

Young Channing strengthened his radical credentials, and the *Messenger*'s, in the next two numbers of the magazine, continuing his attack on the sterile rationalism of his former teachers. The Deity, he wrote in January, is "not a subject *for knowledge* but *for faith*" (6:191). In February he went even farther: "The great truths of the eternal world lie all folded within us" (6:251), an affirmation of the divine capacity of man that within the walls of his alma mater could only have been interpreted as heresy.

Channing and Clarke had written anonymously; that may have saved their reputations for the moment, but it gave their radical statements the appearance of editorial positions. By the beginning of 1839, the *Messenger* remained the sole periodical to treat the Transcendentalists fairly and at length—not because its writers considered themselves members of the new school (though some of them did) but because they shared with the Transcendentalists a fear of human creeds. As their dissatisfaction with New England had led the *Messenger* writers to the open West, so their opposition to reactionary elements within Unitarianism led them toward the "party of hope," of which Emerson was at the moment the most conspicuous member.[62] They defended the Transcendentalists, ironically, not at the expense of their denomination but as progressive leaders of it, a central fact that explains why, even while most vocally opposed to Unitarianism as creed, the magazine still included articles on the Trinity, the atonement, future retribution, and other doctrinal points quite in line with conventional Unitarian thinking. Even so thorough a radical as Cranch remained unconvinced that intuition and "sudden flashes of good feeling" were adequate substitutes for "habitual religion" (5:374). Osgood, still a regular contributor, feared "one sided transcendentalists like R. W. E." who could "not get out of the *me*."[63] There was, in short, no unanimity among the *Messenger*'s contributors on the new philosophy. But they were all veterans of the Western war with the Calvinists, and they were, as a consequence and to a man, thoroughly opposed to human creeds of any form.[64] That opposition, not an endorsement of the new school, shaped the Transcendentalist sympathies of the *Messenger* while tying it on specific points of belief to mainstream Unitarianism. In the strident dialogue that followed Emerson's explosive address in August of 1838, however, such editorial subtleties were lost; as Francis Bowen said, there was simply no room for compromise: "Either one party or the other is entirely in the wrong."[65]

Thus to most Unitarians the *Messenger* appeared an organ of the Transcendentalists. Conservatives like Norton found its outspoken opposition offensive and dangerous; moderates turned to more acceptable publications, the *Register* and the *Examiner.* The *Messenger* suffered as much from neglect as from enmity, as its sagging subscriptions and the tightfistedness of the AUA show. With money scarce and the denomination's funds spread thinly, the AUA spent its missionary allotment elsewhere—largely on missionaries themselves, a record high of twenty-three in 1838–39.[66] Why fund a magazine likely to turn upon its benefactors?

Paradoxically, though, while Unitarians found the magazine's Transcendental defenses unacceptable, the Transcendental group evidently came to regard its Unitarian character the same way. Osgood worried, after reading Clarke's essay on Emerson and the new school, that such "interest in Eastern affairs [is] apt to give a turn to your maga, more interesting to Eastern Transcendentalists, than edifying to readers, who wish to be informed of plain Christian Truth."[67] In a sense his anxiety was well founded, for while Clarke and the rest believed the struggle against creeds a genuinely "Western" issue, the Transcendental controversy itself must have seemed mere parochial squabbling to subscribers in the Ohio Valley, where no other periodical took the least notice of it.[68] But if the magazine's positions lost it readers in the West, there was no corresponding gain in support among the radicals in the East. To be sure, the Transcendental circle read the *Messenger* with interest; some of them—Fuller, Ripley, Brownson, Hedge—subscribed to it; Emerson, grateful no doubt for Clarke's kind words, even parted with some of his verse, the first signed poetry he had ever published, for the magazine's pages.[69] Still, the New England Transcendentalists never threw their support wholeheartedly behind the struggling Western periodical. By late 1838 other magazines seemed equally valuable to them— Brownson's *Quarterly Review* for its radical politics, the *Democratic Review* for its publication of romantic poetry and fiction— and in the end none was a wholly appropriate vehicle for the new philosophy. During a meeting of the Transcendental Club in the spring of 1839, Bronson Alcott lamented that all contemporary magazines save the abolitionist *Liberator* were "destitute

of life, freshness, [and] independence," and by September the
Club turned its attention once again to a magazine of its own,
one free of any political or religious affiliations.[70] Independent
enough to defend the new school, the *Messenger* remained too
Unitarian to actively promote it. And as a literary magazine,
Margaret Fuller told Clarke bluntly, it suffered from an aesthetic ordinariness that even Emerson's poetry could not over-
come.

> About putting beautiful verses in your Magazine, I have no
> feeling except what I should have about furnishing a room. I
> should not put a dressing-case into a parlor, or a book-case
> into a dressing-room, because, however good things are in
> their place, they were not in place there. And this, not in
> consideration of the public, but of my own sense of fitness
> and harmony.[71]

To Clarke all this posed a distressing dilemma, made worse
for the young editor by a crisis in his personal life. Five years
after his arrival in Kentucky, his Louisville congregation still
refused to give him the security of a permanent call, preferring
instead to renew his contract annually. He seemed always to be
seeking their approval, and he had grown convinced that they
would never be wholly responsive to his ministry. On 4 November 1838 he had become engaged to Anna Huidekoper, who
insisted that they postpone the wedding until his future was
more settled.[72] When he returned to Louisville from New England, just before Christmas, Clarke felt pressured both personally and professionally to direct his life toward more stable,
narrowly defined ends.

Editorship of the *Messenger* was the obvious duty to discard.
For three years he had devoted his best energies to it, at the
expense of his pastoral responsibilities and—to some, at least—
his reputation. Serving, he recalled years later, as "publisher,
editor, contributor, proof-reader, and boy to pack up the copies
and carry them to the post-office," he found the work fulfilling
but enervating: for several weeks in September, during the
break between volumes 5 and 6, he had lain bedridden with
"bilious fever" and fatigue.[73] He could look back with satisfaction, if not for the way the *Messenger* was received, at least for

what it had accomplished. But having done as much as he could to support the new philosophy without compromising his personal and editorial opposition to creeds, he felt unrewarded. To most Unitarians he had gone too far; to the Transcendental group, not far enough. His Western readers regarded his emphasis on Eastern affairs as irrelevant or frivolous; his congregation viewed his editorship as an intrusion. Perhaps it was time for a new editor to guide the magazine—Channing or Perkins or Eliot or Christopher Cranch, like-minded men with talent and experience.

Clarke surely talked about his plans when he visited William Channing at Cincinnati on 19 December 1838, just before he arrived back in Louisville, for the transfer of the *Messenger* was much on his mind at year's end. Late in December Edward Cranch suggested returning the magazine to Cincinnati, an offer Clarke greeted "with joy," according to Christopher Cranch.[74] Clarke wrote immediately to William Channing, but the new minister at Cincinnati wanted no part of the editorship, at least not yet. For two months he strenuously resisted, unwilling to take on the added duties unless Clarke absolutely could not bear them. In the meantime Clarke thought more seriously about his future in Louisville (he would soon get offers to settle in Chicago and Charlestown, Massachusetts), and by early February he decided to continue the magazine only until the close of volume 6 in April.[75] Channing relented at last.

To the end Clarke strove to maintain the *Messenger*'s quality; among his final acts as editor was the publication of a generous selection of sonnets by Jones Very, the mystical young writer whose poetry the Transcendentalists highly valued,[76] and he filled the chinks between articles with extracts from Emerson, Coleridge, and George Herbert. Yet his heart was no longer in the work. In mid-March of 1839, almost three years to the day since the *Messenger* was transferred to Louisville, Clarke arrived in Cincinnati to pass the business records and files along to its new editors.[77] The back cover of the April number announced the move officially: henceforth, the *Messenger*'s present editor would be "assisted" by Channing, Perkins, Vaughan, and Edward Cranch, with all correspondence to be directed to Channing at the Cincinnati office. It was a cooperative arrangement

on paper only. Though he continued as a contributor and occasional adviser, Clarke had given up his editorial responsibilities
for good.[78]

Thus the magazine returned to its original home. It had
changed substantially since it left, as had the world in which it
moved; a "living mirror of the times," the *Messenger* under
Clarke bore the stamp of its editor's wide-ranging interests,
from antislavery to church reform to German literature, its
overriding opposition to human creeds leading it finally to defend the religious and aesthetic radicalism of the Transcendentalists. The magazine pledged to be "ultra" in nothing had
become the forum for some of the most innovative ideas of its
time. But as Clarke had shaped its past, so the *Messenger*'s new
editors would direct its future. On the eve of his departure
from the West, Christopher Cranch wrote Clarke a long letter
hinting at the direction the *Messenger* might take. Perkins,
Cranch noted, was entering upon his new duties as minister-at-
large "with the broadest grounds and best hopes."

> He and Vaughan and Channing and a few others—what a
> host they will be—an irresistible phalanx, a select school for
> the development and realization of true democratic ideas.
> The Unitarians here are getting broad awake. Channing is
> pouring life into them by week-fulls, and John C. Vaughan is
> stirring his stumps and the stumps of all around him in the
> great work. Everything looks encouraging.[79]

First Unitarian Church of Louisville. Watercolor by James Freeman Clarke, ca. 1835. *Courtesy of the Filson Club and of the First Unitarian Church of Louisville.*

Cincinnati in 1835. "Fourth Street West of Vine," painting by John Caspar Wild. First Congregational Church (Unitarian) in right center, background. *Courtesy of the Cincinnati Historical Society.*

Ephraim Peabody. *Courtesy of King's Chapel, Boston, Mass.*

James Freeman Clarke, ca. 1840. From Clarke's "Journal 1839–40." *By permission of the Houghton Library, Harvard University.*

James Freeman Clarke. Unitarian Universalist Association archives, Boston, Mass. *Used by permission.*

James Handasyd Perkins. *Courtesy of the Massachusetts Historical Society.*

William Henry Channing. Unitarian Universalist Association archives, Boston, Mass. *Used by permission.*

Harm Jan Huidekoper. *Courtesy of the Crawford County Historical Society.*

William Greenleaf Eliot. From Charlotte C. Eliot, *William Greenleaf Eliot* (Boston, 1904).

Christopher Pearse Cranch, 1843. Sketch by William Wetmore Story. *Collection of Robert D. Habich.*

Samuel Osgood. From *The Knickerbocker* **53 (1859).**

4
1839–1841
"The medium . . . of radical Xn truth"

William Henry Channing was busy. Ordained in Cincinnati on 10 May 1839, with a handsome salary of $1,500 per year, he was expected to earn his keep: preaching every Thursday night and twice on Sundays, visiting his congregation, conducting Sunday School and Bible study classes, baptizing the young into Christian life, and ushering the old out of it. Still, he was an energetic man, on the eve of his twenty-ninth birthday, and the settled regimen of a permanent call proved a refreshing change from his nomadic existence since he graduated from Harvard's Divinity School six years before. "My life passes in a hum drum fashion," he wrote his wife, Julia, "although I am as pleasantly situated as a single man can be."[1]

The lightness of tone, however, belied the anguish caused by Channing's separation from his family. Bad weather and the rigors of travel had kept them apart since his arrival in Cincinnati the previous September, but the reasons for the separation lay deeper. Julia Allen, daughter of a strict New York Episcopalian, had been enjoined by her father not to change her faith after her marriage in 1836, and Channing accepted the call to Cinncinnati knowing that his wife would never countenance his religious opinions. "Do think of this more definitely," he pleaded with her; "do unravel your perplexities. I cannot for my life see why an Episcopalian & Unitarian should not sympathise in far the majority of points and these the essentials. I certainly can with you."[2] But Julia and young Frances remained in New York. For Channing, their absence confirmed personally the divisive sectarian spirit he found so objectionable.

If Channing's personal burden was heavy, his professional one was lightened somewhat by his cousin James Perkins, since February 1939 the minister-at-large in Cincinnati. Inspired by the successful social work of Joseph B. Tuckerman in Boston, Perkins tended to the spiritual and material well-being of the urban poor, regardless of their denominations, and his natural sense of benevolence blossomed in the new role. He visited needy families, lectured to mechanics and laborers, spoke against gambling and drunkenness, and worked to reform prison conditions and public education. Apart from his official duties, Perkins was also a trustee of Cincinnati College, a co-founder of the Society for the Promotion of Useful Knowledge, an active member of the Western College of Teachers, and a leader of the newly formed Ohio Historical Society; in his spare time he gathered material for a projected volume, *The Annals of the West*.[3]

Edward Cranch and John Vaughan, both announced as coeditors of the *Messenger* at the close of volume 6, apparently found themselves occupied with their growing law practice; while each contributed articles from time to time, neither participated formally in the editorial duties. Indeed, when the first number of volume 7 appeared in May 1839, its cover named only Clarke, Channing, and Perkins as editors. Clarke, however, had even less time for the magazine than did the others. Still undecided about his future in the West, he submitted a letter of resignation to the trustees of the Louisville church on 22 April 1839, but was persuaded to stay until a replacement could be found. To his minister's duties he added an appointment as superintendent of Louisville's public schools; his translation of De Wette's *Theodore* for George Ripley's series on German literature was an ongoing project; and in August he and Anna Huidekoper were to be married. "My time is so full," he wrote Anna, "that I am running to and fro from morn till dewy eve."[4] To Channing and Perkins alone, their energies already taxed by pastoral, charitable, and literary work, fell the task of editing the *Western Messenger* in the spring of 1839.

Not surprisingly, then, there was at first little outward change in the magazine under its new editors. Overworked, Channing and Perkins were no doubt grateful for whatever their contributors sent them. From Huidekoper came doctrinal arguments against Calvinist views of sin and innate depravity (7: 100–104, 145–51, 225–33). Clarke contributed an old piece of biblical exegesis (7: 170–71), short German translations, a witty dialogue on modern poets signed "C. F. J." (7: 105–12), and the back matter for May. In the first three numbers of volume 7, nearly one-third of the pages were taken up with sermons, some of them reprinted. There was a flurry of controversy when Christopher Cranch and Thomas Maylin debated Huidekoper on the scriptural evidence for punishment after death (7:197–200, 241–48, 333–41); and the reprinting of Dr. Channing's latest "letter" on slavery (7: 54–67) probably raised some eyebrows among the *Messenger*'s readers. On the whole, though, the volume opened quietly, its contributions not pointed enough to either offend or excite. Dr. Channing sent the new editors his blessing ("Go on, my young friends, with stout hearts & cheerful faith"),[5] but the Boston papers did not even notice the change in command; and neither, it seems, did anyone else.

Even in the placid beginnings of the new volume, however, lay signs of a change in the *Messenger*'s direction. Though the "irresistible phalanx" of radical editors envisioned by Christopher Cranch dissolved, William Channing's and Perkins's commitment to reform appeared early. Opening the May number was Channing's appraisal of "Christian Denominations" (7: 1–8), a sermon that made clear precisely how far he was willing to retain the *Messenger*'s Unitarian affiliation. Sects, he conceded, were "omen[s] of progress," each contributing to the body of doctrine from which reasonable men and women might distill pure truth. But that truth was not embodied in Unitarianism, which was, Channing maintained, "a mere philosophic speculative name" denoting not faith but dogma and "therefore to be shunned by a Christian." In one sense, Channing merely continued Clarke's advocacy of Christian union—a concept most Unitarians endorsed in theory. Yet for Channing, whose experience in the ministry had always been nondenominational, religious union was not a speculative ideal but an achievable goal. Whereas Clarke had been grateful for peaceful coexistence—Unitarians and Presbyterians sharing the platform at an Independence Day celebration—Channing presented plans for the organization of believers called "Christian Brethren," a "true spiritual family, where theoretic quibbles, and speculative differences, and the juggle of creeds is forgotten." The metaphor recalls his longing for a reconciliation with his wife and child; the plan, and the zeal with which he embraced it, testify to his continuing search for a point of stasis in a changing, pluralistic society.

Never much interested in theological debate, and by training unqualified for it, James Perkins confronted problems far more pressing than religious speculation: poverty, unemployment, hunger, crime. Earlier he had argued in the *Messenger* for "Christian Republicanism," the proprietary rule of morally advanced leaders. In 1839, while not abandoning that ideal, he came increasingly to believe enlightened rule insufficient, or at least not imminent enough, to cure the blight of poverty and injustice. Through change in institutions, he realized, would come the opportunity for the regeneration of souls—not the reverse.

The shift in orientation is first noticeable in Perkins's fiction. His short stories, always didactic, had formerly been tales about the misery wrought by acts of individual moral irresponsibility. Increasingly these exempla yielded to fictional dramas about the tragic effects of failed institutions: the unemployed engraver forced into counterfeiting because Cincinnati had no program for relief of the bankrupt (7:235–41), or the "Two Young Thieves" whose story is subtitled "A Tale to Illustrate the Refuge System" (7:395–402). In his essays as well as his fiction he examined various schemes for improving the lot of the poor—work programs for released convicts (7:8–14), "houses of refuge" for delinquent minors (7:279–87). After six months on the job Perkins published his "First Semi-Annual Report of the Minister at Large in Cincinnati" (7:293–307), a compendium of statistics and anecdotes in support of an eclectic reform program. And in August 1839 he broached the subject that would increasingly widen the gulf between the *Messenger*'s traditional supporters among the Unitarians and the radical editors of the magazine—the "view of property in all its relations" that Perkins called "Christian Economy" (7:221–25).

Economic inequity took on a sudden immediacy for Perkins during his tenure as minister-at-large. Yet it is hardly true, as he claimed, that "little [had] been written about it," for since the mid-1830s the rights of propertied versus working (or "producing") classes defined the Democratic and Whig platforms and drove a wedge between liberal and conservative Democrats as well. The organization of trade unions, the food riots of 1837, the rise of the radical Democrats known as "Locofocos" all portended to conservatives the spread of social incohesion and recalled the Jacobin activity during the French revolution. In newspapers and lyceum halls democracy was debated in all its manifestations, and with the presidential election scarcely a year away the voices on each side grew louder and more insistent.[6] In August 1839 the *Messenger* entered the fray.

Perkins was no democrat, at least not in the strict political sense: opposed to any system that did not recognize Christian principles as "the guide of business, the director of every detail, of mercantile, legal, and political action" (7:222), he was no more inclined to throw power to the masses than he was to confine it to the moneyed aristocracy. Still, because he blamed "the present wrongs connected with property" for "the present political and social position of this land," he found the excesses of the democratic movement less objectionable than the corrupt system that gave rise to it.

> Talk as we may of Loco-focoism, and lament as we may the excesses of its prominent friends, it is based on truth, and is strong because so based: it is the form of opposition to the unhallowed influence of wealth, and the unchristian modes of gaining wealth, which the circumstances of our time have called into being. . . . It comes from man's nature, and is one step in the developement of that nature, in the progress of our race. (7:221)

Men's Christian duty was not to oppose that natural impulse, Perkins argued, but to "do what little they may toward guiding and enlightening the spirit of change and overthrow" (7:222).

His practical remarks did not match the fire of his rhetoric: instead of merely accumulating wealth and becoming "idlers," Perkins said tamely, men must "add to the riches of the world, to the means of improvement" (7:224). But to open the subject of property rights, and to speak approvingly of locofocoism, marked a radical departure for the *Messenger* both in position and scope—a trend more clearly defined in the October 1839 number, to which John Vaughan contributed (anonymously) a long essay on "The Chartists" (7:365–95).

Anticapitalistic if not openly socialistic, the British Chartists proposed universal suffrage for all adult males and the abolition of property requirements for membership in the House of Commons. Delegates from labor unions and reform societies gathered in London in 1839, circulated a petition supporting a "People's Charter," and spawned a wave of violent riots after Parliament refused to grant their demands. Vaughan's assessment of the working-class movement, like Perkins's, stopped short of encouraging armed insurrection. But unlike Perkins, Vaughan maintained that the unequal distribution of wealth and of the opportunity to obtain it was ample justification for revolutionary action (7:373–74). Lawlessness, he contended, was merely an intermediate stage in an inevitable progression toward social and economic change: "there are times, indeed, when society needs a strong blast to stir it up." Vaughan found Chartism "not only a glorious sight" but also "a guarantee of a nobler progress of man," for its principles were "moral in character, and bring to those who embrace them moral power" (7:391–92).

With these two essays, both supporting the moral rights of the working-class movement and accepting the legitimacy of its claims, the *Messenger*'s old promise to "speak of all things in a religious spirit" strained to the breaking point its pledge to be "ultra" in nothing. For in a single volume the *Messenger* writers had introduced and approved reform movements that threatened the religious, economic, and political stability of the times. To be sure, the change in orientation was not unforeseen in the magazine that had already spoken favorably of Emerson, Ripley, and other "disorganizers." But the topics must have taken the *Messenger*'s readers by surprise—Chartism defended in a religious monthly?—and the opinions surely appalled many.

The *Messenger* had embarked on its new path as much by design as by evolution, under circumstances that show how thoroughly the magazine could reflect the views of its immediate editor and the needs of the moment. Channing left for his annual visit to the East during the third week of July, leaving Perkins to supervise the second half of volume 7, and for a number of reasons Perkins was impatient to change the magazine's direction.[7] First, he disapproved of the theological articles still appearing in its pages, finding them both irrelevant and counterproductive to Christian union. Second, he wanted an independent source of money to fund the social programs of his ministry; the financial support of the AUA rankled him, for it suggested a denominational affiliation that he was quick to deny.[8] If the magazine could secure a wider readership, the profits might be put to good use. And finally, Perkins had developed views of God and man that destroyed any bond he may ever have had with Unitarian optimism. Calling himself simply a follower of Jesus, he glibly dismissed questions about the Trinity and the doctrines of imputation, grace, and atonement: "I am not told, and care not to ask." The progress of mankind alone interested him, and his views on human nature were enough to make any good Unitarian blanch.[9]

> In the first place, then, with regard to man's nature: I believe this to be, not an imperfect, progressive nature, which tends to develope and perfect itself, and needs only wholesome food, but a diseased or depraved nature, which leads him to seek wrong ends, to desire things evil for him, which makes virtue hard and vice easy, and which must be cured, altered, regenerated. . . .
>
> In the next place, I believe that as we did not make ourselves, and as we do not even now support ourselves, so neither can we regenerate ourselves. . . .
>
> In the third place, I believe Jesus to have been of a nature higher than human nature as it is seen in this world.
>
> And in the fourth place I believe it to be man's duty to keep his diseased condition ever in view, and . . . to work with the Divine Spirit in freeing his nature from its sickness and sin. (7 : 342–43)

Small wonder that Perkins found the reform of institutions more efficacious than regeneration of the soul. He had come to see the liberal faith in human potential as manifestly absurd.

In mid-September 1839, as Perkins put together the last

number of volume 7, he wrote to ask Clarke's opinion of a plan
to make the *Messenger* profitable and to sever formally its connection with organized Unitarianism. He proposed to suspend
publication until the beginning of 1840, thereafter publishing a
smaller monthly issue (48 pages instead of 72) at the reduced
price of $2 annually. During the hiatus Clarke could straighten
out the *Messenger*'s finances ("which cannot be done by any
other mortal man"). Then, Perkins concluded,

> let us have choice matter, no "filling-up," little theology, en-
> tire independence, & we can not only make the maga useful,
> but earn something for ourselves, or for any purpose we may
> ⟨?⟩ please:—e.g. for the printing of a set of tracts to be written
> by us, tried upon the public through the Messr, & afterwards
> flooded out on the world gratis—[10]

"Write me your views," he asked Clarke, but Perkins really did
not want them, for Clarke scarcely had time to reply before
Perkins made the changes public in the October number. In the
future, Perkins pledged, theology would remain "untouched,"
the magazine's focus instead to be "views of vital, practical religion" and Christian perspectives on "science, history, politics,
and society." The *Messenger*'s guiding principles would be "to
seek right" and to promote "christian brotherhood, the sure
and only basis, as we think, of Democracy" (7:436).

Thus as Clarke had four years earlier initiated the *Messenger*
by fiat (and taken Peabody by surprise), so in 1839 Perkins,
quite on his own, again changed the course of the magazine.
Clarke apparently greeted the news coolly, and on 30 October
Perkins tried to justify the act as a consensus.

> Touching the W.M. these are the facts;—Several persons
> here, of various denominations, have said to us 'If you will
> drop sectarian theology your work will be largely taken by
> the public generally'; Vaughan was of this opinion; when Wm
> Eliot was here we talked of it, & he was in favor of ceasing the
> discussion of sectarian theology; I wrote to you, you thro' Dr
> Jarvis, replied you liked the idea; for myself I dont believe in
> your views & wish the only points of discussion to be unsecta-
> rian:—in this state of things—I wrote the closing note to last
> no.

Clearly, though, the reason for the change was Perkins's new sense of the magazine's utility.

> My idea of the W.M. wd be to have it the medium for those extensions of radical Xn truth to all the purposes of life which I regard as the spread of our faith.—The theology of the Gospels in itself I think we shall all agree in, & I have no wish to argue any points beyond.—In showing, by Facts, Essays, Tales, Revs, Poems & Prosings how the religion of Jesus bears upon Politics, Society, Commerce, Art, Science, Literature, Everything—I think we shall find enough to do.

If Clarke and Huidekoper thought "Unitarianism better be stuck to," Perkins said stubbornly, "I stand clear of the whole concern."[11]

Huidekoper indeed wanted his faith "stuck to"; still convinced that the *Messenger's* mission was to spread Unitarianism in the West, he learned of the policy change when he read it in October, and fired off a letter of complaint to Clarke. Theology "was the very subject for the discussion and diffusion of which the work was principally instituted," the older man protested on 19 October. "It is not necessary that the work should be exclusively devoted to Doctrinal discussion. Let the largest part of it be devoted to practical religion; only do not exclude the former." What is more, he found the new emphasis on "Christian democracy" both inappropriate and dangerous; and as a self-made man generous with his money, he resented the implication that the propertied classes were somehow responsible for the misery of the poor. "If the political essay inserted in the last number of the Messenger [Vaughan's on Chartism] be a fair specimen of Christian democracy," he fumed, "I want none of it. The principles of that essay are unsound, hollow and Jacobinical, and its reasoning delusive." To such objections Perkins had a ready (and reductive) answer: "Mr. V's article on Chartists is to many I doubt not 'Jacobinical,' but are we to adopt the Andrews Norton mode of procedure therefore?"[12]

The cooler heads among the magazine's contributors found themselves caught uncomfortably in the middle. Clarke, after six years in Louisville, now considered himself changed "from a sentimental dreamer into a practical man" and apparently sided with Huidekoper. William Eliot, like Clarke a veteran of Western sectarian warfare, thought it foolhardy to silence the bugle before the battle was won. "What do you think of the proposed change in the 'Messenger'?" he asked Peabody in early November.

> For my part, I do not like it at all. It was founded as a Unitarian paper—as such, its mission is not yet accomplished—and to convert it into a general religious magazine is unwise and unwarranted. . . . I am sorry that it ever passed out of Clarke's hands.[13]

If Eliot had indeed favored "ceasing the discussion of sectarian theology," as Perkins claimed, he most likely had in mind a magazine free of vicious denominational attacks, not one in which Unitarian principles themselves would be ignored. Perkins's rash decision alienated perhaps the magazine's two most powerful Western friends: Huidekoper, whose financial aid could easily have buoyed the sinking periodical, and Eliot, who could have canvassed the Unitarian establishment for subscriptions as effectively as he had solicited donations for his new church building—had he been interested in doing so. Clearly, after the close of volume 7, he was not. Eliot's stream of written contributions, already slowed by the end of the decade, trickled now almost to a stop.

Its purposes altered and its future uncertain, the *Messenger* had slipped into limbo by the time Channing returned to the West (still without Julia) in early November 1839. His Eastern tour had been an especially stimulating one. With Emerson, Fuller, Alcott, and other members of the Transcendental Club, he had gathered in September to hear plans for the new journal that would become the *Dial;* later that month he and Fuller met again in Newport, Rhode Island, where he "prophecied a new literature."[14] At the Divinity School commencement in July, Andrews Norton declared in his "Discourse on the Latest Form of Infidelity" that the Transcendentalists were "at war with a belief in Christianity." Channing's friend Ripley countered with his first "letter" on *The Latest Form of Infidelity Examined,* fanning the smoldering miracles controversy once more into flame.[15] The warmth touched Channing: to him the old order seemed everywhere to be breaking apart, the world poised at "the midnight of our present religious or irreligious era," the intellectual community fragmented into seekers after truth. Though satisfied with his preaching, he confessed himself "restless" and spiritually unfulfilled. "I walk in a consciousness of unemployed force," he wrote Fuller on 25 February 1840, "and see not the when nor the how to make a world out of my chaos." His active mind ranged over a number of projects, from replacing the extemporaneous liturgy with formal prayers and chants, to writing an autobiographical "religious novelette" about the groping of a young man toward spiritual truth—a tale he later published in the *Dial* as "Ernest the Seeker."[16]

Meanwhile, the January deadline for resuming the *Messenger* came and went. Rumors reached New England that the magazine had at last fallen into bankruptcy, "so oppressed with debt" (as Sarah Clarke put it) "that it has resolved upon suicide to escape from its embarrassments."[17] Neither James Clarke nor his brother Samuel in Boston had had much success trying to settle the magazine's finances, and a testy exchange of letters with James Munroe Co. over old accounts in New England seemed to underscore the futility of any further attempts.[18] Clarke had little time for the task anyway, for on 5 February he resigned again from his pulpit in Louisville, this time for good. By May he planned to be on his way to a new church, perhaps in Boston.[19] Like Channing, Clarke had been approached by Margaret Fuller to contribute to the projected *Dial*, but with the apparent demise of the *Messenger* fresh in their minds, neither man responded with much more than cautious interest.

In early February, at last, came word of the *Messenger*'s fate. The *Christian Register* (8 February 1840) carried an open letter "To Friends of the Western Messenger" that confirmed their suspicions of insolvency. "Although our debts are small our private means are smaller," claimed Channing and Perkins, and "our old accounts are not yet settled." But the magazine, though down, was not yet out. Under the new title the *Sower* it would be resumed in the spring, the editors announced, "to cast abroad whatever germs of Truth, Goodness, Beauty we can gather," provided the magazine was clear of debt.

To what extent the *Sower* would simply continue the old *Mes-*

senger under a new name cannot be determined, for the new magazine never appeared. It is highly improbable that Channing and Perkins would have attempted a second periodical while trying so unsuccessfully to keep the first alive. Most likely the *Sower* was merely to be old wine in a new bottle, not an entirely separate magazine, as some scholars have assumed.[20] When Perkins sent the prospectus to Clarke for insertion in the Louisville papers, he spoke hopefully of the *Messenger*'s renewal.

> If we deal lightly with Theology, & keep our high ground of Religion we may get many subscribers out of your Unitarian Goat flock.—Many now, Episcopal, Presbyn., Baptist, & Methodist stand ready to befriend us if we will not be *too anti.*—

Privately the editors were much less sanguine about the magazine's prospects. "I fear much that we shall be obliged to give up our publication here," Channing confided to Fuller just a few weeks after the prospectus appeared. There seemed neither sufficient interest nor immediate need for the *Messenger* to resume.[21]

The necessary stimulus came in April 1840—not from the editors but from the congregations in Louisville and Cincinnati. For years the Western missionary effort had been shaped by its dependence upon New England for funds, for material, for ministers themselves. By the end of the 1830s, there were no less than a dozen Unitarian societies in the West, but to a great extent they remained satellites of the AUA in Boston; when money grew scarce or Eastern interest waned, as happened frequently after the depression of 1837, the Western congregations suffered first and most severely.[22] Ministers lost were hard to replace: Peabody and Osgood had returned East in 1837, Silsbee and Farley in 1838, Cranch in 1839, Huntoon and Clarke in 1840. If the Western societies were to survive, they would have to sustain themselves and provide their own preachers.

There grew, as a result, a sudden interest in a "Western Agency" to coordinate the various congregations and in a regional divinity school to turn out the ministers that Harvard

seemed less and less able to supply.[23] On 1 April 1840 the Louisville Unitarian Association for the Extension of Christian
Knowledge met for the first time, followed by the Union of
Christian Brethren in Cincinnati on 9 April. Together they
pledged support for a regional agency and theological school,
both to be established, they hoped, by June. On 10 April the
Louisville group sent a letter to each of the Western societies,
and some of the Eastern ones, inviting them to form local chapters to further the cause (8:44–47). Within a month they had
raised $300.[24]

It was hardly the groundswell of popular sentiment the
ministers had longed for; probably the five "managers" constituted the entire membership of the Louisville group. But it
was a start, an encouraging sign of renewed spirit, and though
the groups began in Unitarian congregations, their avowed interest was nonsectarian enough—to promote "not correct
speculation . . . but a life of love" (8:44–45)—to encourage men
like Perkins and Channing. Appealing, too, was the sense of
organization: constitutions, officers, dues, and budgets
heralded the type of concrete planning long absent from the
Western effort. Most important, the movement needed an organ to advance the "new bond of sympathy among men"
(8:44). With the *Messenger* teetering between suspending publication and resuming it, the movement apparently provided
enough reason to tilt the balance. In April Perkins and Channing hurriedly assembled material and rushed a new number
through the press.

That first number of volume 8 appeared in mid-May 1840,[25]
with Channing back in the editor's chair. Still deeply in debt, in
a fit of pique he threatened to "publish the names of non-
paying subscribers, and expunge them from our list." But when
he outlined the *Messenger*'s goals in his prefatory note, his tone
was overwhelmingly optimistic. Never before had he felt "so
strong a conviction of the importance of this periodical, nor so
good a hope for its success." Henceforth, he announced, the
magazine would be devoted to "a diffusion of the *Spirit of Jesus*"
and the "inculcation of a spirit of Life—individual and social
Life." Toning down Perkins's injunction against theological discussions (which he nonetheless regarded as "subordinate to re-

ligious convictions"), he was adamant about the magazine's affiliation with the "mere scholastic title" of Unitarianism: "the Western Messenger ought never to be the organ of a sect." Channing departed as well from Perkins's hard-boiled pessimism about human nature. "Man is moral," he affirmed; "the kingdom of God will come by the renewal of spiritual life in individual souls" and by applying the spirit of Jesus to "all social relations." To this end the *Messenger* was consecrated: Brotherhood. "We would seek to conceive and realise," Channing concluded rhapsodically, "an Ideal of Humanity" (8:1–7).

Just how much of this "new" *Messenger* was really new? To be sure, its commitment to the nonsectarian exploration of truth continued a longstanding editorial policy, as did the open invitation to all sincere contributors—if anything, the *Messenger* had been overly accommodating in publishing its critics. So too the call for "a spirit of Life," little more than a rejection of the dry scholasticism that Clarke had earlier called "a dead weight in the mind" (6:40). And the goal of brotherhood, then as now, had a long history and few critics. In all, Channing's dedication repeated most of the policies already in place since Clarke took over the editorship in 1836, as well as some conventional Unitarian pieties. The *Christian Register* (6 June 1840) broke its two-year silence and welcomed back the "clear decisive, penetrating voice" of the *Messenger,* commending its promotion of "liberality, truth and righteousness."[26]

Yet there was a barb in this otherwise smooth opening of volume 8. To "conceive" an Ideal of Humanity was one thing, to "realise" that Ideal quite another, especially in 1840, when visions of social reform hung heavy in the air and animated the planners of new societies: Adin Ballou at Hopedale, George Ripley at Brook Farm. "We are all a little wild here with numberless projects of social reform," Emerson wrote Carlyle wryly in October. "Not a reading man but has a draft of a new Community in his waistcoat pocket." Associationism, Fourierism, Perfectionism, Non-Resistance, Christian Socialism—there were schemes to fit every pocket.[27]

With such a potpourri of plans available to them, the *Messenger* writers, particularly the younger ones, hot with the fever of reform, often fell prey to an infatuation with mere novelty. As

Cranch put it, the times called men to "leave then the old for the old, and take what is good and true out of the new" (8:120). But if the young liberals writing for the magazine did the first with enthusiasm, they sometimes were incapable of exercising the judgment necessary for the second. Edward Jarvis heralded the founders of the New England Non-Resistance Society as "true coadjutors in the Christian reform" (8:201), noting only as an afterthought their radical anarchism. In Perkins's essay "Associations, a Vital Form of Social Action" (8:271–76), "all Governments, and social arrangements" were brushed aside as "but the outer skin" of society. ("If the skin die," Perkins shrugged, "it sloughs off, and a new one comes.") Even some of the longer pieces, notably Vaughan's three-part review of Carlyle's *Chartism* (8:87–90, 108–15, 162–68), showed an intellectual frothiness that set conservatives' teeth on edge. Vaughan flatly refused to "refute or criticise" *Chartism* (8:168), despite his own reservations about some parts of it. So moved was he by the essay's "kindling, generous love of liberty" (8:168) that he overlooked its fundamental attacks on laissez-faire capitalism and legal means of reform.[28] Partly, such excessive tolerance was fostered by the *Messenger*'s policy of opening its pages to all views expressed "strongly, candidly and kindly" (8:8); in part, the exigencies of monthly publication made sustained investigation of current topics an unaffordable luxury. Still, the magazine opposed to dogma of all sorts often praised new "isms" as a matter of course, without much attention to their weaknesses or implications. Channing and the *Messenger,* Huidekoper grumbled to his son, had succumbed to "the ultra spirit of the times."[29]

Thus Huidekoper was especially dismayed when the *Messenger*'s attention returned to the most dangerous manifestation of the ultra spirit, socialism. Democracy, "the disease of the young and the theoretic," he felt confident would be cured by age;[30] but economic socialism had a particular urgency in 1840, and if the other *Messenger* writers were willing—indeed eager—to fill the magazine's pages with tales of working-class oppression, Huidekoper would not stand idly by and let the charges go unanswered. Dr. Channing, it was true, had recently aired his views on the struggles of the laboring classes, in a pamphlet generously abstracted in the May and June numbers (8 : 35–42, 59–63). For the laborer, argued Channing, what was needed was not social or political advancement but "Elevation of Soul," the "inward and real change" without which other reforms were irrelevant. But Dr. Channing's call for self-culture did nothing to counter charges like Vaughan's that laid the blame for poverty squarely on the immorality of the rich. So in the summer of 1840 Huidekoper published in the *Messenger* his justification of capitalism as a moral activity, "The Right and Duty of Accumulation" (8 : 145–49). Because "excess of earnings" reward honest labor and prudence, Huidekoper maintained, accumulation of wealth is a moral right; and because wealth, properly used, represents "power to do good and be useful," to deny a man the opportunity to accumulate riches "beyond what is necessary to supply the wants of himself and his family" is a moral wrong, robbing the poor of the motivation for industriousness and the wealthy of the means of benevolence.

Appearing that same summer, though, was the essay on social and economic injustice before which Channing's piety and Huidekoper's measured logic would pale: Orestes Brownson's explosive "The Laboring Classes," published in the July *Boston Quarterly Review.*[31] Scoffing at the futility of self-culture, Brownson scored the middle class for locking wage-earners in a "slave system, without the expense, trouble, and odium" of literal bondage. Only radical and sweeping reforms, he argued, could break the hold of the propertied masters: destruction of the priesthood, who discouraged this-worldly change; legal measures to ensure the equitable distribution of wealth; separation of the federal government from the banking system; and abolition of the hereditary descent of property. And those reforms would come only through revolution, "the war of the poor against the rich."

The reaction to Brownson's essay was swift and correspondingly passionate. Democrats, whose party Brownson had recently embraced, scrambled to exorcise the devil in their midst; delighted Whigs cast him as the representative locofoco; and "Brownsonism" became the epithet of convenience for any kind of subversive heresy. Dr. Channing found the essay "shocking or absurd," while newspapers and magazines poured out abuse. From all sides, it seemed to Brownson himself, resounded "one universal scream of horror."

Not quite *all* sides. For one publication, at least, rallied to Brownson's defense—the *Messenger.* In the back matter of the October 1840 number Perkins carefully divorced the magazine from Brownsonism itself.

> As respects the spirit of Mr. B.'s article, and the mode of action he proposes, we are in the strongest opposition to him: we think his spirit unchristian, and his plan of action unwise.

Yet the issue of "Man against Property" Perkins considered the question of the day, and Brownson had addressed it with "clearness, vigor and boldness" in an essay "worthy of careful study." "Right or wrong," Perkins wrote, Brownson "has a mind of his own," and his freedom of expression must not be suppressed (8:288).[32]

All things considered, Perkins's modest defense of Brownson seems a moderate enough response. But in the din that greeted "The Laboring Classes" all things were not considered, and no response short of outright condemnation was thought moderate. After its perceptible drift toward radical causes, and following its similar defenses of Emerson, the *Messenger*'s treatment of Brownson certified its position as a standard-bearer of ultraism. Huidekoper voiced his outrage in the November issue. Seditious, false, and in principle "totally destructive of the whole of our present social system," he called Brownson's essay—an inflammatory appeal to the same ignorant "passions and prejudices" that guided the ugly course of the French Revolution (8:316–30). Even worse, Huidekoper wrote, was the liberality of the educated.

> The danger arising from this source would be vastly less, if these new opinions were subjected to the same severe scrutiny which the old ones are undergoing. But this appears frequently not to be the case. Either from the love of novelty, from the fear of appearing to be behind the age, or from a blind partiality for the innovator, these new opinions are often treated with a criminal indulgence. What cannot be

openly approved, is either passed by in silence, or is excused under the plea of good intentions. Now this indulgence is treason to the community. (8:316)

There can be little doubt that Huidekoper was referring to the "criminal indulgence" of the *Messenger.*

Perkins published the essay with a cool disclaimer—"not because we agree altogether with its sentiments and arguments, but because we deeply respect its author"—and invited "any views on the opposite side" (8:330). He received instead a spate of angry criticism from readers as appalled as Huidekoper. When Channing returned in November 1840 from his Eastern visit, he found subscribers in a fury, and he answered them in kind. "How unfortunate! that we should thus oppose public opinion!" he wrote. "Oh respectable friends! Pity our misfortune, that, having entered the cave of this Cyclops, we did not find him so hideous as represented, and saw no human bones" (8:383). Brownson was "quite as pure in purpose and sound in judgment" as his critics and deserved a fair hearing, but on the *Messenger*'s policy there could be no debate.

> One thing, friends, we would have you fully understand: We became editors of this periodical, supposing ourselves to be freemen, and the Western Messenger an organ of Freedom; and, so long as we continue editors, we shall assuredly act on this supposition. (8:384)

Ironically, without having recommended Brownson's essay or even reprinting it—indeed, while condemning its "spirit and mode of action" and providing a platform for one of its staunchest critics—the *Messenger*'s editors found themselves at year's end allied with the most notorious radical of the time and locked in an angry standoff with their own readers.

Nor was the magazine's developing radicalism confined to social issues. The Ideal of Humanity was as much religious as social; for Channing, in fact, the two were inseparable. Under his guidance, the Union of Christian Brethren at Cincinnati had expanded its purposes to "the great work of promoting *Christian Union*" (8:490), seeking to transform religion from "a little nook in the broad field of life" to "*the essential indwelling spirit of human existence in all its details"* (8:492). "My idea in beginning the Association of Christian Brethren had this aim, *social reformation,"* confessed Channing to a parishioner. "I am as sure, as if heaven whispered it to me, this is the *great idea* of our time and land. Deeper than to theological truth, must go the reform."[33]

"Religion the social principle," as Channing termed it (8:499), was of course no new idea; nor was it one that most Unitarians would have found objectionable. But in volume 8 the *Messenger* continued to cast conventional Unitarians—and with them the religion of mere convention—as impediments to progress. Organized Unitarianism, conceded an "Eastern Correspondent" in the July 1840 number, "has made headway as a sect."

> But has it penetrated more deeply into Truth itself? Has it taught or ever learnt any new secrets of spiritual life? Has it gone on to marry into each other the religious and intellectual life. . .? Unless we speak of the *New School,* now rising like a phoenix out of the ashes of old Unitarianism, which as a sect seems to have had its day, I think we must say no. If we look at Mr. Norton, and some few who sympathise with him, we must say, that Unitarianism has stopped short at the overthrow of technical error; that it did not exterminate the seeds of error; and consequently the Unitarian Church has become as formal, as lifeless, nay, as bigoted as any other church. (8:133–34)

With Brownson calling for an end to priestcraft, and with Ripley and Norton waging their pamphlet war in full public view, the *Messenger's* criticism in 1840 fueled an already enflamed situation. Norton had more than a few sympathizers, and they had been pronounced dead once too often. The reviewer for the *Christian Register* (25 July 1840) protested the magazine's violations of both truth and clarity, calling the remark about Norton "as inconsistent with the laws of justice as of kindness and correct taste"—but forgave the lapse in view of the magazine's general "mission of usefulness."

It was too late, though, for olive branches. In the August issue Clarke attacked the denomination once more, accusing conservative Unitarians of "loudly singing the praises of charity and liberality" only when tolerance suited them. The miracles question, he charged, showed the denomination's true colors.

> Mr. Emerson they know and acknowledge to be a singularly pure-minded, devout and conscientious person. But what do some of them do? They cry out more loudly against him than ever they were attacked by the orthodox. They scruple not to call him an ATHIEST,—him, whose life, if the tree be known by its fruits, is the life of one walking with God. They denounce him, and all who are supposed to think with him; and they get up a popular excitement, and a terror of dreadful heresies, and talk about the "latest form of Infidelity," and ask indignantly or sorrowfully, "what are we coming to?" using, in short, the same means to create a vague terror which have been used about themselves. (8:187–88)

A month later Channing mocked those who tried to drive "Kant and Bronson Alcott, Coleridge and Waldo Emerson, Carlyle and Mr. Brownson" into a "common fold, there to be slaughtered at their leisure by orthodox metaphysicians of the good old sensuous school" (8:227). After four years of bitter squabbling over the Transcendental heresies, the *Messenger* writers had clearly grown frustrated, and by the end of 1840 there was little point in keeping up the charade of civility. By its continuing hostility toward the spiritual philosophy, the old school had proved itself incapable of any meaningful role in the religious reform the younger men thought inevitable. "Shall we never learn to tolerate any heresy but our own?" Clarke asked in disgust (8:188).

With rapprochement out of the question, the *Messenger*'s editors at last took a definite stand in the miracles controversy. Beginning with the first number of volume 8 they reprinted in installments James Martineau's "The Bible: What it is, and What it is not," an examination of the historical foundations of Scripture that concluded miracles to be "simply awakening facts" and not proofs of Christianity's validity; such proof, said Martineau, lay "in the moral doctrine as established by our reason and conscience, not in the preternatural act displayed before our senses" (8:209–10).[34] Following Martineau came the equally radical "Relation of the Bible to the Soul" from Theodore Parker, who also asserted the primacy of "Conscience and

Reason," relegated Scripture to the mere "historical form" of Christianity, and declared the Gospel subordinate to the inner voice of the Soul (8:339, 396). No less than his famous "Discourse of the Transient and Permanent in Christianity," delivered six months later, Parker's "Relation" celebrated intuitive moral truths and dismissed creeds and Scripture as ephemeral.

No editorial disclaimer followed Martineau's sermon or Parker's essay, for by early 1841 Channing had joined Cranch and Clarke in open sympathy with the new school. He admitted as much in February, when he reprinted "at the request of a highly respected friend" (perhaps Huidekoper) a passage by Joseph Priestley attacking "the vain and delusive imagination of an *immediate and supernatural* communion with God," then followed it with a rhapsody by an unnamed writer on the divinity of the soul.[35] "For ourselves," Channing announced, "we far prefer the cloudy raptures of the mystic to the dry clearness of the philosopher. . . . These mystics are the gleams of a coming morning, the songs before the dawn of an eternal day. Oh! for a prophet—a TRUE MAN" (8:452–61).

To men like Huidekoper (who could not read Emerson, and who thought Alcott "worthy of the lunatic asylum") such reveries were proof that the *Messenger* had advanced beyond recall into the fuzzy realm of religious ultraism. Channing, Huidekoper decided, suffered from a "constitutional tendency toward the vague and the mystic."[36] Publicly the response to the magazine was only slightly less severe. The *Christian Register* (9 January 1841) cited Parker's essay as evidence that the magazine's contributors "sometimes err in respect to what is most needed for the furtherance of the cause of Christ in the West." A local Episcopal minister found in it proof of Unitarian infidelity. And more subscribers bolted. Channing himself, "gently reprimanded and bitterly scolded, according to the taste of readers," insisted once more that "this periodical *is not the organ of a sect*" (8:520). But the irony of the situation did not escape him: in a climate of suspicion and extremism, independence was costing the magazine dearly—in subscriptions, in reputation, in influence.

"Were men invited to lay aside prejudice and party spirit, and exclusiveness of every kind," Channing had written the summer before, "the charge of 'fanaticism' would be immediately brought forward" (8:492). By early 1841 the accuracy of that prediction had become painfully apparent. Trinitarians remained impervious to his calls for Christian Union; in late fall of 1840 the Young Men's Bible Society, which seemed to Channing about to break the bonds of sectarianism (8:381), stunned him by voting to expel Unitarians from its membership (8:475–88). Within his congregation, too, there was friction. Channing preached on abolitionism "oftener than his unwilling congregation liked" (according to the church historian), offered the church building for meetings of antislavery societies, and openly supported the Liberty Party's candidate for president, James G. Birney—the same Birney whose abolitionist press had been destroyed by a Cincinnati mob in 1836.[37] He could count on little support within his own denomination, having already alienated the Eastern clergy by his alliance with Parker and facing the intransigence of "Channing liberals" like Huidekoper, who insisted on saving men from the "delusion of looking to social reform for the amelioration of their condition" (8:448). Even his closest friends were remote. James Clarke was gone now, back in Boston to organize his Church of the Disciples. James Perkins showed more interest in reforming schools and prisons than in regenerating souls, and he had lately begun coediting and writing for the *Family Magazine,* a popular "Abstract of General Knowledge" published out of Boston, New York, and Cincinnati.[38] Most of all there was Channing's absent wife, to whom his religious speculations would never be acceptable. Personally he found Cincinnati a pleasant place to live (he had felt more "free" in the pulpit there than in any other place he had ever preached[39]) but intellectually he was not at home. And the frustrations of his mental life were mirrored in his role as editor of the *Messenger,* where his heartfelt convictions on religious reform and social improvement had been met by readers with indignation, misunderstanding, or outright disdain.

These public and private pressures coincided with a severe crisis in Channing's inner life—and surely helped to precipitate it. Sometime in the late winter of 1840–41, his already tenuous sense of mission gave way to an agonizing skepticism about his profession and about Christianity itself. Spiritually he came unmoored; overwhelmed by "a deluge, an upheaving, a downsinking" of religious sentiment, as he confessed to Margaret Fuller, he lost touch with his "true inward life."[40] A year later, his vision less clouded, he would isolate the source of his confusion as a profound doubt of Jesus' divinity; at the moment, though, early in 1841, he could no longer remain in the pulpit. In an open letter to his congregation, he announced his intention to resign, and the reasons for the decision.

> Health of mind and health of body,—unfitness to be your spiritual guide,—unwillingness to remain in the ministry as a profession, and to receive from a salary a support,—discontent with the present organization of the Church,—speculative views which separate me from the great body of Christians,—and last and chief, a desire, for *silence and rest,* in which to seek for deeper truth and larger wisdom on all subjects.

The break was amiable but irrevocable. By 15 April he could report to Fuller, "The words are spoken. The stag is free"; two months later he was on his way back to Cambridge, there to spend several months in seclusion and meditation in his mother's home.[41]

To what extent did the reaction to the *Messenger*'s radicalism contribute to Channing's departure? Given his mercurial temperament and idealistic bent, his crisis of the soul was probably inevitable. Surely, though, the *Messenger*'s failure was vivid and measurable evidence of the "present organization of the Church," for the magazine's pages had provided a forum for his "speculative views." The disintegration of the *Messenger*'s support objectified his own intellectual and spiritual collapse. And if his chief desire was for silence and rest, the editorship had afforded him little of either. The *Messenger* was a yardstick to gauge the reception of his ideas, and the numbers were not good. Even with the magazine in publisher's hands, the final responsibility for its solvency fell to Channing; and though he held the *Messenger* steady on its editorial course for two years, he could not keep it from bankruptcy. Despite repeated calls for overdue payments, and even with the inclusion of advertising, the *Messenger* was still over $200 in debt.[42]

A year earlier, Channing had pledged to continue the magazine "till some more efficient organ of Truth supplies its place" (8:1). In the April 1841 number, the *Messenger*'s last, he offered several successors: the *Practical Christian* and the *Future* were trumpeting the virtues of Christian Socialism; Fuller's *Dial* seemed to Channing "the wind-flower of a new spring," unequaled in "profound thought, a pure tone of personal and social morality,—wise criticism,—and fresh beauty." Hopeful to the end, Channing congratulated his readers on "the bright signs of the times," anticipating even as he wrote the *Messenger*'s final pages the "transition from the present Utilitarian and Selfish Era, to a later state of Justice and Peace, the Era of Individuality" (8:570–72). But amid the prophecies lay a tempering reminder of the price of vision. "Must we be always wholly opposed to or wholly in favor of measures or men?" he wondered. "The true wisdom is to gather the gold from all streams" (8:570–71). To the *Western Messenger,* a victim at last of intolerance, neglect, and economic failure, it was less a cry of optimism than an apostrophe to despair.

5
The Achievement of the
Western Messenger

Even in a culture routinely given to local hagiolatry, James Freeman Clarke in his old age enjoyed a special veneration. One of New England's most beloved ministers and popular scholars, at 75 he could look back with satisfaction at a life well lived: he had known almost everyone worth knowing, traveled widely at home and abroad, and weathered the stormy half century that spanned Jacksonianism and Reconstruction. Yet when a historian of Unitarianism wrote Clarke in 1885 for his reminiscences, he skipped over his mature career and recalled his youthful experiences in the Ohio Valley with "our poor little 'Western Messenger' . . . in which we put the best life we had."[1]

On the surface it is a curious statement, for the "best lives" of the men who directed the *Messenger*'s course seem to have begun after the magazine's collapse in 1841. Of those who returned East in the 1830s, Ephraim Peabody accepted the pastorate of Boston's King's Chapel, serving there with distinction until he died of tuberculosis in 1856; Samuel Osgood spent two decades as minister of the famed Church of the Messiah in New York City until his ordination as an Episcopal priest in 1870; and Christopher Cranch, after publishing a book of poems in 1844, left the ministry to become a painter and translator, spending many of his remaining years in Europe. Of those who stayed in the West, William Eliot settled permanently in St. Louis, founded the Eliot Seminary (now Washington University), and promoted civic reforms; it remained for his grandson, Thomas Stearns Eliot, to make the odyssey eastward. Harm Jan Huidekoper continued until his death in 1854 to encourage the growth of rational Unitarianism in the Ohio Valley. And as tirelessly as Huidekoper labored in service of the denomination, James Perkins battled against it. He agreed to preach "temporarily" after Channing left Cincinnati in 1841 and remained in the pulpit for five years, resigning over the congregation's insistence upon the name *Unitarian* in 1846. A year later he was back, this time officially ordained; and in October 1848, encouraging his flock to abandon "the whole ground of sectarianism," he attempted to revive the Union of Christian Brethren, which had folded soon after Channing's departure. The experiment was destined to be tragically short-lived; for on 14 December 1849, distraught over the disappearance of his two young sons (who turned up safe), Perkins boarded the river ferry, quietly set down his cloak and memorandum book, and stepped off the deck into the rushing waters of the Ohio.[2]

Perkins's submission to despair stands in sharp contrast to William Channing's abiding optimism. Emotionally elastic, Channing hit bottom in 1841 but rebounded quickly, fortified by a resolute faith in human progress that lends itself to parody in a more skeptical age. "He always felt, when he rose from his bed, that the 'one divine far-off event' might well occur before he sat down to breakfast," claims Van Wyck Brooks.[3] After some months in seclusion, Channing returned to the pulpit, first in Nashua in 1842, later in New York City, West Roxbury, and Rochester. But what led him "out of the dusty twilight shadow," he recalled years later, was the promise of action, "the Great Social Reforms of Anti-Slavery &c, ending in Christian Socialism at Brook-Farm." Along the "spiral ascending path" of his life in the 1840s were other stops: the North American Phalanx in New Jersey; Sing Sing and Blackwells Island in New York, to awaken the spirits of the prisoners; the Religious Union of Associationists in Boston. To the unsympathetic, Channing's restless flirtations with reform activities show "an overenthusiasm and lack of definiteness well calculated to wreck any project dependent on him alone to shape its course." But his impatience with the shortcomings of human efforts in fact affirmed his singular commitment to their goals—social progress and religious union. Inept at practical affairs, Channing lived a life of earnest seeking, confident always in the "Divine Presence over, & through, & in Humanity."[4]

For James Clarke, the *Messenger*'s prime mover, the seeking was no less earnest; but he channeled it largely into the development of a single institution, his Church of the Disciples. Organized in 1841, the church experienced quick success; more moderate in its principles than, say, the group that gathered around Theodore Parker, it was progressive enough in its polity—active participation by the laity in services, voluntary contributions rather than the sale of pews to the wealthy— to attract those who found conventional Unitarianism too rigid but Transcendentalist reform too amorphous. Clarke's ministry provided him both the opportunity for social projects and the leisure to write over thirty books and hundreds of essays and sermons, many of them forays into comparative religion. His was the life of the activist, and not without its moments of courage. Clarke was among the few who consented to exchange pulpits with the outcast Parker in the mid-1840s; he drafted the antislavery protest signed by 173 Unitarian ministers and sent to Congress after the annexation of Texas in 1845. But no longer was he the firebrand who baited Andrews Norton or pronounced his colleagues dead of complacency.[5]

While their greatest public achievements came after 1841, however, it is neither fair nor accurate to conclude that the *Messenger* writers "crawled back to Boston" and left "no memorials or continuing mission" in the Ohio Valley.[6] As the vanguard of Unitarian liberalism in the West, they took a beating, the more so because support from the rear was sporadic or lukewarm. But by 1841 they had established a network of congregations whose beliefs had been anathema before they came—the rock upon which later Unitarians built their Western church. In 1844 the dream of a Western seminary was realized, when Huidekoper and his son Frederic opened the Meadville Theological School; the plan to coordinate the regional missions bore fruit in 1852, with the establishment of the Western Unitarian Conference.[7] And as the *Messenger* writers left their mark on the West, so the frontier experience left its mark on them. In the West their theological commitment to Christian union was put to the test. Well might Nathaniel

Frothingham boast at Boston's First Church that he had never spoken the word *Unitarian* in his pulpit—he didn't have to, and no one would have cared if he had.[8] But the Western ministers enjoyed no such tolerance. Forced to defend their beliefs in a suspicious, sometimes hostile, environment, to acknowledge an intellectual pluralism that Boston had never known, to seek a common ground, they distilled their speculations into fundamentals and discarded the dogma and conventions. By the time their own denomination tried to rally against the Transcendental heretics, the *Messenger* writers had learned their lesson well. Western necessity had become principle: sectarianism was heresy, tradition and civility notwithstanding. Those of the *Messenger* group who went West and stayed concerned themselves with nonsectarian benevolence and public improvements. Those who returned East—notably Cranch, Channing, and Clarke—did not return "to the fold, chastened, subdued."[9] Schooled in an open society, they could coexist with conservative Unitarianism but never fully conform to it. For the *Messenger* writers, the habits of mind and patterns of response forged in the West were the themes on which their later careers were largely variations. Intellectually they had indeed lived their "best lives" in the Ohio Valley.

In all, they were a remarkable group, distinguished less for the novelty or depth of their thought than for the energy with which they pursued their commitment to truth. Not surprisingly, their efforts continued to be literary; and for the editors proper, the *Messenger* marked not the end but the beginning of their work in periodicals. Peabody wrote often for the *Examiner* and the *North American Review,* then assumed the editorship of the *Christian Register* in 1849.[10] In his diary for November 1840, just when the *Messenger* reached its crisis over Brownson and Parker, Clarke outlined his plans for "the establishment of a newspaper—or editing the Christian Register." Though the second goal never materialized, the first did, when in 1847 he became editor of the *Christian World* in Boston.[11] William Channing, too, built upon his experiences with the *Messenger.* From 1843 to 1844 he edited the *Present,* a wide-ranging monthly of literature and social commentary undergirded by his developing interest in Fourierism and devoted to "union and growth in Religion, Science, and Society." Just as ephemeral was his aptly named *Spirit of the Age* (1849–50), a weekly paper that promoted a wildly ambitious reform program. It folded, Channing admitted, because "I am brainsick—and it does not pay."[12]

This continuing attraction to periodical publication suggests that, whatever their disappointments with the *Messenger,* the editors did not regard the venture as a failure. Certainly, the facts of the magazine's publication would bear them out. At its peak, in early 1837, the subscription list numbered between five hundred and six hundred—a considerable readership in a market so glutted that the prestigious *Christian Examiner* could attract only about eight hundred subscribers, the *Dial* never more than three hundred.[13] The *Messenger*'s longevity was also impressive, especially since the magazine enjoyed no sustained denominational support and weathered the financial doldrums of 1837 to 1840. Of the other periodicals associated with the Transcendental group by midcentury, none lasted more than four years, and one—Elizabeth Peabody's *Aesthetic Papers* (1849)—folded after a single issue. For Western magazines, the mortality rate was even higher, the life expectancy considerably less. The wonder is not that the *Messenger* collapsed when it did, but that it did not cease much sooner.

Besides its mere staying power, the magazine was remarkable for the breadth and quality of its contents. Periodicals of the time often were dreary affairs, collocations of sentimental verse, partisan essays, and reprinted material. When the *Messenger* fit that description, as it did on more than one occasion, it was at least no worse than its competitors. But at its best, the *Messenger* had no competition. What other American periodical could claim first printings of Emerson, Dr. Channing, Keats, Holmes, Parker, and Margaret Fuller; review-essays on Coleridge, Wordsworth, Shelley, Tennyson, Carlyle, and Irving; original translations of Goethe, Schiller, Richter? Less scholarly than the *Examiner,* not so stodgy as the *North American Review,* the *Messenger* gained in immediacy and sharpness what it sacrificed in prestige. For the Transcendental group in particular, other avenues of publication being closed to them, the *Messenger* provided space for experimentation: Emerson's first signed poetry, Fuller's earliest literary criticism, Parker's "heretical" essay on the Bible and the soul as well as his trenchant satires on fellow ministers and misty-eyed reformers (4:402–5; 8:397–402).

Still, it is the *Messenger*'s trials and ultimate collapse that interest and instruct. Had the magazine truly been "crying in the wilderness, unheard," as some scholars have suggested,[14] it might have lived longer but not so well, an inoffensive document deservedly forgotten. But the *Messenger*'s history provides ample testimony that readers indeed "heard" its cries—important, perceptive readers whose support, denial, or indifference accounted for both the magazine's death and the tenor of its life.

In part they responded to fundamental changes in the *Messenger* writers' view of the West. When the magazine was established in 1835, it confronted a world big with promise but without direction. Confident of the possibilities that lay in chaos in the West, the magazine's founders sought to give shape to a formless culture. That they had misplaced their confidence soon became apparent. Perkins's essays on horse-racing, Eliot's on land speculation, and Clarke's on dueling and gambling show that the *Messenger* writers found some of the weeds in the Western garden too ugly to tolerate but too deep in the soil to pull out by the roots. After three years in Kentucky, Clarke revised his expectations of the frontier masses. "A deep reverence for truth, a profound respect for law, a ready submission to right, a loyal allegiance to duty," he wrote in 1836, were all that were yet required to "make the western character as perfect as humanity can ever hope to become." Significant omissions, those—and Clarke knew it; sometimes he felt "choked by custom" in the "moral miasma" of Louisville. Cranch thought the West "a desert in more respects than one." And in 1838 Perkins pinpointed the essential failure of the Western people. Still convinced that the absence of "an iron armor of faith" fitted the West for liberalism, he recognized in the *Messenger*'s continuing financial troubles a larger truth about frontier openness.

It was thought that many persons, who were dissatisfied with prevalent forms of religious worship, and who knew of none

more suitable to their ideas, would learn, by means of the
Messenger, that a form of faith did exist with which they
could sympathize. Many such persons were found, but they
were, in general, little disposed to pay for the new faith that
was offered them, though they might be very willing to re-
ceive it; in other words, they had no particular objection to
Unitarianism, but cared very little for religion at all.[15]

Just as discouraging was the continuing resistance of those
who *did* care. Sectarianism proved a more intransigent force
than the *Messenger* writers had anticipated. The expulsion of
Unitarians from the Young Men's Bible Society was an act of
bigotry repeated elsewhere—by the Presbyterians who imposed
a "spiritual quarantine" on a minister who had spoken from a
Unitarian pulpit (7:126–27), by the Indiana college president
who refused to let Clarke deliver an invited address before the
students (8:150–52). Worst of all was the aborted promise of
the nondenominational Disciples of Christ, whose growth in
the early 1830s augured such a bright future for Western religion. Slow to discard the vestiges of Baptist ceremony and insistent upon a literalist interpretation of Scripture, the Disciples
proved uneasy allies for Unitarian liberals who more and more
saw the Bible as suggestive rather than prescriptive. The same
Alexander Campbell whom Clarke had hailed as a brother in
1835 ridiculed Unitarianism as "no better than Deism" in
1840.[16] "He has founded a large sect, and doubtless thinks the
time has nearly come for him and his to be admitted to the
fellowship of the orthodox," Clarke concluded bitterly (8:129–
30).

Socially, intellectually, and religiously, the West failed to meet
the high expectations the Unitarians had set for it. As that
failure became ever clearer, the *Messenger*'s purpose shifted,
from organizing a world in chaos to reorganizing a culture
suddenly grown rigid. The West had quite simply cohered fas-
ter than the Eastern ministers had expected, and in quite the
wrong ways. Their response was a profound ambivalence to
their adopted culture: their remaining faith in its possibilities
made them reluctant to condemn Western corruption, but their
growing recognition of it made silence impossible. Clarke's position on slavery illustrates the awkwardness of the *Messenger*'s
social criticism. Appalled by the manifest evil of the slavery

system, he remained convinced that its end could best be achieved through the natural development of the West's democratic potential; as a result he condemned slavery but not slaveholders, and the position angered almost everyone.

At the same time that Western culture showed evidence of closing, the East was breaking wide open. Frustrated with the West's failed promise, the *Messenger* writers now saw signs of productive chaos in the very region they had fled because of its earlier rigidity. Paradoxically, New England seemed more "western" than the West: its opinions suddenly in flux, its traditions challenged, its social structure under fire from reformers of all kinds. As the battle for religious and intellectual freedom, apparently unwinnable in the West, returned to New England, the *Messenger* writers turned their attention increasingly there—not because the region was familiar to them but because, suddenly and happily, the familiar was falling away.

Clearly the *Messenger*'s part in the Transcendental controversy was not welcomed by all Eastern Unitarians. But the dispute, dominated as it was by the shrillest and most extreme voices, makes it difficult to see precisely why the magazine so irritated its New England readers, or at least makes it too easy to explain the problem in simple terms. Recent scholarship has begun to rescue conservative Unitarians from their undeserved reputation as vindictive pedants compulsively shouting down their high-minded opponents.[17] The *Messenger*'s history shows how tolerant they actually were. Even after three years of indecorous criticism of their orthodoxy, hypocrisy, and leading ministers, the Eastern clergy remained remarkably patient with the *Messenger*, twice voting it financial support and withholding the public censure that the magazine seemed to warrant.[18] Subscription records, admittedly fragmentary, show no single position that caused a mass defection of subscribers; rather, it appears that the magazine's New England support withered away gradually. Eighty percent of New England's subscribers were already delinquent with their payment by the close of the first volume in 1836, a loss recouped only after Clarke's tour late in the year. But the list shrank again at the end of 1837, even before Clarke's sweeping condemnation of the Unitarian denomination, and toward the end of 1839 it grew even smaller. At that time Samuel Clarke reported that from March to September only 23 New England subscribers had renewed for volume 8—down from 126 three years before.[19] Probably the economic depression and the *Messenger*'s impolitic criticism contributed equally to the falling off of support in the East.

One thing, however, is clear: the easy conclusion that the *Messenger* failed because it championed Transcendentalism simply has no basis in fact. For by volume 8, when the *Messenger* at last came out in favor of Parker's biblical speculations and endorsed the epistemological "mysticism" of the Transcendentalists, the damage had already been done. In the West the *Messenger* had lost readers because of its position on slavery, its attention to the parochial quarrels in New England, its flagging interest in native literature, and its promotion of Unitarian theology in a region dominated by Calvinists. In the East it offended readers with its potshots at leading clergy, its evenhanded treatment of radicals like Alcott, Brownson, and Emerson, its failure to adhere to the missionary purposes for which it had been founded. As the *Messenger* shifted its emphasis from forming its world to reforming it, the magazine became more stridently critical and appeared—to its readers and to some of its contributors—to have abandoned its original purpose; instead of encouraging cohesion it was sowing dissent by promoting principles "destructive of our social order."[20] Overall, the *Messenger* moved in directions opposed to the cultural and political counterrevolution that began in the mid-1830s and culminated in the Whig triumph of 1840. During that time, as Arthur M. Schlesinger, Jr., shows in convincing detail, Jacksonianism was largely replaced in the popular imagination with a social philosophy based on three points: (1) the identity of class interests, (2) an idyllic view of the workingman, and (3) the efficacy of internal reform, or self-culture.[21] The *Messenger,* on the other hand, increasingly addressed class conflict, reminded its readers of the miserable condition of the urban poor, and advocated external reform, or institutional change. Thus, besides alienating specific segments of its audience, the magazine was fundamentally out of step with the spirit of its age. By 1841 the *Messenger* had lost its readers, but not because they protested its endorsement of Transcendentalist views. Loud and

revealing though they were, the howls that greeted the defenses of Parker and Brownson in late 1840 and early 1841 did
not signal a mass desertion of subscribers: for the most part
they had abandoned the magazine two years earlier. The *Messenger*'s nonsectarian independence, not its advocacy of Transcendentalist ideas or economic radicalism, was its fatal illness.

What, then, of the *Messenger*'s reputation as a Transcendentalist periodical? The Pennsylvania minister who in 1841
blamed the magazine's downfall on its close association with the
"wild and crude notions" of New England's "*new Illuminati*"
stands at the head of a long line of critics to reach the same
verdict. The grounds for the decision, though, have never been
quite clear. For naming the members of the new school is far
easier than identifying the ties that bound them. So reluctant
were the Transcendentalists to admit a common intellectual de-
nominator, and so long have others tried to find one, that the
search for who the Transcendentalists were or what they believed usually ends in a set of qualified assumptions, some too
easy, but some more accurate. Biographical criteria include the
sense of community evidenced by the Transcendental Club or
Brook Farm, or by shared projects such as the *Dial;* as an epistemological touchstone, most scholars cite as "Transcendental"
the belief in the primacy of intuitive knowledge; the most accepted ontological "test" is what William H. Channing called
the "vague yet exalting conception of the godlike nature of the
human spirit."[22] Whatever the criteria, the consensus has been
overwhelming: the *Western Messenger,* according to received wisdom, is the first periodical of American Transcendentalism. But
with the full history of the magazine in view, the facts point to a
different conclusion.

First of all, the *Messenger* writers occupied a broad spectrum
of opinion, and most of them would have balked at being called
Transcendentalists. At one extreme is Huidekoper, who found
the spiritual philosophy gobbledygook and Emerson's sanity
questionable;[23] at the other is William Henry Channing, whose
many allegiances to radical causes make "Transcendental" only
one of a number of equally accurate titles. Somewhere in the
middle are Osgood, stirred by Emerson's *Nature* but convinced
after his "Divinity School Address" that men who speak such

language "ought not to be suffered to preach in any Christian Church"; Ephraim Peabody, to whom "all that German philosophy" was "a mistake," since humanity acted only on sensation, never on principle; Perkins, who casually compared the miracles controversy to a debate over "whether the key stone of an arch supports the flanks, or the flanks the keystone" (7:435); and Eliot, a fence-straddler on every issue but the nature of miracles.[24] Even Clarke never outgrew his early doubts about transcendental epistemology: the distinctions between Reason and Understanding, he told Fuller in 1833, were merely "a new form of words" and should "always be left in the schools with the desks & globes."[25] Of the *Messenger*'s major contributors, only Christopher Cranch actively cultivated a reputation as a Transcendentalist.[26] None of the others felt wholly comfortable as members of the new school; most can be placed there only partially or incidentally; several would have choked at the very thought.

Nor was the Transcendental circle particularly eager to embrace the Western writers or their magazine. The New England group's offerings to the *Messenger* were small recompense for the magazine's defenses, and while Emerson, Brownson, Ripley, Alcott, and Fuller are known to have read the magazine with interest, not once did the New England radicals as a group offer more than lukewarm support to the struggling editors. Emerson never even subscribed. When in 1839 the *Messenger* found itself all but friendless in New England, the members of the new school kept their distance and planned a magazine free of denominational reputation and more suitable to their literary inclinations. For under Perkins and Channing, social issues crowded out literary ones. By the end of volume 7 Fuller no longer considered the *Messenger* "a fit receptacle" for a series of essays she was planning on the fine arts in America. "It seems scarcely right to put them there merely for the sake of seeing them in print," she thought.[27]

The connection between the Western writers and the New England Transcendentalists was thus a tenuous one, always compromised and qualified by an independence of mind that made figures like Emerson or Brownson inspiring thinkers while precluding a slavish adherence to their ideas. Not until the very end, after reducing the Transcendental controversy to the difference between the "cloudy raptures" of mysticism and the "dry clearness" of philosophy (8:452), did the *Messenger* firmly endorse the intuitive epistemology that can be identified indisputably as "transcendental." Up to that time the magazine had defended only the Transcendentalists' right to think independently—never the absolute rightness of a Transcendental position. Indeed, the *Messenger*'s editors would have been hard pressed to find such a position even had they wanted to defend it, for the Eastern members of the new school could hardly agree among themselves on much besides their "common opposition to the old school." Their shared faith in man's greater potential led to two antithetical modes of response to the world, the individual and the social: by the founding of Brook Farm in 1841, the practical consequences of the division had already become apparent. William Henry Channing early suspected Emerson of "somewhat exclusive and unsympathetic contemplativeness" in *Nature* and wished him "more fully warmed to the great social idea of our era."[28] Brownson declared that "no man can deny that the realization of the good of all beings is something superior to the realization of the good of the individual."[29] For his part, Emerson affirmed the need for radical selfhood, the asocial quest to "be alone with the Alone," and he distrusted what he considered the inevitable degeneration of any organized social reform into "a little shop, where the article, let it have been at first never so subtle and ethereal, is now made up into portable and convenient cakes."[30]

Much has been made—perhaps too much—of this division of the Transcendentalists into two camps.[31] The fact remains, however, that from the first the term *new school* has been a designation of convenience, not accuracy. Certainly there was no "school" of thought to which the members of the circle would assent, no philosophy that bound them, no system or creed broad enough to encompass them all.[32] Even the name *Transcendentalist* was imposed upon them, a term of derision that stuck despite their vocal protests that it had no meaning. They talked together, but never with one voice; at bottom they shared only the intensity of their commitment to the new. In the Transcendentalists' fervor the *Messenger* writers found a compelling vitality, an iron string to which their hearts, too, could vibrate.

But as even Christopher Cranch was quick to point out, "union in sympathy differs from union in belief."[33] The *Western Messenger* was not intended to be, nor did it ever become, an organ of Transcendentalist doctrine—or any doctrine, for that matter. Its consistent editorial opposition to human creeds made the advocacy of a transcendental "ism" impossible.

And yet, the *Messenger* was indeed a Transcendental periodical—not because the new school offered a coherent and attractive credo but precisely, and paradoxically, because it did not. The stimuli for the Transcendental controversy were the miracles issue and the challenge of idealism; but the *Messenger* writers recognized in the debate the more fundamental issue that had animated them for years: the restriction of individual truth-seeking by the boundaries of doctrine. As others strove to untie the tangled threads of "Germanism" and "Idealism" and "Transcendentalism," the *Messenger* writers treated the knot as Gordian, and simply cut it; for them the debate boiled down to the issue of intellectual freedom. In fact, there is ample evidence that they were right. For so thoroughly was the Transcendental controversy pervaded by charges of "bigotry" and "exclusiveness" that it is often hard to distinguish voices.

> By the exclusive principle, I mean the assumption of the right for an individual, or for any body of individuals, to make their own private opinions the measure of what is fundamental in the Christian faith. . . .
>
> But the doctrine which lies at the foundation of your whole Discourse is a signal manifestation of the exclusive principle. You propose your own convictions,—and convictions, which it will appear in the sequel of this letter, are directly at war with the prevailing faith of the Church,—as the criterion of genuine Christian belief.[34]

The author? Not Andrews Norton accusing the new school of intellectual assumption, but George Ripley accusing the old school of precisely the same thing. Freedom from human creeds, the theoretical goal that most Unitarians found intolerable in practice, became for the Transcendentalists the precondition for knowing God, man, and nature. If there is a Transcendental spirit, it is captured in Emerson's bold claim in "Circles": "No facts are to me sacred; none are profane; I sim-

ply experiment, an endless seeker with no Past at my back."[35] By
definition, Transcendentalism was undefinable, an assertion of
the need to seek truth unfettered by tradition, by creeds, by
imposed or received "isms."

This spirit of boundless inquiry constitutes the point of intersection between the Eastern Transcendentalists and the major
writers for the *Messenger.* Frustrated by the West's failed promise of intellectual independence, then betrayed by the dogmatism of their brethren in New England, the *Messenger* writers
located in Transcendentalism what they had sought for years—
"that fresh, earnest, truth-loving and truth-seeking SPIRIT,"
Cranch wrote effusively, "that heart's-thirst . . . after something
always new and lovely and true,—something always adapted to
the soul's deep demands."

> I allude, I repeat, not to any system, or creed, or philosophy,
> or party, or sect—to no men or speculations, except so far as
> such are types of a free, earnest, and humble love of
> Truth. . . . The true Transcendentalism is that living and
> always new *spirit* of truth, which is ever going forth on its
> conquests into the world, and leading all captivity captive.
> (8:407)

For six years the *Western Messenger* had pursued truth in the
same "free, earnest, and humble" spirit, declaring its allegiance
to originality rather than conformity, to a living and organic
faith instead of the lifeless formalities of creeds—to an intellectual independence that was essentially as well as literally transcendental: a pursuit of "something beyond" the conventions of
literature, religion, and social organization.

The irony was that the New England group failed to appreciate the *Messenger.* Well might Channing have looked skep-
tically on Margaret Fuller's plans for the *Dial:*

> There are no party measures to be carried, no particular
> standard to be set up. . . . It were much if a periodical could
> be kept open to accomplish no outward object, but merely to
> afford an avenue for what of free and calm thought might be
> originated among us by the wants of individual minds.[36]

Fully as well as the *Dial,* and for two years longer, the *Messenger*
had represented "the constant evolution of truth, not the pet-

rifaction of opinion"[37] and had been met with confusion, opposition, and finally abandonment. Heir to the *Messenger*'s mission, the *Dial* would also be heir to its fate. As completely as the *Messenger*'s readers had failed to respond to the magazine's vitality, the founders of the *Dial* ignored the lesson of its demise.

In 1849, some three years after flames consumed the phalanstery at Brook Farm, William Henry Channing stood amid the rubble and reflected upon the experiment in socialism. "Posterity will remember it," he decided. "And never did I feel so calmly, humbly, devoutly thankful that it has been my privilege to fail in this grandest, sublimest, surest of all human movements."[38] Though the *Messenger*'s end had come with no fiery drama, Channing's words stand as a fitting epitaph for the magazine as well. Like Brook Farm, the *Messenger* was an experiment, not without its successes, but one that collapsed under the combined weight of disagreements among its friends, resistance from its enemies, and the unsuitability of its ideals to its culture. Like Brook Farm too, the magazine testified to a bold faith in progress beyond the meager bounds of convention. Its opposition to creeds and to the "party spirit" was a manifestation of the same Transcendentalist impulse that drove Emerson to trust his own genius, Thoreau to "speak somewhere *without* bounds," Whitman to "steer for the deep waters only":[39] nonsectarianism was the religious analogue of self-reliance. The *Messenger* kept open the Unitarian liberalism that was rapidly closing in upon itself; provided a forum for "honest truth seekers" in an age that did not honor its prophets; and embodied, in its pages and in the responses it drew, the tension inherent in American Romanticism between the seductions of conformity and the rewards of independence. For its nonconformity the world had whipped it. Yet, as Channing well knew, there was a kind of glory even in failure, when the attempt was a noble one. Ultimately the *Messenger*'s achievement lies in the quality of its seeking and in the persistence with which it asserted the possibilities of progress. The *Western Messenger* is quintessentially a romantic document, in its pages affirming the need for bold searching, in its history exemplifying the dangers of the quest.

Notes

Preface

1. James Kay to Clarke, Northumberland, Pa., 14 July 1841, MHi. Kay (1777–1847) was minister from 1822 until his death to the congregation founded by Joseph Priestley (Riverview Cemetery records, Northumberland County, Pa.; Herbert C. Bell, ed., *History of Northumberland County* [Chicago: Brown, Runk and Co., 1891], p. 539). Throughout this study I have reproduced quoted material exactly. For manuscripts, the following conventional symbols have been used: opposed arrows to enclose a writer's insertions, angle brackets to enclose cancellations, and square brackets to enclose editorial insertions.

2. "Western Examiner," *Christian Register*, 21 March 1835. Clarke wrote and distributed this prospectus (Peabody to Harm Jan Huidekoper, Cincinnati, [ca. 7] March 1835, MH-AH). For the change in title, see chapter 2.

3. James Clarke, "The Messenger's Affinities," *WM* 1 (November 1835):357. Citations to the magazine appear parenthetically in the text, by volume and page numbers. For the complete contents of the *Messenger*, including dates, titles, and authors, see my "Annotated List of Contributions to the *Western Messenger*," *Studies in the American Renaissance 1984*, ed. Joel Myerson (Charlottesville: University Press of Virginia, 1984).

4. Judith A. Green summarizes the written contributions of the editors and main writers in "Religion, Life, and Literature in the *Western Messenger*" (Ph.D. dissertation, University of Wisconsin-Madison, 1982).

5. Peabody to Clarke, Cincinnati, 25 June 1835, MH–AH.

6. Clarke to William H. Venable, Jamaica Plain, Mass., 19 February 1886, in Venable, *Beginnings of Literary Culture in the Ohio Valley* (Cincinnati: Robert Clarke, 1891), p. 74; Venable, p. 72; Frank Luther Mott, *A History of American Magazines 1741–1850* (1930; rpt. Cambridge: Harvard University Press, Belknap Press, 1966), p. 663; Clarence L. F. Gohdes, *The Periodicals of American Transcendentalism* (Durham, N.C.: Duke University Press, 1931), p. 27; John Wesley Thomas, *James Freeman Clarke: Apostle of German Culture to America* (Boston: Luce, 1949), p. 79.

7. The single exception is Charles E. Blackburn, "JFC," pp. 134–238.

8. Elizabeth R. McKinsey, *The Western Experiment: New England Transcendentalists in the Ohio Valley* (Cambridge: Harvard University Press, 1973), pp. 42, 48–49; Octavius Brooks Frothingham, *Transcendentalism in New England* (1876; reprint, Gloucester, Mass.: Peter Smith, 1965), p. 105.

9. Channing to William Greene, Rondout, N.Y., 1 October 1840, OCHP.

10. Channing to Frothingham, London, 10 January 1982, PSt.

11. Venable first cited the *Messenger* as "a harbinger of the famous Boston *Dial*," noting that the two periodicals shared at least ten contributors (p. 80). Gohdes calls the magazine "a full-fledged organ of transcendental thought" (*Periodicals*, p. 18), a judg-

ment repeated verbatim in John G. Greene, *"The Western Messenger," Journal of Liberal Religion* 4 (1942):53. McKinsey says that the *Messenger* "stands as the first of all Transcendentalist periodicals" (*Western Experiment*, p. 7).

12. Fuller to Caroline Sturgis, Providence, 16 November 1837, in *The Letters of Margaret Fuller*, ed. Robert N. Hudspeth (Ithaca, N.Y.: Cornell University Press, 1983–), 1:314; Robert D. Habich, "James Freeman Clarke's 1833 Letter-journal for Margaret Fuller," *ESQ: A Journal of the American Renaissance* 27 (1981):54; Brownson, Review of *Two Articles from the Princeton Review, Boston Quarterly Review* 3 (1840):270.

13. "Historic Notes of Life and Letters in New England," *The Complete Works of Ralph Waldo Emerson*, ed. Edward W. Emerson, 12 vols. (Boston: Houghton, Mifflin, 1903–1904), 10:342.

14. Gohdes, *Periodicals*, p. v.

15. J36–39, entry for 26 November to 1 December 1838. According to Clarke, the others arguing for the new school were George Ripley, Cyrus A. Bartol, and himself; the old school was represented by Francis Parkman (father of the historian), Ezra Stiles Gannett, and F. W. P. Greenwood.

16. Anne C. Rose, *Transcendentalism as a Social Movement, 1830–1850* (New Haven: Yale University Press, 1981), p. 71. That even so careful a scholar as Rose can succumb to such an inaccurate metaphor illustrates how easily we can slip from fact to hyperbole.

17. For a list of representative works, as well as a cogent assessment of the trend, see David Robinson, "Unitarian Historiography and the American Renaissance," *ESQ: A Journal of the American Renaissance* 23 (1977): 130–37.

18. Lawrence Buell, *Literary Transcendentalism: Style and Vision in the American Renaissance* (Ithaca, N.Y.: Cornell University Press, 1973), p. 38. Frothingham suggests a less direct debt, claiming that Unitarians "opened the door to the new speculation" by being "friends of free thought in religion" (*Transcendentalism*, pp. 114–15).

19. McKinsey, *Western Experiment*, p. 21.

Chapter 1. The Ohio Valley in 1835

1. Josiah Stoddard Johnston, ed., *Memorial History of Louisville*, 2 vols. (Chicago and New York: American Biographical Publishing Co., [1896]), 1:77, 89–90; "Louisville: 1837," *Western Monthly Magazine and Literary Review*, n.s. 1 (1837): 139–40; *JFCAuto*, p. 68. For vivid descriptions of Western travel and of Louisville, see James Freeman Clarke, "George D. Prentice and Kentucky Thirty-five Years Ago," *Old and New* 1 (1870): 739–44.

2. Benjamin Drake, "Cincinnati, at the Close of 1835," *Cincinnati Mirror*, 13 February 1836; Francis P. Weisenburger, *The Passing of the Frontier 1825–1850*, vol. 3 of *The History of the State of Ohio*, ed. Carl Wittke (Columbus: Ohio State Archaeological and Historical Society, 1941), pp. 82–85; *Cincinnati Mirror*, 19 March 1836; Frances Trollope, *Domestic Manners of the Americans* (1832; rpt. New York: Vintage, 1949), p. 88.

3. According to Harriet Beecher, his daughter (*The Autobiography of Lyman Beecher*, ed. Barbara M. Cross, 2 vols. [Cambridge: Harvard University Press, Belknap Press, 1961], 2:82).

4. General histories of the Unitarian movement are abundant. An excellent brief study is *A Stream of Light: A Short History of American Unitarianism*, ed. Conrad Wright (Boston: Unitarian Universalist Association, 1975).

5. Weisenburger, *Passing of the Frontier*, p. 148; quoted in William W. Sweet, *Religion in the Development of American Culture, 1765–1840* (New York: Scribners, 1952), p. 117.

6. William W. Sweet, *The Presbyterians* (New York: Harper and Brothers, 1936), p. 107.

7. Niels H. Sonne, *Liberal Kentucky 1780–1828* (New York: Columbia University Press, 1939), pp. 260 and passim.

8. Tiffany, *HJH*, pp. 197–244. Huidekoper (1776–1854), a Dutch immigrant who made a fortune as an agent for the Holland Land Company, embraced Unitarianism in the early 1820s. His daughter Anna (1814–97) married James Freeman Clarke. For Unitarianism in Meadville, see also Earl M. Wilbur, *A Historical Sketch of the Independent Congregational Church, Meadville, Pennsylvania 1825–1900* (Meadville, Pa.: n.p., 1902).

9. Ephraim Peabody to Rhoda Abbot Peabody, Meadville, 2 July 1830, quoted in Tiffany, *HJH*, pp. 208–9.

10. Prospectus of the *Unitarian Essayist*, quoted in Tiffany, *HJH*, p. 221.

11. In October 1832 Peabody offered to resume editorship of the *Essayist*, but in December he changed his mind, writing Huidekoper that "it would not be advisable to publish it here at this time" (Peabody to Huidekoper, Cincinnati, December 1832, MH–AH).

12. *MemJHP*, a eulogistic portrait by Perkins's cousin, includes selections of Perkins's historical writings, poetry, and tales.

13. Clarke, "Journal of Myself," entry for 24 May [1832], MHi.

14. Clarke, "Journal Louisville" (for Sarah A. Clarke), entries for 17 March 1834, 4 April 1834, MHi; Clarke, "Louisville Journal/March 1835" (for Sarah A. Clarke), entry for 30 March 1835, MHi. Sarah Anne Clarke (1808–96) was an amateur painter and a friend of Emerson and Margaret Fuller (Joel Myerson, "'A True & High Minded Person': Transcendentalist Sarah Clarke," *Southwest Review* 59 [1974]: 163–72).

15. Eliot to Clarke, Boston, 12 October [1833], MoSW; Clarke to Eliot, Louisville, 4 December 1833, MH bMS Am 1569 (325). The only biography is Charlotte C. Eliot, *William Greenleaf Eliot: Minister, Educator, Philanthropist* (Cambridge, Mass.: Houghton, Mifflin, 1904).

16. Eliot, *William Greenleaf Eliot*, p. 10.

17. This is a generous estimate. After three years of preaching, Eliot still could count on no more than "twenty-five or thirty in pleasant weather" (Eliot, *William Greenleaf Eliot*, p. 29).

18. Eliot to Dr. James Freeman, [St. Louis], 30 December 1834, in Eliot, *William Greenleaf Eliot*, pp. 21–22.

19. Ephraim Peabody, "Memoir and Writings of J. H. Perkins," *Christian Examiner* 50 (1851): 160.

20. Clarke to Fuller, Louisville, 15 December 1834, in *Letters of JFC*, p. 86; Clarke to Eliot, 4 December 1833; Clarke to Channing, Buffalo, 17 June 1834, MH bMS Am 1569 (287). In a published letter of 4 April 1835 Clarke called the West "all in a ferment, a perpetual boiling up and over—we overturn, and overturn, and overturn—nothing is stable, nothing fixed" ("Liberal Christianity in the West," *Boston Observer*, 23 April 1835).

21. Clarke to Fuller, Louisville, 15 December 1834; Ephraim Peabody to Rhoda Abbot Peabody, 2 July 1830; Clarke, "Louisville Journal/March 1835," entry for 30 March 1835.

22. Trollope, *Domestic Manners*, pp. 108–9. For summaries of the major sects, written by leaders of each, see I. Daniel Rupp, comp., *An Original History of the Religious Denominations at Present Existing in the United States* (Philadelphia: J. Y. Humphreys, 1844).

23. See John B. Boles, *The Great Revival, 1787–1805* ([Lexington]: University of Kentucky Press, [1972]) and Sydney E. Ahlstrom, *A Religious History of the American*

People (New Haven: Yale University Press, 1972), pp. 429–54. A contemporary account of the "bodily agitations" witnessed at Cane Ridge appears in Elder John Rogers, *The Biography of Eld. Barton Warren Stone* (1846; reprint, New York: Arno, 1972), pp. 39–42.

24. Louis B. Wright, *Culture on the Moving Frontier* (Bloomington: Indiana University Press, 1955), p. 68.

25. Quoted in Sweet, *Religion in the Development,* p. 171.

26. Caleb Atwater, *A History of the State of Ohio, Natural and Civil* (Cincinnati: Glezen & Shepard, 1838), p. 304; Trollope, *Domestic Manners,* p. 76.

27. Weisenburger, *Passing of the Frontier,* pp. 158–60. See also William H. Venable, *Beginnings of Literary Culture in the Ohio Valley* (Cincinnati: Robert Clarke, 1891), pp. 197–226, for an analysis of the effect of sectarianism on periodical literature. R. Carlyle Buley captures the spirit of the moment: "So numerous and complex were the schisms and crossings over and so illogical were many of them, that groups and sects not infrequently found themselves back in the fold whence they had started" (*The Old Northwest. Pioneer Period: 1815–1840,* 2 vols. [Bloomington: Indiana University Press, 1950], 2:419.

28. Lyman Beecher, *A Plea for the West,* 2d ed. (Cincinnati: Truman & Smith, 1835), pp. 12, 185.

29. Atwater, *History of Ohio,* p. 304.

30. Simon Clough, "The Christian Denomination," *Christian Examiner* 4 (1827): 184. Information on the Christian Connexion is taken from Alexander Campbell, *The Christian System* (1836; 4th ed., 1866; reprint, New York: Arno, 1969); Winfred E. Garrison and Alfred T. DeGroot, *The Disciples of Christ: A History,* rev. ed. (St. Louis: Bethany Press, 1958); Rogers, *Biography of Stone,* passim; and Ahlstrom, *Religious History,* pp. 445–52.

31. Campbell, *Christian System,* pp. 18, 71, 72; Rogers, *Biography of Stone,* pp. 193, 203, 208.

32. Conrad Wright, "Introduction," *A Stream of Light,* p. xiii; Campbell, *Christian System,* p. 103. See also Rogers, *Biography of Stone,* p. 231.

33. Quoted in Sweet, *Religion in the Development,* p. 224.

34. Ahlstrom, *Religious History,* pp. 446, 451; Alice Felt Tyler, *Freedom's Ferment* (1944; reprint, New York: Harper, 1962), p. 201.

35. Ahlstrom, *Religious History,* p. 452; Garrison and DeGroot, *Disciples of Christ,* pp. 328–29. The Disciples claimed 325,000 "communicants" and over 500,000 persons of "their general views" by 1844, figures that are surely inflated but that nevertheless indicate how widespread the movement was thought to be (Rupp, *Original History,* p. 170).

36. Clarke to Charles Briggs, Louisville, 23 June 1835, AUA Letterbooks, MH-AH.

37. George W. Cooke argues that "a few of the leaders saw the opportunity, but the churches were not ready to respond to their appeals" (*Unitarianism in America* [Boston: American Unitarian Association, 1902], pp. 153–54); Elizabeth R. McKinsey, *The Western Experiment: New England Transcendentalists in the Ohio Valley* (Cambridge: Harvard University Press, 1973), p. 4.

38. See, for example, Daniel Walker Howe, "'At Morning Blest and Golden-Browed': Unitarians, Transcendentalists, and Reformers, 1835–1865," in *A Stream of Light,* pp. 58–60.

39. Quoted in Cooke, *Unitarianism,* p. 133; "Constitution of the American Unitarian Association," in *Sixteenth Report of the American Unitarian Association* (Boston: James Munroe, 1841), p. 42.

40. Cooke, *Unitarianism,* pp. 126–27. Among the founders of the AUA were James

Walker (1794–1874), a Divinity School graduate in 1817 and later president of Harvard; Henry Ware, Jr. (1794–1843), who enrolled in but did not graduate from the Divinity School, class of 1817; John Gorham Palfrey (1796–1881), a graduate in 1818 and later dean of the Divinity School; Jared Sparks (1789–1866), also an 1818 graduate and later president of Harvard; and Alexander Young (1800–1854), a graduate in 1824 *(DivCat)*.

41. Built into the Unitarian system was a commitment to tolerance—as Dr. Channing put it, "the duty of candor, charitable judgment, especially toward those who differ in religious opinion" ("Unitarian Christianity," in *The Works of William E. Channing, D.D.* [Boston: American Unitarian Association, 1896], p. 382). That ideal, understandably, was sorely tested in practice; broadmindedness made Unitarians reluctant to promote their beliefs as a sectarian doctrine, but it did not prevent them from actively arguing the truth as they saw it. "Our object," wrote James Walker, "is not to convert men to our party, but to our principles; and to our principles, not because they are ours, but because they are the truth" ("Difficulties in Parishes," *Christian Examiner* 9 [1830]: 18).

42. *First Annual Report of the Executive Committee of the American Unitarian Association* (Boston: Isaac R. Butts, 1826), pp. 10–11; *Second Annual Report of the American Unitarian Association* (Boston: Bowles and Dearborn, 1827), pp. 75, 82.

43. *Second Annual Report*, p. 14; Clough, "Christian Denomination," pp. 189–90, 186, 185, 191.

44. Howe, "'At Morning Blest and Golden-Browed,'" pp. 33–34.

45. Cooke, *Unitarianism*, p. 144. Briggs (1791–1873), a Divinity School graduate in 1818, served as Secretary until 1847 *(DivCat)*.

46. Henry Ware, Jr., "An Address delivered before the Ministerial Conference in Berry Street, May 27, 1835," *Christian Examiner* 19 (1835): 102–3.

47. *Tenth Report of the American Unitarian Association* (Boston: Charles Bowen, 1835), pp. 30–31, 50.

48. *Eleventh Report of the American Unitarian Association* (Boston: L. C. Bowles, 1836), pp. 34, 38–39. James William Thompson (1805–81) was minister at Salem *(DivCat)*.

49. Blackburn, "JFC," p. 55; McKinsey, *Western Experiment*, p. 51. Scholars have insisted upon immense cultural gaps between East and West as the reasons for Unitarianism's relative ineffectiveness in the West. For instance, McKinsey concludes that the missionaries could never reconcile the "two Wests—their ideal and the rough-and-tumble frontier reality" (p. 53). Blackburn places part of the blame on the Unitarians' "Eastern accent" (p. 92). Ralph L. Rusk views Unitarianism as "handicapped by the unpopularity of its religious creed" in the West (*The Literature of the Middle Western Frontier*, 2 vols. [New York: Columbia University Press, 1925], 1:184). However true these claims may be for the later years of the Unitarian missionary movement, it is incorrect to make them for the year 1835, as I have attempted to show.

50. Useful discussions of the Transcendentalist controversy include Clarence Faust, "The Background of Unitarian Opposition to Transcendentalism," *Modern Philology* 35 (1938): 297–324; William R. Hutchison, *The Transcendentalist Ministers* (New Haven: Yale University Press, 1959); and Alexander Kern, "The Rise of Transcendentalism 1815–1860," in Harry Hayden Clark, ed., *Transitions in American Literary History* (Durham, N.C.: Duke University Press, 1953), pp. 247–314.

51. Clarke to Fuller, [Louisville], 12 April 1835, in *Letters of JFC*, p. 91.

52. Clarke to Fuller, Louisville, 15 December 1834, in *Letters of JFC*, pp. 86–87.

53. Earl Morse Wilbur, *A History of Unitarianism*, 2 vols. (Cambridge: Harvard University Press, 1946–52), 2:441–42; Blackburn, "JFC," pp. 276–77 (a useful chart of AUA expenditures from 1826–1850); Lawrence Buell, *Literary Transcendentalism*

(Ithaca, N.Y.: Cornell University Press, 1973), p. 23. For a partial list of Unitarian periodicals, see Cooke, *Unitarianism*, pp. 447–52.

54. Hedge to Fuller, Cambridge, 20 February 1835, MH-AH bMS 384/1 (17). Follen (1796–1840) was the first professor of German literature at Harvard, 1825–35. Furness (1802–96) was minister at Philadelphia and an accomplished German scholar. Marsh (1794–1842), president of the University of Vermont, wrote an influential preface to his 1829 edition of Coleridge's *Aids to Reflection.*

55. Emerson to Carlyle, Concord, 12 March 1835, in *The Correspondence of Emerson and Carlyle,* ed. Joseph Slater (New York: Columbia University Press, 1964), pp. 119–21; Alcott, "Life, Speculative and Actual" [Journal for 1835], entry for March 1835, p. 104, MH 59M–308 (8); Carlyle to Emerson, London, 13 May 1835, in *Correspondence,* pp. 129–30. See also Joel Myerson, *The New England Transcendentalists and the "Dial"* (Rutherford, N.J.: Fairleigh Dickinson University Press, 1980), pp. 31–36.

56. Sarah Clarke wrote to James on 28 February 1835, acknowledging receipt of the prospectus for his Western magazine, and told him of the "*Transcendental Journal* which is projected by the supernal coterie" (MH bMS Am 1569.3 [12]).

57. Stanley M. Vogel, *German Literary Influences on the American Transcendentalists* (New Haven: Yale University Press, 1955), p. xvi. René Wellek argues that "the minor Transcendentalists show only slight contacts with German philosophy proper" but affirms the effect of German literature on their thinking ("The Minor Transcendentalists and German Philosophy," *New England Quarterly* 15 [1942]: 652–80).

58. Walter Sutton, *The Western Book Trade, 1796–1880* (Columbus: Ohio State Historical Society, 1961), p. 67; Frank L. Mott, *A History of American Magazines 1741–1850* (1930; reprint, Cambridge: Harvard University Press, 1966), p. 386; Rusk, *Literature of Middle Western Frontier,* 1:156. For a listing of a "representative selection" of Western periodicals to 1840, see idem, 2:145–84.

59. Quoted in Venable, *Beginnings of Literary Culture,* p. 67.

60. Thomas, *Apostle,* p. 76.

61. "A Chapter on Autography," in *The Complete Works of Edgar Allan Poe,* ed. James A. Harrison, 17 vols. (New York: Thomas Y. Crowell, 1902), 15:223. For details on Gallagher's active literary career, see Rusk, *Literature of Middle Western Frontier,* 1:339–43, and Venable, *Beginnings of Literary Culture,* pp. 436–70.

62. John T. Flanagan, *James Hall: Literary Pioneer of the Ohio Valley* (Minneapolis: University of Minnesota Press, 1941), pp. 197 and passim.

63. John P. Foote, *Memoirs of the Life of Samuel E. Foote* (Cincinnati: Robert Clarke, 1860), pp. 177–79. New Englanders made up a relatively small part of Cincinnati's population, but as Weisenburger notes, "a New England background served as a passport to good society and to favorable business contacts" (*Passing of the Frontier,* p. 48).

64. Channing to Julia Allen Channing, Cincinnati, 12–14 January 1839, MH bMS Am 1755 (150). See also Louis L. Tucker, "The Semi-Colon Club of Cincinnati," *Ohio History* 73 (1964): 13–26. A sampling of the pieces read at Semi-Colon meetings is printed in Foote, *Memoirs,* pp. 242–87.

65. Other discussion clubs included the Cincinnati Lyceum, founded in 1830 "for scientific and literary improvement" and, also in Cincinnati, the "Inquisition," devoted to "the public discussion of questions, orally and through papers submitted" (Henry A. Ford and Kate B. Ford, *History of Cincinnati, Ohio, with Illustrations and Biographical Sketches* [Cleveland: L. A. Williams, 1881], p. 219). Clarke's J34–36 and J36–39 reveal random meetings of an unnamed club whose participants included George Keats, Francis E. Goddard, and other prominent citizens of Louisville.

66. See, for example, Rusk, *Literature of Middle Western Frontier,* 1:179 and Thomas,

Apostle, p. 61.

67. Octavius B. Frothingham, *Boston Unitarianism 1820–1850* (New York: Putnam's, 1890), p. 1. The fullest discussions of Unitarian aesthetics and the value placed on "genteel" literature are Daniel W. Howe, *The Unitarian Conscience: Harvard Moral Philosophy, 1805–1861* (Cambridge: Harvard University Press, 1970), pp. 174–204, and Buell, *Literary Transcendentalism,* pp. 23–54.

68. Dr. William Ellery Channing, "Remarks on National Literature," in *Works,* pp. 124, 126.

69. William Charvat, *The Origins of American Critical Thought 1810–1835* (Philadelphia: University of Pennsylvania Press, 1936), pp. 13–17.

70. [James Hall], "Literature and Religion," *Western Monthly Magazine* 1 (1833): 545. Hall devoted his magazine "chiefly to elegant literature" but intended it to be "useful" as a "medium for disseminating valuable information and pure moral principles" ("To the Reader," *Western Monthly Magazine* 1 [1833]: 1).

71. Peabody to Clarke, Cincinnati, 26 January 1835, MH-AH.

Chapter 2. 1835–1836: "The leading western magazine"

1. J34–36, entry for 13 November 1834.

2. Peabody to Clarke, Cincinnati, [24] and 26 January 1835, MH–AH. Albert Clarke Patterson (1809–74), son of Enoch and Mary Adams Patterson of Boston, was graduated from Harvard's Divinity School in 1833 and ordained at Buffalo on 13 August 1834. He resigned his ministry in May 1836, became a Protestant Episcopal priest in 1839, and served a number of Episcopal churches in New York and Massachusetts before his death in Buffalo (*DivCat; NEHGR* 37 [1883]: 153–54; *WM* 2 : 419–22).

3. It is interesting to speculate about the effect on the *Messenger*'s financial health had Peabody lowered the subscription price and tried to sell all 750 copies at $1.30 per year, a bargain in 1835.

4. J34–36; Peabody to Clarke, [Cincinnati], 14 March [1835], MH–AH.

5. "Western Examiner," *Christian Register,* 21 March 1835.

6. J34–36, entry for February 1835.

7. Clarke to Fuller, Cincinnati, 20 February 1835, in *Letters of JFC,* pp. 88–89; Clarke to Davis, [Cincinnati], 20 February 1835, in *JFCAuto,* p. 108.

8. Clarke and Peabody to Whitman, Cincinnati, 19 February 1835, AUA Letterbooks, MH–AH.

9. Peabody to Huidekoper, Cin[cinnati], [7] March 1835, MH–AH, dated from postmark.

10. Peabody to Huidekoper, Cincinnati, December 1832, MH–AH; Peabody to Clarke, Cincinnati, [22 March 1835], MHi, dated from postmark.

11. Peabody to Clarke, 14 March [1835].

12. Peabody to Clarke, 22 March 1835; J34–36, entries for 4 March, 18 March 1835.

13. Peabody to Clarke, 14 March 1835, 22 March 1835.

14. J. W., [Letter to the Editor], *Christian Register,* 4 April 1835. Clarke thanked Whitman for his remarks in a letter of 20 April 1835, AUA Letterbooks, MH–AH; "The Western Examiner," *Christian Examiner* 18 (1835): 271. The prospectus also appeared in the *Boston Observer,* whose editor encouraged an "efficient subscription" to the magazine on 23 April 1835.

15. Clarke to Palfrey, Louisville, 24 April 1835, MH bMS Am 1569 (573); Sarah

Clarke to J. F. Clarke, [Boston?], 28 February 1835, MH bMS Am 1569.3 (12). Osgood (d. 1863), a Harvard M.D. (1817), was a subscriber to the *Messenger* (*HarCat;* SubBook). In his "Louisville Journal/March 1835," MHi, Clarke responded, "What Dr. Osgood says about our Maga may be very true—yet we shall have a great deal of help as we are not to confine ourselves to theology by any means."

16. Peabody to Clarke, [Cincinnati], 20 May 1835, MH–AH.

17. Clarke to Fuller, Louisville, 24 June 1835, in *Letters of JFC*, p. 98; Peabody to Huidekoper, Cincinnati, 3 July 1835, MH–AH.

18. Peabody to Clarke, 22 March 1835.

19. "Louisville Journal/March 1835," entry for 30 March 1835; Clarke to Fuller, Lexington, 14 June 1835, in *Letters of JFC*, p. 95.

20. Clarke to Briggs, Louisville, 23 June 1835, AUA Letterbooks, MH–AH; Peabody to Clarke, Cincinnati, [24] June 1835, MH–AH. Clarke felt a responsibility to care for his mother and sister, both of whom later joined him in Louisville.

21. Peabody to Clarke, 14 March 1835; Peabody to Huidekoper, Cincinnati, October 1832, MH–AH; Peabody to Clarke, [Cincinnati], 25 May 1835, MH–AH; Peabody to Clarke, 3 July 1835.

22. Peabody to Clarke, Cincinnati, 25 June 1835, MH–AH; Peabody to Clarke, Cincinnati, 19 and 23 June 1835, MH–AH. In a letter of 6 July 1835 Clarke responded peevishly, "'Grave, witty, articles,' my dear friend, do not grow on every bush" (MH bMS Am 1569 [599]).

23. Huidekoper's "correspondent" was Rev. Nathaniel West (1820–64), an Irish Presbyterian who came to Meadville in September 1834 (S. J. M. Eaton, *History of the Presbytery of Erie* [New York: Hurd and Houghton, 1868], pp. 331–34).

24. On Beecher's heresy trial see *The Autobiography of Lyman Beecher*, ed. Barbara M. Cross, 2 vols. (Cambridge: Harvard University Press, Belknap Press, 1961), 2:261–72.

25. An English abolitionist, Maylin ran a school in Cincinnati and served as Treasurer of the Western Literary Institute, and College of Professional Teachers (*Cincinnati Directory, for 1836–1837* [Cincinnati: J. H. Woodruff, 1836]).

26. For a summary of anti-Catholic incidents and publications, see Alice Felt Tyler, *Freedom's Ferment* (1944; reprint, New York: Harper, 1962), pp. 363–77.

27. A Mesopotamian diviner, Balaam uncontrollably spoke the words of God (Num. 22–23).

28. Peabody to Clarke, Cincinnati, 29 June 1835, MH–AH.

29. Peabody to Clarke, [Cincinnati], 7 July 1835, MH–AH; J34–36, entries for 28 and 29 July 1835; Peabody to Huidekoper, 3 July 1835, 26 December 1835, MH–AH.

30. Peabody to Clarke, Cincinnati, 9 November 1835, MH–AH. Howe (1811–88), son of Samuel and Susan Tracy Howe of Worthington, Mass., married Sarah Templeton Coolidge (b. 1814) of Boston in Cincinnati on 21 September 1835. In 1846 he moved to Detroit, there serving as treasurer of the Michigan Central Railroad and engaging in the manufacture of iron, until his return to Cambridge in 1859 (Daniel Wait Howe, *Howe Genealogies*, 2 vols. [Boston: New England Historic Genealogical Society, 1929], 2:295; *Index to the Probate Records of the County of Middlesex*, 2d series [Cambridge, Mass.: n. p., 1912]).

31. Charles E. Blackburn, "Some New Light on the *Western Messenger*," *American Literature* 26 (1954): 326–27; Clarke to Peabody, Louisville, 5 November 1835, MH bMS Am 1569 (600).

32. Robert S. Peabody and Francis G. Peabody, *A New England Romance: The Story of Ephraim and Mary Jane Peabody* (Boston: Houghton, Mifflin, 1920), pp. 91–95; Peabody to Huidekoper, 26 December 1835. Peabody's son Samuel (1834–35) died on 1 October

in Watertown, Mass. (*Christian Register,* 17 October 1835). Mary Jane Derby (1807–92), whom Peabody had married on 5 August 1832, found her blindness only temporary (*New England Romance,* pp. 38, 80, 164). Peabody's personal trauma was compounded when in early January 1836 the American novelist and critic John Neal accused him of plagiarizing the Phi Beta Kappa poem, "stolen piece-meal . . . and republished in Boston for original!—*with impunity*" (J. N., "Stop Thief!" *New-England Galaxy,* 2 January 1836). In a blistering defense of Peabody, Perkins replied that no one could claim credit for Neal's poetry "without calling down upon himself the pity and condemnation of the whole world, for so degrading and disgracing himself as to lay claim to such volumes" (*Cincinnati Mirror,* 6 February 1836).

33. Clarke left for Mobile and New Orleans on 10 December 1835, returning to Louisville on 16 February 1836 (J34-36). His replacement was George W. Hosmer (1803–81) of Northfield, Mass., who would later replace Patterson at Buffalo, serve as president of Antioch College, and fill the pulpit at Newton, Mass. (*DivCat*).

34. Peabody to Huidekoper, 26 December 1835; *Cincinnati Mirror,* 25 July, 8 August, 12 September 1835; *Western Monthly Magazine* 4 (1835): 136–37; *Christian Register,* 17 October, 24 October 1835; *Christian Examiner* 19 (1835): 268–70.

35. Clarke to Whitman, Louisville, 20 April 1835, AUA Letterbooks, MH–AH.

36. Peabody to Clarke, 3 July 1835. Peabody opposed reprinting sermons, not because he objected to "preaching" in the magazine, but because he thought sermons "always badly written—& the thought is generally blotted out like bars of iron in a rolling mill" (Peabody to Clarke, 20 May 1835).

37. See Perkins, "Reasons for Leaving the Law," *WM* 1:859–60.

38. Clarke to Peabody, 6 July 1835.

39. Peabody to Clarke, 20 May, 29 June, 3 July 1835.

40. Peabody to Clarke, 7 July 1835.

41. Clarke to Peabody, Louisville, 5 November 1835; Peabody to Clarke, [Cincinnati], 9 November 1835, MH–AH.

42. On 23 May 1835, for instance, he complained to Clarke that of the material on hand for the first number "there are but 5 articles that are Western": the reports of Campbell and the Western Literary Institute, the reviews of Beecher's *Plea* and Riddell's *Synopsis,* and the column on regional poetry.

43. Clarke to Fuller, 20 February 1835, December 1833, in *Letters of JFC,* pp. 88, 67.

44. Peabody to Clarke, 3 July 1835.

45. Ralph L. Rusk, for example, in *The Literature of the Middle Western Frontier,* 2 vols. (New York: Columbia University Press, 1925), 2:179–80, explains the column's demise by quoting an unsigned notice (by Clarke) of Gallagher's *Hesperian* in April 1838: "Our people, perhaps, have as yet no literature because they have nothing to say" (*WM* 5:71). Clearly though, since Peabody found "our poetical aspirants too numerous" (*WM* 1:272), the problem was not a shortage of verse but a scarcity of the *type* of poetry he found valuable.

46. James Hall edited the *Western Souvenir, a Christmas and New Year's Gift for 1829* (Cincinnati: N. and G. Guilford, [1828]), the first annual devoted exclusively to Western literature. Other anthologies include William D. Gallagher, ed., *Selections from the Poetical Literature of the West* (Cincinnati: U. P. James, 1841); William T. Coggeshall, *The Poets and Poetry of the West* (Cincinnati: Follett, Foster, 1860); Emerson Venable, ed., *Poets of Ohio* (Cincinnati: Robert Clarke, 1909); and Willard R. Jillson, *Early Kentucky Literature 1750–1840* (Frankfort: Kentucky State Historical Society, 1931).

47. Daniel Walker Howe, *The Unitarian Conscience: Harvard Moral Philosophy 1805–1861* (Cambridge: Harvard University Press, 1970), p. 194.

48. *JFCAuto*, p. 39.

49. Huidekoper to Peabody, [Meadville], October 1832, in Tiffany, *HJH*, pp. 263–64; Peabody to Huidekoper, 26 December 1835.

50. Robert D. Habich, "James Freeman Clarke's 1833 Letter-journal for Margaret Fuller," *ESQ: A Journal of the American Renaissance* 27 (1981): 47–56; Clarke, "Journal of Myself," MHi, entry for May 1833, p. 137. On the same page, in an entry dated April 1837, Clarke recalls his decision not to publish his first response to Norton: "I acted upon [the?] above reasoning and did not publish my article. [But?] afterwards I was sorry. . . . Mr Emerson told me he [though]t me wrong in not publishing. 'When we feel strong conviction' said he 'we should believe ourselves put there by Providence to speak, whether men hear or forbear.'"

51. J34–36, undated entry, p. 104; Clarke to Fuller, Louisville, 16 March 1835, in *Letters of JFC*, p. 89; Clarke to Eliot, [Louisville], 24 February 1834, MH bMS Am 1569 (326). Blackburn, "JFC," provides a cogent discussion of Clarke's Louisville sermons, pp. 74–88.

52. Clarke, "Journal Louisville" (for Sarah Clarke), entry for 17 March 1834, MHi; J34–36, p. 75 (sermon notes for Mobile); Ephraim Peabody to Rhoda Abbot Peabody, Meadville, 2 July 1830, in Tiffany, *HJH*, p. 209; Clarke to Channing, Louisville, 4 October 1833, MH bMS Am 1569 (283).

53. J34–36. The transfer took several days, for Clarke did not return to Louisville until 15 March. Peabody contributed occasionally to the *Messenger* after relinquishing control, but his health prevented his staying in the West. He left Cincinnati in May 1836, preached in Dayton and Mobile, then returned to New England in the summer of 1837, serving the Unitarian churches in New Bedford from 1838 to 1845 and in Boston (King's Chapel) from 1846 until his death in 1856 (*DivCat; Heralds*, 3 : 297–303).

54. Because the February 1836 number had appeared late (*WM* 1 : 588), and to allow time to change editors, there was no March 1836 number.

55. Even under Peabody's editorship Clarke's sectarian pieces were motivated not so much by theological as by personal disagreements, or because he detected a spirit of dogmatism. His "Three Witnesses" (*WM* 1 : 175–82), for instance, an argument against the authenticity of the Trinitarian proof text in the seventh chapter of John, was written "to cut up the jackass in the New York Rev.," a Reverend Hunt of Amherst (Clarke to Peabody, 6 July 1835).

56. "Tests—Affinities," *Baptist Cross and Journal*, 24 July 1835.

57. Clarke, "General Preface to Vol. I and Prospectus of Vol. II," *WM* xii, x. Though bound at the beginning of the first volume in most sets of the *Messenger*, this is clearly an introduction to the second volume.

58. See also Samuel Osgood's "Dark Side of Our National Prosperity" (*WM* 2 : 171–76).

59. Peabody had encouraged Clarke to "write what you will in a German spirit" but found him indiscriminate in his taste for Goethe and Schiller (Peabody to Clarke, 3 July 1835). Clarke thought "a regular supply of articles short & long—trans. & criticisms on & from Germany" appropriate to the *Messenger* (Clarke to Peabody, 6 July 1835).

60. Osgood (1812–80), son of Thomas and Hannah Stevens Osgood, was graduated from Harvard in 1832 and from the Divinity School in 1835; he remained in the West from June 1836 to March 1837, returned to New England, and filled Unitarian pulpits in Nashua, N.H., Providence, and New York City's Church of the Messiah. An able German scholar and a frequent contributor to periodicals, he lacked in his preaching "the genius to inspire," according to O. B. Frothingham; discouraged with his failure to achieve distinction in the Unitarian denomination, he became a Protestant Episcopal

priest in 1870. A member of the New-York Historical Society and later editor of the "Easy Chair" column in *Harper's Magazine,* he coedited the *Christian Inquirer* from 1850 to 1854. On 24 May 1843 he married Ellen Murdock of Boston (*DivCat; NEHGR* 36 [1882]: 113–22; J. B. Moore, "Rev. Samuel Osgood, D. D.," *Magazine of American History* 5 [1880]: 399–400; Frothingham, *Recollections and Impressions* [New York: G. P. Putnam's, 1891], pp. 94–99).

61. Using publication data, newspaper reviews, and booksellers' records, Rusk claims that Scott and Byron were the most popular British Romantics in the West at this time; Wordsworth, Coleridge, Keats, and Shelley were "little noticed" (*Literature of Middle Western Frontier,* 2 : 10–11). Louis B. Wright adds Southey, Thomas Moore, and Felicia Hemans to the list of well-known writers (*Culture on the Moving Frontier* [Bloomington: Indiana University Press, 1955], p. 74). Saul Hounchell notes that, of the nine leading literary magazines in the West before 1840, only the *Messenger* reviewed Wordsworth and Tennyson ("The Principal Literary Magazines of the Ohio Valley to 1840" [Ph.D. dissertation, George Peabody College for Teachers, Nashville, Tenn., 1934], p. 334).

62. Clarke and Peabody to Whitman, 19 February 1835; Clarke to Peabody, Louisville, 30 May [1836], MH bMS Am 1569 (601); Clarke to Peabody, 6 July, 5 November 1835.

63. Sarah Clarke to J. F. Clarke, Newton, 3 March 1836, MH bMS Am 1569.3 (12); Clarke to Peabody, 30 May 1836.

64. Clarke to Fuller, Louisville, 28 March 1836, in *Letters of JFC,* pp. 116–17; Sarah Clarke to J. F. Clarke, [Newton], 7 May 1836, MH bMS Am 1569.3 (12); "Report of the Executive Committee," *Eleventh Report of the American Unitarian Association* (Boston: L. C. Bowles, 1836), pp. 17, 21. The *Christian Register* had printed extracts from the *Messenger* four times since the beginning of 1836, on 16 January, 30 April, 14 May, and 3 September, but had not reviewed or promoted the magazine itself.

65. Clarke to Peabody, 30 May 1836; Clarke to AUA Executive Committee, Louisville, 13 June 1836; AUA Letterbooks, MH–AH; Osgood to Clarke, [Cincinnati], 5 July [1836], MHi; Sarah Clarke to J. F. Clarke, Newton, 11 July 1836, MH bMS Am 1569.3 (12).

66. In the fullest treatment of the subject, *Patterns of Antislavery Among American Unitarians* (Rutherford, N.J.: Fairleigh Dickinson University Press, 1977), Douglas C. Stange traces the activities of individual Unitarians but claims that "it is not possible to define precisely the denomination's position on anti-slavery" (p. 177).

67. Caleb Atwater, *A History of the State of Ohio, Natural and Civil* (Cincinnati: Glezen & Shepard, 1838), p. 324; Lowell H. Harrison, *The Antislavery Movement in Kentucky* (Lexington: University Press of Kentucky, 1978), p. 10; Henry A. Ford and Kate B. Ford, *History of Cincinnati, Ohio* (Cleveland: L. A. Williams, 1881), p. 87. Gilbert Barnes, *The Antislavery Impulse 1830–1844* (New York and London: A. Appleton-Century Co., 1933) remains the definitive study of the religious foundations of antislavery movements.

68. James Clarke, "George D. Prentice and Kentucky Thirty-Five Years Ago," *Old and New* 1 (1870): 743. See also Clarke's letter to the *Christian Register,* 3 September 1836, on colonization efforts in Kentucky, and Clarke, *Anti-slavery Days* (New York: R. Worthington, 1884), pp. 22–30, for anecdotal evidence of the sentiments of slaveholders in the state.

69. In New England Dr. Channing found himself in a similar predicament, his *Slavery* appeasing neither the abolitionists nor their opponents (Arthur W. Brown, *Always Young for Liberty* [Syracuse, N.Y.: Syracuse University Press, 1956], pp. 228–31).

70. Clarke spoke from the pulpit of Channing's Federal Street Church about 2 October and again on 9 October 1836 and from Mellish Motte's pulpit at the South End Church, Boston, on 16 October (*Christian Register,* 8 October, 15 October 1836). An

anonymous listener summarized the first of these discourses in "Religious Wants of the West," *Christian Register,* 8 October 1836.

71. Clarke collected $100 "subscribed in State Street" and $105 from Motte's congregation specifically for the *Messenger.* The Ladies of the Benevolent Association of Danvers donated $150, recommending that all but 25% of that sum be sent to Eliot for use in St. Louis. But since Clarke records in J36–39 (1 December 1836) that he sent only $50 to Eliot, he evidently took liberties with the recommendation and kept $100 for the magazine.

72. In addition to raising money, Clarke's visit to New England put the *Messenger* back in the good graces of the local press. On 23 October the *Christian Register* printed its first favorable notice of the *Messenger* in a year, citing its "pleasing variety of articles" (especially Huidekoper's on "The Unitarianism of the First Three Centuries") and encouraging Easterners to subscribe.

73. The Transcendental Club met at Ripley's home on 19 September, its first real meeting, and at Alcott's on 3 October (Joel Myerson, "A Calendar of Transcendental Club Meetings," *American Literature* 44 [1972]: 200). Clarke recorded his attendance in J36–39 (9 October 1836), following that entry with a summary of his conversations with Dr. Channing.

74. *The Transcendentalists: An Anthology* (Cambridge: Harvard University Press, 1950), p. 94.

Chapter 3. 1837–1839: "A living mirror of the times"

1. Of the vast literature on the period, probably no single work captures the spirit of the decade better than Arthur M. Schlesinger, Jr., *The Age of Jackson* (Boston: Little, Brown, 1945).

2. Here, and elsewhere, the significant distinction between the size of the subscription list and the number of paying subscribers should be noted. The *Messenger*'s editors rarely knew the exact state of accounts. If Peabody's early estimate of 300 subscribers is accurate (Peabody to Huidekoper, Cincinnati, 3 July 1835, MH–AH), then the third volume began with a subscription list of at least 600 names. But since Clarke's records show a monthly press run of 550 from March to July 1837, the actual number of copies distributed to subscribers was probably closer to 500 (MHi).

3. Clarke to Peabody, Louisville, 21 February 1837, MH bMS Am 1569 (604).

4. Samuel Barrett [Assistant Secretary, AUA] to Clarke, Boston, 23 January 1837, MHi; *Twelfth Report of the American Unitarian Association* (Boston: James Munroe, 1837), p. 4. The donation to the *Messenger* is listed, without a date, in the annual statement of the AUA's accounts for 24 May 1836 to 30 May 1837. Clarke's disappointment with the organization during the previous winter makes it likely that the money was appropriated sometime in early spring, perhaps after Briggs's return to Boston in March 1837.

5. Clarke arrived in Cincinnati on 17 December 1836 and left on 26 January 1837; Osgood remained in Louisville from 23 November to 3 February (J36–39).

6. Though Osgood insisted he was not "fishing for a call," he wrote Clarke on 23 January from Louisville (MHi) to ask whether the Cincinnati congregation truly wanted him back. "I offer [my services] to our cause," Osgood explained huffily, "but do not wish to obtrude them anywhere." He returned to Cincinnati briefly, but by 27 March he was in Louisville, on his way to Mobile and Augusta, Georgia, before returning to New England, where he settled at Nashua, N.H., in September 1837 (J36–39; Osgood to Clarke, Nashua, 30 September 1837, MHi).

7. *Fourteenth Report of the American Unitarian Association* (Boston: James Munroe, 1839), p. 15; *Twelfth Report,* p. 31. Benjamin Huntoon (1792–1864), a Dartmouth

graduate in 1817, filled the Cincinnati pulpit until May 1838, then preached at Peoria, Ill., until August 1840, when he returned to Massachusetts (George A. Thayer, *The First Congregational Church of Cincinnati (Unitarian): A History* [Cincinnati: n.p., 1917], p. 18; *NEHGR* 19 [1865]: 176–78).

8. William Pitkin Huntington (1804–85), a graduate of Harvard's medical school in 1835, was ordained as an evangelist at Plymouth on 26 April 1837 and served in Hillsborough, Ill., through the mid-1840s, later becoming an Episcopal priest (*The Huntington Family in America* [Hartford, Conn.: Privately printed, 1915], pp. 729–30; Harvard University archives; *Christian Register,* 6 May 1837; *WM* 7:218). Charles Andrew Farley (1806–87), who graduated from Harvard's Divinity School in 1832, preached at Alton from 1836 to 1838, then served in Maine, Connecticut, and California before leaving the ministry in 1851 (*DivCat; Heralds,* 3:197).

9. James Thurston (1806–72) arrived in Louisville on 4 June 1837 for a Western tour, but within a year he was back in the East, where he was ordained at Windsor, Vt., on 27 June 1838 (J36–39; *DivCat; NEHGR* 26 [1872]: 445). William Silsbee (1813–90) left the West in September 1837, then returned to serve at Pittsburgh in the summer and fall of 1838. He was ordained at Walpole, N.H., on 1 July 1840 (Silsbee to Clarke, Louisville, 10 August 1837, MH bMS Am 1569 [1045]; *WM* 5:409; *DivCat*).

10. Miller, "CPC," pp. 34–46; C. P. Cranch to E. P. Cranch, Quincy, 26 September, 30 September, 15 October 1835, WyU. The seventh child of William and Anna Greenleaf Cranch, Edward Pope Cranch (1809–92) attended Columbian College in Washington, D.C., and moved in 1831 to Cincinnati, where he read law with Salmon P. Chase. A poet and an essayist as well as a lawyer, he contributed frequently to the early numbers of the *Messenger* (*NEHGR* 1 [1847]: 79; *New York Times,* 21 August 1886; manuscript records of the First Congregational Church of Cincinnati, OCHP).

11. J36–39, entry for 1 December 1836; Miller, "CPC," pp. 54–56.

12. C. P. Cranch to E. P. Cranch, St. Louis, 6 December 1836, in Miller, "CPC," p. 65; Francis B. Dedmond, "Christopher Pearse Cranch: Emerson's Self-appointed Defender Against the Philistines," *Concord Saunterer* 15 (1980): 6–19.

13. Ripley's *Discourses* developed the theories that Spirit alone is permanent and that man in his natural state participates in the Divine; the reviewer in the *Christian Register,* 3 December 1836, recommended the book "to every reader who is conscious to himself of possessing a spiritual nature not made for earth alone." The same issue of the *Register* noticed Brownson's *New Views,* which predicted the synthesis of Protestant "materialism" and Catholic "spiritualism" in the "Church of the Future," as "abundant material for thought and reflection." In his review of *Remarks* (which Perry Miller has called "a prosaic *Nature*"), M. L. Hurlbut worried over the "*tendency* of Mr. Furness's theory" but felt confident that Furness himself "would disavow any such purpose" (Miller, *The Transcendentalists: An Anthology* [Cambridge: Harvard University Press, 1950], p. 124; Hurlbut, Review of *Remarks on the Four Gospels* by W. H. Furness, *Christian Examiner* 22 [1837]: 104). For an overview of the miracles controversy see Miller, *The Transcendentalists,* pp. 157–246, and William R. Hutchison, *The Transcendentalist Ministers* (New Haven: Yale University Press, 1959), pp. 52–97.

14. Miller, *The Transcendentalists,* p. 168.

15. *The Complete Works of Ralph Waldo Emerson* [Centenary Edition], ed. Edward W. Emerson, 12 vols. (Boston: Houghton, Mifflin, 1903–4), 10:342–43.

16. George Ripley, [Letter to Andrews Norton], *Boston Daily Advertiser,* 9 November 1836. Ripley put the Transcendentalist position succinctly: "The evidence of miracles depends upon a previous belief in Christianity, rather than the evidence of Christianity on a previous belief in miracles." He hoped Norton would in the future "desire to elicit truth by discussion rather than to silence it by authority."

17. Dr. William Ellery Channing, "Likeness to God," in *The Works of William E. Channing, D.D.* (Boston: American Unitarian Association, 1896), p. 293.

18. Joel Porte notes the significant coincidence of Emerson's "heretical" Divinity School Address and the 200th anniversary of Anne Hutchinson's excommunication from the First Church of Boston (*Representative Man: Ralph Waldo Emerson in His Time* [New York: Oxford University Press, 1979], pp. 98–99).

19. Francis Bowen, Review of *Nature* by Ralph Waldo Emerson, *Christian Examiner* 21 (1837): 371–85; idem, "Locke and the Transcendentalists," *Christian Examiner* 23 (1837): 170–94; Octavius B. Frothingham, *Boston Unitarianism 1820–1850* (New York: Putnam's, 1890), p. 59.

20. Clarke to Emerson, Louisville, 18 January 1835, in *The Letters of Ralph Waldo Emerson*, ed. Ralph L. Rusk, 6 vols. (New York: Columbia University Press, 1939), 1:425; Parker to Convers Francis, West Roxbury, 8 February 1845, in Gary A. Collison, "A Critical Edition of the Correspondence of Theodore Parker and Convers Francis, 1836–1859" (Ph.D. dissertation, Pennsylvania State University, 1979), p. 440.

21. Andrews Norton, [Letter to the Editor], *Boston Daily Advertiser*, 5 November 1836. Norton insisted that he had "no wish to interfere with the rights of free discussion" but maintained that those rights are "sometimes misunderstood."

22. Clarke apparently received a copy of *Remarks* when he visited Furness in Philadelphia on 12 and 13 September 1836, for it was not available for sale in Boston until 12 November, after Clarke had left New England for Kentucky (J36–39; *Christian Register*, 12 November 1836).

23. Ralph Waldo Emerson, *The Collected Works of Ralph Waldo Emerson*, ed. Alfred R. Ferguson et al. (Cambridge: Harvard University Press, Belknap Press, 1971–), vol. 1, *Nature, Addresses, and Lectures*, ed. Robert E. Spiller (1971), pp. 29–30.

24. See *WM* 1:223–25, 365–66, and 629–48. Clarke attempted Alcott's methods with his Sunday School children on 12 February 1837 (J36–39).

25. For the reception of Alcott's *Conversations* see Larry A. Carlson's introduction to "Bronson Alcott's Journal for 1837: An Edition, With Notes and an Introduction" (Ph.D. dissertation, Pennsylvania State University, 1979), pp. 36–51, and Odell Shepard, *Pedlar's Progress: The Life of Bronson Alcott* (Boston: Little, Brown, 1937), pp. 180–218.

26. Osgood to Clarke, Charlestown, 20 July 1837, MHi.

27. Ripley to Clarke, Boston, 16 January 1837, MHi. Clarke's translation was published as volumes 10 and 11 of the series in 1841.

28. Carlson, "Bronson Alcott's Journal," p. 184. In his journal for May, Alcott acknowledged Clarke's second defense as "having done me good justice" (p. 280).

29. Printed in Arthur M. Schlesinger, Jr., *Orestes A. Brownson: A Pilgrim's Progress* (Boston: Little, Brown, 1939), p. 59n.

30. Miller, *The Transcendentalists*, pp. 171–73; Hutchison, *Transcendentalist Ministers*, pp. 58–64.

31. Clarke to Fuller, Louisville, 16 March 1835, in *Letters of JFC*, p. 89.

32. Frothingham (1793–1870) delivered the sermon at the First Church of Boston on 15 March 1835, the twentieth anniversary of his ordination.

33. Osgood to Clarke, Charlestown, 20 July 1837, MHi. Ripley was probably right about Clarke's personal reasons for the slanderous comments: emboldened by the geographical distance between Boston and Louisville, Clarke cultivated a reputation for "Western habits of recklessness" (see chap. 1, n. 14). And convinced, moreover, that true Unitarianism was in essence tolerant and progressive, he tended to isolate conservative "orthodoxy" as individual aberrations—"Nortonism," for instance—rather than as an inertia within the denomination. The issue that separated true from false

Unitarians, he told the assembled members of the AUA in 1841, was "whether we were willing to modify our opinions for the sake of progress, or determined to resist progress rather than alter our opinions" (*Sixteenth Annual Report of the American Unitarian Association* [Boston: James Munroe, 1841], p. 39). Thus the remarks on Frothingham, though ill-timed and discourteous, were consistent both with Clarke's temperament and with his view of the denomination: by seeming to oppose "progress," Frothingham had violated the spirit of Unitarianism, and to Clarke's way of thinking the pastor deserved to be upbraided.

34. Clarke to Fuller, Louisville, 26 July 1837, in *Letters of JFC*, p. 125; J36–39. Clarke arrived in Boston on 29 August (J36–39).

35. Silsbee to Clarke, 10 August 1837; Jarvis to Clarke, Louisville, 31 August 1837, MHi. Edward Jarvis (1803–84), who remained in the West until 1843, was a tireless reformer, an amateur historian, and a prolific writer on the treatment of the insane.

36. C. P. Cranch to Margaret Cranch, Louisville, 14 October 1837, in Miller, "CPC," pp. 71–72.

37. Admitted to the bar at Charleston, S.C., in 1829, John Champion Vaughan (1806–92) settled permanently in Cincinnati in December 1837, unable to countenance the slavery in his home state. An active supporter of reform movements, he edited several abolitionist newspapers in the 1840s and became, with James G. Birney and Salmon P. Chase, a leader in the Free Soil Party (Samuel Bernshein, "John Champion Vaughan," OCHP).

38. For another subscriber's response to Maylin, see *WM* 4:212–13. Dana declared in the November number that by excluding the topic of slavery the *Messenger* "advocates too crippled a system of Religion to suit the wants of this age, and of this people" (*WM* 4:214). On 18 September 1837 Maylin wrote Clarke to protest the publication of his private letter. (Clarke in turn published the second letter in February 1838 [*WM* 4:397–400]). Maylin apparently reconsidered his position, for he contributed again to the *Messenger* in 1840 and 1841.

39. The writer was probably James G. Birney, editor of the *Philanthropist*.

40. Clarke, miscellaneous accounts, MHi. Beginning in April 1837, the *Messenger* was printed by Morton & Smith (later Morton & Griswold).

41. Clarke to William H. Venable, Jamaica Plain, Mass., 19 February 1886, in Venable, *Beginnings of Literary Culture in the Ohio Valley* (Cincinnati: Robert Clarke, 1891), p. 74; Samuel C. Clarke to J. F. Clarke, Newton, 14 November 1837, MH bMS Am 1569 (822). The eldest of the Clarke brothers, Samuel (1806–97) sailed to South America and the East Indies from 1833 to 1835, contributed travel sketches and translations of Spanish poetry to the *Messenger,* and later established himself as a druggist (William W. Johnson, *Clarke-Clark Genealogy* [North Greenfield, Wis.: Privately printed, 1884]).

42. Samuel C. Clarke to J. F. Clarke, Newton, 25 November 1837, MH bMS Am 1569 (823); Samuel C. Clarke to J. F. Clarke, Newton, 16 December 1837, MH bMS Am 1569 (824).

43. Clarke to Charles Briggs, Louisville, 15 December 1837, AUA Letterbooks, MH–AH. Clarke listed some approximate numbers of subscribers outside of New England: Louisville (80); Cincinnati (70 or 80); Buffalo (30); St. Louis (20 or 30); Alton, Ill., and Mobile, Ala. (12 each); Chicago, Lexington, Meadville, Nashville, and Pittsburgh (8 or 10 each).

44. Henry Rice, treasurer of the AUA, complained in 1837 about the "severe pressure for money" that had left many of the group's contributors "reduced and unable to pay" the money they had pledged (*Twelfth Report*, p. 5). For the scope of the economic failure—food shortages, mass bankruptcies, widespread unemployment, and the dan-

ger of workingmen's riots—see Samuel Rezneck, "The Social History of an American Depression, 1837–1842," *American Historical Review* 40 (1935): 662–87.

45. A New Hampshire subscriber, for instance, reluctantly continued his subscription despite "some displeasure (not exactly the word neither) at your course encouraging the 'New Views,' as Mr Brownson would say, of Mr. Emerson, and others" (John Prentiss to Clarke, Keene, N.H., 15 January 1838, MHi).

46. Peabody took particular offense at Clarke's free use of personal letters. *"Do not & do not ever put any thing from my letters into the Messenger unless I give you directions to,"* he wrote from Dayton on 20 June 1836 (MH–AH). Another reader, Charlotte Wilby, was furious when Clarke published a letter from her (*WM* 2:349–51) and signed it "a close student of 'Sartor Resartus'" (Wilby to Clarke, Boston, 12 January 1837, MHi).

47. The full exchange involved Clarke, James Hall, and Mann Butler, Hall's rival in the field of regional history. Reviewing Hall's *Sketches of History, Life, and Manners in the West* (Cincinnati, 1834–35) in the May 1836 *Messenger,* Butler pronounced the work "too *lightly* deduced from original authority, and in many important matters, utterly *contradictory* to it" (*WM* 1:677). Clarke repeated the charge of inaccuracy in the *North American Review* 43 (1836): 2–3. Hall answered both in the preface to his *Statistics of the West* (Cincinnati, 1837), accusing Clarke of parroting Butler's review in "an obscure periodical called the *Western Messenger*" (p. vii). "Those charges," Clarke responded, "are none the less likely to be true, for being made by two witnesses instead of one" (Review of *Statistics of the West* by James Hall, *North American Review* 45 [1837]: 235).

48. Farley to Clarke, Alton, Ill., 5 February 1838, MHi.

49. Osgood to Clarke, Louisville, 5 January 1837, MHi; Silsbee to Clarke, 10 August 1837. Arthur S. Bolster discusses in detail the continuing negotiations between Clarke and his congregation in "The Life of James Freeman Clarke" (Ph.D. dissertation, Harvard University, 1953), pp. 201–5.

50. Osgood to Clarke, Nashua, N.H., 28 February 1838, MHi.

51. Quoted in Sarah Clarke to Amos Bronson Alcott, 2 May 1838; copy in Alcott's "Autobiography 1838," MH 59M–306 (22).

52. Clarke to Fuller, Louisville, 6 August 1838, in *Letters of JFC,* p. 133.

53. *Christian Register,* 23 December 1837; *WM* 4:411. On 25 April 1838 Sarah Clarke reported the "anxious concern your friends have manifested" after James's "last loud shriek for assistance" in the *Messenger* (MH bMS Am 1569.3 [12]). Huidekoper enclosed his donation in a letter of 23 February 1838 (Bolster, "Life of Clarke," p. 206).

54. Holmes to Clarke, [Boston], 17 March 1838, in John T. Morse, Jr., *Life and Letters of Oliver Wendell Holmes,* 2 vols. (Boston: Houghton, Mifflin, 1897), 2:272–77.

55. "The Divinity School Address," in *Collected Works,* 1:84, 90.

56. Julia Power posits three reasons for Shelley's poor reception in New England through 1850: "He was rejected by most of his admirers after their period of youth was over; he was superseded by Goethe; he was banned as an atheist and an immoral character" (*Shelley in America in the Nineteenth Century* [Lincoln, Neb., 1940], p. 69).

57. Emerson, for instance, found Shelley a "uniformly imitative" poet, though "evidently a devout & brave man" (*The Journals and Miscellaneous Notebooks of Ralph Waldo Emerson,* ed. William H. Gilman et al., 16 vols. [Cambridge: Harvard University Press, Belknap Press, 1961–82], 7:316). Margaret Fuller, on the other hand, admired the beauty of Shelley's poetry but regretted "that the unhappy influences of early education prevented his ever attaining clear views of God, life, and the soul" (*The Letters of Margaret Fuller,* ed. Robert N. Hudspeth [Ithaca, N.Y.: Cornell University Press, 1983–], 1:144).

58. The point was anticipated by Dr. Channing, who in 1828 thought Shelley "a man

lost to religion through the folly, hypocrisy, and intolerance of its 'friends' " (William Henry Channing, *Memoir of William Ellery Channing*, 3 vols. [Boston: Crosby and Nichols, 1848], 2 : 346).

59. J36–39, entries for 2, 3, 12, 13, 15, and 16 October 1838; Clarke to Briggs, Louisville, 8 October 1838, AUA Letterbooks, MH–AH.

60. J36–39, entries for 22 and 24 October 1838; Cranch to Clarke, Cincinnati, 10 October 1838, Cranch Papers, MHi. Channing came to Cincinnati between 10 and 23 October; Cranch arrived in Louisville on 28 October (C. P. Cranch to E. P. Cranch, Louisville, 28 October 1838, WyU). The son of Francis Dana and Susan Higginson Channing and nephew of the famous Dr. Channing, William Henry (1810–84) was Clarke's classmate at the Divinity School at Harvard and James Perkins's cousin. After a year of European travel, William Henry Channing tried to establish a workingmen's church in New York City, leaving the project in August 1837. An active reformer, he remained in Cincinnati until April 1841, then began a series of social experiments including another ministry in New York and a brief sojourn at Brook Farm. In 1854 he sailed for England, where he resided—except for a period as chaplain to the House of Representatives during the Civil War—for the rest of his life. In 1836 he married Julia Allen (1813–89) of Rondout, N.Y. The only full-length study is *MemWHC*.

61. Minister at King's Chapel since 1824, Francis William Pitt Greenwood (1797–1843) gave his "Discourse Preached before the Society for the Promotion of Theological Education in Harvard University" on 3 January 1830 at Dr. Channing's Federal Street Church in Boston; the sermon was published as *The Theology of the Cambridge Divinity School* (Boston, 1830) in the first series of AUA tracts (*DivCat; Christian Register*, 9 January, 6 February, 13 February 1830).

62. In *The American Adam: Innocence, Tragedy, and Tradition in the Nineteenth Century* (Chicago: University of Chicago Press, 1955), R. W. B. Lewis argues that "the entire program of the party of Hope was religious in temper. It represented a concerted effort to renew immediate contact with the root source and begetter of things. . . . It revealed the perennial Protestant impulse toward unmediated communication with divinity" (p. 175). The term is properly Emerson's, from his 1841 lecture "The Conservative," in which he explores the "primal antagonism" between the forces "of Past and Future, of Memory and Hope, of the Understanding and the Reason" (*Collected Works*, 1 : 184).

63. Osgood to Clarke, Nashua, 8 October 1838, MHi.

64. Huidekoper, in many ways the most conservative of the group, significantly took the most panoramic view of the evil of human creeds—they were, he said, the sole impediment to the progress of man toward spiritual perfection (*WM* 6 : 391–94).

65. Bowen, "Locke and the Transcendentalists," p. 183.

66. *Fourteenth Report*, p. 15. The AUA's financial statement lists only nineteen of the missionaries by name in 1838–39; of a total expenditure of $6,257.21, $1,344.31 went to fund missionary activities (pp. 4–5).

67. Osgood to Clarke, Nashua, 5 December 1838, MHi.

68. Ralph L. Rusk, in his exhaustive study of the periodical literature of the Ohio Valley, concludes that aside from the articles on Emerson in the *Messenger* "there is, perhaps, no other evidence that he was known at all on the frontier" (*Literature of the Middle Western Frontier*, 2 vols. [New York: Columbia University Press, 1925], 2 : 37).

69. Responding to Clarke's request of the previous spring, Emerson sent his poem "To the Humble-Bee" on 7 December 1838 (O. W. Holmes, *Ralph Waldo Emerson* [Boston: Houghton, Mifflin, 1884], pp. 128–29). From Margaret Fuller, Clarke received copies of Emerson's "Good-bye, Proud World" and "The Rhodora," which Emerson also permitted him to publish (*JFCAuto*, pp. 124–25; Holmes, *Emerson*, pp. 130–31).

The poems were printed in February (*WM* 6:239–41), April (*WM* 6:402), and July 1839 (*WM* 7:166), respectively, with a fourth contribution, "Each in All," appearing in February (*WM* 6:229–30).

70. Joel Myerson, "A History of the Transcendental Club," *ESQ: A Journal of the American Renaissance* 23 (1977): 31; idem, *The New England Transcendentalists and the "Dial"* (Rutherford, N.J.: Fairleigh Dickinson University Press, 1980), pp. 31–38. For the transcendental character of the *Quarterly Review* and the *Democratic Review*, see Clarence L. F. Gohdes, *The Periodicals of American Transcendentalism* (Durham, N.C.: Duke University Press, 1931).

71. Fuller to Clarke, Groton, Mass., 8 January 1839, in *Letters of Margaret Fuller*, 2:34.

72. J36–39. On 2 November Clarke proposed, but Anna deferred accepting until two days later, after consulting her father on the matter. Clarke was prepared to marry her in six weeks; she preferred to wait a year (J36–39). The wedding actually took place on 15 August 1839.

73. Clarke to Joseph Henry Allen, Jamaica Plain, 17 February 1885, in *JFCAuto*, pp. 380–81; J36–39, entry for 10–24 September 1838.

74. J36–39; Clarke to Anna Huidekoper, [Louisville], 29 December 1838, in *JFCAuto*, p. 124; C. P. Cranch to E. P. Cranch, Louisville, 1 January 1839, WyU.

75. Clarke to Anna Huidekoper, Louisville, 22 January, 3 February 1839, in *JFCAuto*, pp. 125–26. The Unitarian Society of Chicago offered Clarke $1000 per year—the same salary he received in 1839 at Louisville (Trustees, Unitarian Society of Chicago, to Clarke, Chicago, 7 February 1839, MH bMS Am 1569 [1073]). Osgood reported on 6 March 1839 (MHi) that the church at Charlestown was considering calling Clarke to the pulpit.

76. Later in the year, Emerson edited a selection of Very's poems. Groups of Very's religious sonnets appeared in the *Messenger* in March (*WM* 6:308–14) and April 1839 (*WM* 6:366–73), and single poems appeared throughout volumes 7 and 8.

77. Clarke was in Cincinnati by 18 March (*JFCAuto*, pp. 128–29).

78. At least some of the *Messenger*'s readers viewed Clarke's departure with regret. According to Sarah Clarke, when Emerson announced the news among some friends "it was received with much resistance: they said that you were eminently fitted for the task, and doing it so well, and had all the right qualities, and ——— had none of them, etc." (Sarah Clarke to J. F. Clarke, [ca. April 1839], MH bMS Am 1569.3 [12]). The deleted name is surely William Channing's.

79. Cranch to Clarke, Cincinnati, 16 February 1839, in Leonora Cranch Scott, *The Life and Letters of Christopher Pearse Cranch* (Boston: Houghton, Mifflin, 1917), p. 44. Cranch left for Washington, D.C., about 2 March 1839 (Francis B. Dedmond, "Christopher Pearse Cranch's 'Journal. 1839'," *Studies in the American Renaissance 1983*, ed. Joel Myerson [Charlottesville: University Press of Virginia, 1983], p. 144).

Chapter 4. 1839–1841: "The medium . . . of radical Xn truth"

1. *MemWHC*, p. 145; W. H. Channing to Julia Channing, Cincinnati, 17 June 1839, MH bMS Am 1755 (154).

2. *MemWHC*, pp. 109, 142–43; W. H. Channing to Julia Channing, Boston, 2 October 1836, MH bMS Am 1755 (115). Octavius B. Frothingham minimizes the problem: "The difference in religious opinion, instead of being a bar of separation, was an occasion of charity, generosity, and patience" (*MemWHC*, p. 110).

3. *MemWHC*, p. 146; *MemJHP*, pp. 113–14, 210, 243–44.

4. Trustees, Unitarian Society of Louisville, to Clarke, Louisville, 25 April 1839, MH bMS Am 1569 (1074); Clarke to Anna Huidekoper, Louisville, 30 May, 25 July 1839, in *JFCAuto,* p. 131.

5. Dr. William Ellery Channing to Clarke, Boston, 14 May 1839, MH bMS Am 1569.7 (105).

6. Arthur M. Schlesinger, Jr., in *The Age of Jackson* (Boston: Little, Brown, 1945), pp. 132–266, provides a detailed and sympathetic view of the labor reform movement and its political implications from 1835 to 1840.

7. W. H. Channing to Julia Channing, Wheeling, 26 July 1839, MH bMS Am 1755 (155). Perkins saw the August number through the press and edited the issues for September and October 1839.

8. A year later Perkins still found it necessary to tap the AUA's coffers, but on 25 August 1840 he insisted to Charles Briggs that "if this ministry cannot now support itself here it does not deserve support from abroad" (AUA Letterbooks, MH–AH).

9. Huidekoper's response (*WM* 8 : 16–18) is representative of conventional Unitarian views on the subject.

10. Perkins to Clarke, Cin[cinnat]i, 18 September 1839, MH bMS Am 1569.7 (507).

11. Perkins to Clarke, Cincinnati, 30 October 1839, MH bMS Am 1569.7 (508).

12. Huidekoper to Anna Huidekoper Clarke, Meadville, 19 October 1839, MH bMS Am 1569 (1); Perkins to Clarke, 30 October 1839. Huidekoper, no less than Perkins, was interested in "vital" rather than merely "scholarly" religion; but because he considered doctrinal speculations "very useful auxiliaries towards the formation of Christian character," he wrote Clarke on 19 December 1839, the *Messenger* was obligated to continue "controverting the prevailing opinions" in the West (Tiffany, *HJH,* p. 209).

13. Clarke to Anna Huidekoper, Louisville, 21 July 1839, in *JFCAuto,* p. 131; Eliot to Peabody, St. Louis, 4 November [1839], MoSW.

14. Perkins to Clarke, 30 October 1839; Fuller to Channing, Jamaica Plain, 1 January 1840, in *The Letters of Margaret Fuller,* ed. Robert N. Hudspeth (Ithaca, N.Y.: Cornell University Press, 1983–), 2 : 111. Channing attended meetings of the Transcendental Club on 16 and 18 September 1839, the second being devoted to the new journal (Joel Myerson, "A Calendar of Transcendental Club Meetings," *American Literature* 44 [1972]: 204–5).

15. On the important pamphlet war among Norton, Ripley, and others, see Charles Crowe, *George Ripley: Transcendentalist and Utopian Socialist* (Athens: University of Georgia Press, 1967), pp. 97–123. Convenient excerpts appear in Perry Miller, *The Transcendentalists: An Anthology* (Cambridge: Harvard University Press, 1950), pp. 210–46.

16. Channing to Fuller, Cincinnati, 25 February 1840, in *MemWHC,* pp. 167–68; Channing to Clarke, Cincinnati, January 1840, in *MemWHC,* pp. 169–70. "Ernest the Seeker" appeared in the *Dial* 1 (1840): 48–58 and 233–42.

17. Sarah Clarke to J. F. Clarke, Newton, 30 January 1840, MH bMS Am 1569.3 (12). "I think it is just as well that the *Messenger* should died [*sic*] young," she wrote philosophically, "and not live to be superannuated."

18. On 3 February 1840 one of Munroe's representatives charged Clarke $39 for subscriptions already paid or never authorized when the Boston firm became the *Messenger's* agent in 1836, adding tactfully "it was understood when we bought your list, that we were buying bona fide subscriptions, and we doubt not the same was presumed by yourself" (MHi). In a nasty reply on 21 February, Clarke accused Munroe of dishonest accounting and refused to pay (autograph copy in "Tables. Nov. 1839–[January 1840]," MHi). Munroe answered on 4 March, calling Clarke's letter "sufficiently offensive, as you doubtless intended it to be" and enclosing copies of the past bills to support the charges (MHi).

19. J. F. Clarke to Sarah Clarke, Louisville, 8 February 1840, MH bMS Am 1569 (1148). For the full circumstances see Arthur S. Bolster, Jr., *James Freeman Clarke: Disciple to Advancing Truth* (Boston: Beacon, 1954), pp. 121–26, and Blackburn, "JFC," pp. 122–29.

20. *MemWHC,* p. 169; Charles E. Blackburn, "Some New Light on the *Western Messenger,*" *American Literature* 26 (1954): 333–34.

21. Perkins to Clarke, [Cincinnati], [ca. March 1840], MH bMS Am 1569.7 (505); Channing to Fuller, 25 February 1840.

22. For an example of Eastern Unitarians' wavering attitude toward the Western missions at this time, see the *Christian Register,* 10 August 1839, in which "A Layman" recommends keeping AUA funds in the East instead of "throwing away money by endeavoring to force our religious views on [Westerners]." Two weeks later "Another Layman" countered that Western apathy was in fact cause to increase the financial support there (*Christian Register,* 24 August 1839).

23. Of the twenty-five graduates of Harvard's Divinity School from 1837 through 1840, only two settled in the West: Rufus P. Stebbins (Class of 1837), minister at Meadville from 1844 to 1856, and John Healy Heywood (Class of 1840), Clarke's successor at Louisville from 1840 to 1880 *(DivCat).*

24. Clarke to Charles Briggs, Louisville, 12 May 1840, AUA Letterbooks, MH–AH. On 22 April Channing wrote Briggs, proposing Clarke as the head of the agency (AUA Letterbooks, MH–AH).

25. It carried an obituary, reprinted from the *Cincinnati Chronicle,* for Harvard's president John T. Kirkland, who had died in Boston on 26 April. Allowing for mailing and printing time, the number must have appeared no earlier than the second week in May. Volume 8 was published by John Brooks Russell (1801–91), a Boston-born printer and member of Channing's congregation who moved to Cincinnati in 1839 (obituary clipping file, OCHP).

26. The *Register* had last noticed the *Messenger* on 18 August 1838, though it had reprinted several pieces from the Western periodical in the intervening months.

27. Emerson to Carlyle, Concord, 30 October 1840, in *The Correspondence of Emerson and Carlyle,* ed. Joseph Slater (New York: Columbia University Press, 1964), p. 283.

28. Carlyle had no faith in piecemeal reform laws, which he called in *Chartism* "not things but shadows of things" (*Works,* 30 vols. [London: Chapman and Hall, 1896–99], 29:188); he proposed instead mass education and emigration to North America.

29. H. J. Huidekoper to Frederic Huidekoper, [Meadville], 7 January 1841, in Tiffany, *HJH,* p. 281.

30. Huidekoper to Anna Huidekoper Clarke, Meadville, 21 February 1840, quoted in Blackburn, "Some New Light on the *Western Messenger,*" p. 336.

31. The essay appeared in the *Boston Quarterly Review* in two parts, one in July (3:358–95) and a second in October (3:420–512). A detailed analysis appears in Arthur M. Schlesinger, Jr., *Orestes A. Brownson: A Pilgrim's Progress* (Boston: Little, Brown, 1939), pp. 89–108; for the essay's reception, see idem, *Age of Jackson,* pp. 272–75, 299–304.

32. The reaction to Perkins's defense of Brownson's intellectual liberty points out the sensitivity of public opinion toward both the man and the issues. Modern scholars have also overestimated the intrinsic importance of the defense, as well as misreading it. Perry Miller, for instance, attributes it to Channing and calls it, perhaps too dramatically, "an unsung deed of courage in the annals of American journalism" (*The Transcendentalists,* p. 447). Charles Blackburn, who also assumes Channing's authorship, finds in the defense "warm words of praise" for Brownson's essay ("Some New Light on the *Western Messenger,*" p. 334).

33. Channing to William Greene, Rondout, N.Y., 1 October 1840, OCHP. Channing's sermon, preached on 2 August 1840, was published the following March in the *Messenger* as "The Death and New Birth of the Church."

34. Minister at Liverpool and brother of the reformer Harriet, James Martineau (1805–1900) published in 1836 *The Rationale of Religious Inquiry*, a book warmly received among the American Transcendentalists. Martineau had a reputation for radicalism, his view of miracles being especially suspect, and in 1840 he was a leader of the liberal wing within British Unitarianism (Earl M. Wilbur, *A History of Unitarianism*, 2 vols. [Cambridge: Harvard University Press, 1945–52], 2:367–71).

35. Signed "S. D. R.," the reprinted passages on the soul were surely the work of the Rev. Samuel Dowse Robbins (1812–84), a classmate of Clarke's and Channing's at the Divinity School *(DivCat)*. Using another piece by Robbins, Clarence Gohdes establishes him as "an enthusiastic member of the New School" in "Some Remarks on Emerson's *Divinity School Address*," *American Literature* 1 (1929): 27–31.

36. Huidekoper to [Clarke?], [Meadville], 10 March 1843; H. J. Huidekoper to Frederic Huidekoper, 7 January 1841, in Tiffany, *HJH*, pp. 280–81.

37. George A. Thayer, *The First Congregational Church of Cincinnati (Unitarian): A History* (Cincinnati: n. p., 1917), pp. 20–22.

38. Charles Cist, *Cincinnati in 1841: Its Early Annals and Future Prospects* (Cincinnati: Privately printed, 1841), p. 95.

39. Channing to Greene, 1 October 1840.

40. Channing to Fuller, Cincinnati, 15 April 1841, in *MemWHC*, pp. 164–66. In a letter to his friend and biographer many years later, Channing recalled three times when it had "befallen me to pass out of the glory of the Christian Religion into the shadow-regions of Sceptical Unbelief, or Half-Belief,—first in company with the *Deists* while at the Cambridge Divinity-School; secondly, with the Transcendentalists at Cincinnati, in mid-manhood; lastly, with the Students of Comparative Religions, in quest of the *Synthetic Religion*, here, in London" (Channing to Octavius B. Frothingham, London, 10 January 1882, PSt).

41. *MemWHC*, pp. 151–53; Channing to members of the First Congregational Church of Cincinnatti, [Cincinnati], [ca. April] 1841, OCHP.

42. According to a yellow slip bound into the last number. The *Messenger* had begun carrying advertising for school books and local teachers in the December 1840 number.

Chapter 5. The Achievement of the *Western Messenger*

1. Clarke to Joseph Henry Allen, Jamaica Plain, 17 February 1885, in *JFCAuto*, p. 380.

2. George A. Thayer, *The First Congregational Church of Cincinnati (Unitarian): A History* (Cincinnati: n. p., 1917), p. 24; *MemJHP*, pp. 256, 306–309; *New-York Tribune*, 17 December 1849.

3. Van Wyck Brooks, *The Flowering of New England 1815–1865* (New York: E. P. Dutton, 1936), p. 251.

4. Channing to Octavius B. Frothingham, London, 10 January 1882, PSt; Lindsay Swift, *Brook Farm: Its Members, Scholars, and Visitors* (New York: Macmillan, 1900), p. 217.

5. *JFCAuto*, p. 226. For discussions of Clarke's later activities within the denomination, as well as the history of the Church of the Disciples, see William R. Hutchison, *The Transcendentalist Ministers* (New Haven: Yale University Press, 1959), pp. 144–52, and

Arthur S. Bolster, Jr., *James Freeman Clarke: Disciple to Advancing Truth* (Boston: Beacon, 1954), pp. 127–56.

6. Elizabeth R. McKinsey, *The Western Experiment: New England Transcendentalists in the Ohio Valley* (Cambridge: Harvard University Press, 1973), p. 48.

7. Bruce M. Stephens, "Liberals in the Wilderness: The Meadville Theological School 1844–1856," *Pennsylvania History* 42 (1975): 291–302; Charles H. Lyttle, *Freedom Moves West: A History of the Western Unitarian Conference* (Boston: Beacon, 1952).

8. Earl Morse Wilbur, *A History of Unitarianism*, 2 vols. (Cambridge: Harvard University Press, 1945–52), 2:439.

9. McKinsey, *Western Experiment*, p. 49.

10. With three other ministers, Peabody began coediting the *Register* on 13 October 1849. It is a testimony to Peabody's spirit, if not to his good sense, that several months after he relinquished control of the *Messenger* he was ready to try again. Still weak from his bout with tuberculosis and uncertain about his future, he wrote Clarke from Dayton, Ohio, on 8 August 1836 (MH–AH) about a plan "to establish a Quarterly Review— Literary Mercantile & Political—to be published simultaneously at New Orleans— Natchez, St. Louis, Louisville & Cincinnati—to get into partnership with some business man—set up a Printing Press—in some one of those places—& publish that & print other things." A week later Clarke advised him to drop the scheme: "Of the plans you mention, I like the Quarterly the *least*. I find hard[ly any]thing in its favour" (Clarke to Peabody, Louisville, 15 August 1836, MH bMS Am 1569 [602]).

11. "Notes & Reflections 1839 & 1840," entry for November 1840, MHi. First issued in January 1843, the *Christian World* represented the views of the Church of the Disciples; Clarke published over 200 articles and poems in the paper and served as editor from November 1847 through May 1848 (Bolster, *James Freeman Clarke*, p. 164).

12. Clarence L. F. Gohdes, *The Periodicals of American Transcendentalism* (Durham, N.C.: Duke University Press, 1931), pp. 83–100, 132–42.

13. *Christian Register*, 29 February 1840; Joel Myerson, *The New England Transcendentalists and the "Dial"* (Rutherford, N.J.: Fairleigh Dickinson University Press, 1980), p. 74. The geographical distribution of the *Messenger*'s subscribers, like the precise number of readers, is an important point about which the editors' shoddy records provide little exact information. In "JFC," Charles E. Blackburn speculates that one-fourth to one-third of the subscribers lived "in the East" (p. 290). The magazine's subscription book (newly discovered among Clarke's papers at the Massachusetts Historical Society) helps to pin down the figures, though the list is undated (it seems to have been kept current from 1835 to the end of 1838) and several subscribers' names, confirmed in other sources, do not appear. The list includes 100 names from New England (Massachusetts, Maine, New Hampshire, and Vermont); 380 from elsewhere in the East, West, and South; and 13 periodicals with which the *Messenger* was "exchanged." The largest concentrations of readers were in Cincinnati (105), Louisville (93), Buffalo (40), Boston (39), and Cambridge (18); the list includes readers in 60 other towns and cities, 42 of them outside New England. Many of the names have been canceled, and the list probably includes errors. As a rough guide, though, its proportions show the magazine's relative popularity among Western readers.

Why the *Messenger*'s editors printed so many extra copies—Clarke's account books reveal a monthly run of 700 during volume 6 (MH bMS Am 1569.2 [6])—cannot be determined; certainly the number of paying subscribers never reached that figure. In the mid-1840s Perkins sold a "great pile" of unmailed copies to a Cincinnati bookseller (William H. Venable, *Beginnings of Literary Culture in the Ohio Valley* [Cincinnati: Robert Clarke, 1891], p. 72).

14. McKinsey, *Western Experiment,* p. 52.

15. Clarke, "Western History," *North American Review* 43 (1836): 28; Cranch to Catherine Myers, Peoria, 29 March 1837, in Leonora Cranch Scott, *The Life and Letters of Christopher Pearse Cranch* (Boston: Houghton, Mifflin, 1917), p. 32; Perkins, "The Western Messenger," *Christian Examiner* 25 (1838): 37–42.

16. After 1844 there was a brief alliance of Unitarians and Disciples of Christ in the West: the AUA funded several Campbellite missionaries, and the Meadville Theological School admitted students from the Disciples. Relations soured, however, by the early 1850s (Stephens, "Liberals in the Wilderness," pp. 298–301; Blackburn, "JFC," pp. 37–43).

17. See for example Hutchison, *Transcendentalist Ministers,* p. 21, and Daniel Walker Howe, *The Unitarian Conscience* (Cambridge: Harvard University Press, 1970), pp. 21–23, 92.

18. William R. Hutchison argues convincingly that the conservatives' reluctance to battle the Transcendental heresy in public before 1837 derived in part from their sense of the impropriety of debating theology in the newspapers (*Transcendentalist Ministers,* pp. 56–59).

19. Samuel C. Clarke to J. F. Clarke, Newton, 22 September 1839, MH bMS Am 1569 [826]; James Munroe & Co. to J. F. Clarke, Boston, 4 March 1840, MHi.

20. H. J. Huidekoper to Frederic Huidekoper, [Meadville], 7 January 1841, in Tiffany, *HJH,* p. 281.

21. Arthur M. Schlesinger, Jr., *The Age of Jackson* (Boston: Little, Brown, 1945), pp. 267–82.

22. William Henry Channing, in *Memoirs of Margaret Fuller Ossoli,* 2 vols. (Boston: Phillips, Sampson, 1852), 2:13. For recent scholarly attempts to define Transcendentalism, see Gohdes, *Periodicals,* pp. 1–16; Hutchison, *Transcendentalist Ministers,* pp. 22–34; Perry Miller, *The Transcendentalists: An Anthology* (Cambridge: Harvard University Press, 1950), especially pp. 7–12; Lawrence Buell, *Literary Transcendentalism* (Ithaca, N.Y.: Cornell University Press, 1973), pp. 2–7; and Anne C. Rose, *Transcendentalism as a Social Movement, 1830–1850* (New Haven: Yale University Press, 1981), chap. 2.

23. Tiffany, *HJH,* p. 286.

24. Osgood to Clarke, Nashua, N.H., 4 September 1838, MHi; Peabody to Clarke, [Cincinnati], 7 July 1835, MH–AH.

25. Robert D. Habich, "James Freeman Clarke's 1833 Letter-journal for Margaret Fuller," *ESQ: A Journal of the American Renaissance* 27 (1981): 54. Charles E. Blackburn concludes that while Clarke was "no less a transcendentalist" than Emerson or Alcott, he differed with them in "direction" and deserves to be known primarily for his work as a Unitarian ("JFC," pp. 239–72). In "James Freeman Clarke: A Practical Transcendentalist and his Writings" (Ph.D. dissertation, Washington University, 1953), Derek Colville argues his thesis most cogently on pp. 17–64.

26. Francis B. Dedmond, "Christopher Pearse Cranch: Emerson's Self-appointed Defender Against the Philistines," *Concord Saunterer* 15 (1980): 6–19.

27. Undated entry [ca. early September 1839] in "Notebook S. M. Fuller 1840," MH fMS Am 1086 (Box D).

28. [William H. Channing], Review of *An Oration, Delivered Before the Phi Beta Kappa Society . . .* by R. W. Emerson, *Boston Quarterly Review* 1 (1838): 107. Channing's authorship is confirmed by the marginalia in Theodore Parker's copy of the periodical (Gohdes, *Periodicals,* p. 74).

29. Orestes A. Brownson, Review of *An Address, Delivered Before the Senior Class in Divinity College, Cambridge* by R. W. Emerson, *Boston Quarterly Review* 1 (1838): 505.

30. Emerson to Fuller, Concord, 29 August 1840, in *The Letters of Ralph Waldo Emerson*, ed. Ralph L. Rusk, 6 vols. (New York: Columbia University Press, 1939), 2:328; "The Transcendentalist," in *The Collected Works of Ralph Waldo Emerson*, ed. Alfred R. Ferguson et al. (Cambridge: Harvard University Press, Belknap Press, 1971–), vol. 1, *Nature, Addresses and Lectures*, ed. Robert E. Spiller (1971), p. 211.

31. See, for example, Gohdes, *Periodicals*, pp. 11–12, and Schlesinger, *Age of Jackson*, pp. 382ff. Anne C. Rose takes an opposite position, that the Transcendentalists as a group "engaged wholeheartedly in the reforms of their day" (*Transcendentalism*, p. viii).

32. In "The Transcendentalist" Emerson was careful to qualify his generalizations: "You will see by this sketch that there is no such thing as a Transcendental *party*" (*Collected Works*, 1:205).

33. C. P. Cranch to William G. Cranch, Quincy, Mass., 11 July 1840, in Scott, *Life and Letters*, p. 51.

34. George Ripley, *The Latest Form of Infidelity Examined* (1839), in Miller, *The Transcendentalists*, p. 216.

35. Emerson, *Collected Works*, vol. 2, *Essays: First Series*, ed. Joseph Slater (1979), p. 188.

36. Fuller to Channing, Jamaica Plain, 22 March 1840, in *The Letters of Margaret Fuller*, ed. Robert N. Hudspeth (Ithaca, N.Y.: Cornell University Press, 1983–), 2:126.

37. Prospectus for the *Dial* (probably written by Ripley), reprinted in Thomas Wentworth Higginson, *Margaret Fuller Ossoli* (Boston: Houghton, Mifflin, 1884), p. 152.

38. *MemWHC*, pp. 245–46.

39. Henry David Thoreau, *Walden*, ed. J. Lyndon Shanley (Princeton, N.J.: Princeton University Press, 1971), p. 324; Walt Whitman, "Passage to India," in *Leaves of Grass: A Textual Variorum*, ed. Sculley Bradley et al., 3 vols. (New York: New York University Press, 1980), 3:574.

Bibliographic Essay

The most valuable primary sources used in this study of the *Western Messenger* are the largely unpublished letters, diaries, and other documents left by its editors and major contributors. Of those collections, by far the most extensive are the papers of James Freeman Clarke at the Massachusetts Historical Society and the Houghton Library, Harvard University. The first group, part of the Society's Perry-Clarke collection, contains approximately one hundred letters to Clarke from subscribers. Clarke's journals include several from the Western years. J34–36 and J36–39 are useful, for in them Clarke recorded almost daily his correspondence, his sermons, his travels and conversations, his visits to friends and parishioners, and, in J36–39, a nearly complete list of his contributions to the magazine through the December 1838 number. Fragmentary letter-journals to his sister Sarah in 1834 and 1835, as well as brief diaries kept intermittently during his last years as a Divinity School student, provide some understanding of the reasons for Clarke's move West and for his ambivalence toward his new surroundings. Also in this collection is the only known subscription book for the *Messenger,* inscribed "Simeon S. Goodwin" but written in Clarke's hand. The Society has prepared an in-house guide to the collection.

The Clarke papers at the Massachusetts Historical Society are complemented by those at the Houghton Library, which include hundreds of letters by Clarke and to him. The James Freeman Clarke papers (bMS Am 1569), the largest of the Houghton groups, are especially notable for the correspondence about the magazine, including letters on business affairs from Samuel C. Clarke and on the magazine's Eastern reception from Sarah A. Clarke. Useful, too, are the letters between Harm Jan Huidekoper and his daughter, Anna Huidekoper Clarke, which record Huidekoper's gradual disenchantment with the *Messenger.* The library has a finding list for the collection. Leonard Neufeldt provides the most complete inventory of the Clarke manuscripts in "James Freeman Clarke: Notes toward a Comprehensive Bibliography," *Studies in the American Renaissance 1982,* ed. Joel Myerson (Boston: Twayne, 1982), pp. 209–26.

None of the other manuscript collections is as large or as revealing, but taken together the records are impressive. Useful for tracing the complex relationship between the *Messenger* and the American Unitarian Association are the bound letter-books of the AUA at the Andover-Harvard Theological Library, Harvard University. Also at the Divinity School is a folder of letters on the *Messenger* from Ephraim Peabody to Clarke and Huidekoper. William Greenleaf Eliot's letters, many of them to Clarke and Peabody, are in the Washington University Archives (microfilm item 100/00/3). Small groups of Christopher Pearse Cranch's letters from the period are in the American Heritage Center, University of Wyoming, and in the Cranch Family papers at the Massachusetts Historical Society. Most of William Henry Channing's manuscripts have been lost; but useful to a study of the Western years are the Channing letters in the William Greene Collection, Cincinnati Historical Society, and in the Channing Family papers at the Houghton, especially those from Channing to his wife, Julia (bMS Am 1755). A substantial collection of Samuel Osgood's papers is located at the New-York Historical Society, though most of them are post-1841. James Handasyd Perkins's papers at the Massachusetts Historical Society are of limited value for an examination of the *Messenger.*

The text of the *Western Messenger* presents few problems, for there is no evidence that more than one impression exists for each number. I have used the nearly complete run in the Pennsylvania State University Libraries, supplemented by those at the Houghton Library and the Massachusetts Historical Society. Convenient but incomplete are the microfilm and microfiche editions of the magazine, in the American Periodicals Series and the Library of American Civilization, both of which omit a number of pages and fail to include some of the paper wrappers that provide tables of contents and notices to subscribers. Perry Miller includes excerpts from the magazine in his collection *The Transcendentalists: An Anthology* (Cambridge: Harvard University Press, 1950).

Contemporary evaluations of the magazine are, of course, crucial for understanding its reception and eventual demise. The *Christian Register,* published biweekly in Boston, frequently noticed the *Messenger* and often printed responses to individual articles. Boston's bimonthly *Christian Examiner* printed several essays by Perkins, Clarke, and Peabody and occasionally responded to the magazine. Factual data about subsidies and other financial aid for the Western cause, as well as a record of the organization's proceedings, appear in the annual reports of the AUA, published (under various titles) following the yearly meetings in late May. Contemporary Western periodicals provide a counterbalance to these Eastern responses; most useful are the *Cincinnati Mirror,* the *Hesperian,* and the *Western Monthly Magazine.* Individual reactions to the magazine appear throughout the letters and journals of the major and minor Transcendentalists, especially Emerson, Margaret Fuller, Bronson Alcott, Theodore Parker, and George Ripley, all of whose papers are cited in the notes.

II

Like most American periodicals of the nineteenth century, the *Western Messenger* has been often mentioned, if little examined. There are two useful bibliographies to the secondary scholarship. Edward E. Chielens provides helpful annotations in *The Literary Journal in America to 1900: A Guide to Information Sources* (Detroit: Gale, 1975), the single best listing of published books and articles about the magazines of the century. More current, and more focused, is the essay by Donald F. Warders in *The Transcendentalists: A Review of Research and Criticism,* ed. Joel Myerson (New York: Modern Language Association, 1984), an evaluation of scholarship on the *Messenger* and ten other magazines conducted by the Transcendentalist circle.

The *Messenger* has been examined in two unpublished doctoral dissertations. Charles E. Blackburn, in "JFC," traces in detail the intellectual biography of James Freeman Clarke during his Western years and covers Clarke's part in the magazine on pp. 134–238. Working from manuscript sources, Blackburn presents new information on the magazine's history, identifies its editors, and examines some aspects of its business affairs. But his focus is upon Clarke; he treats the *Messenger* as "one tangible 'artifact' of Clarke's years as a Unitarian missionary"; and he does not make use of Clarke's Western journals and subscriptions records, Eliot's and Channing's letters, the correspondence of the AUA, and other key documents. Blackburn's work is summarized in "Some New Light on the *Western Messenger*," *American Literature* 26 (1954): 320–36. Less analytic is Judith A. Green, "Religion, Life, and Literature in the *Western Messenger*" (Ph.D. dissertation, University of Wisconsin-Madison, 1982), a lengthy summary of the written contributions of the three main editors and five other major contributors.

Except for Green, no one before me has devoted an entire work to the *Western Messenger*, but the magazine has always found a place in American literary histories. The earliest of these to report reliably on the magazine is William H. Venable, *Beginnings of Literary Culture in the Ohio Valley* (Cincinnati: Robert Clarke, 1891), which includes a letter from Clarke and a discussion of the magazine's publishing history. Considerably more complete, though lacking in the firsthand anecdotal evidence of Venable's book, is Ralph L. Rusk's two-volume *Literature of the Middle Western Frontier* (New York: Columbia University Press, 1925). Rusk discusses the literary merits of the *Messenger*, summarizes the range of its contents, and identifies some of the minor Western figures connected with it. Also useful for comparing the magazine with other periodicals of the region is Saul Hounchell, "The Principal Literary Magazines of the Ohio Valley to 1840" (Ph.D. dissertation, George Peabody College for Teachers, Nashville, Tenn., 1934), though it is restricted to "non-religious content only." Kathleen Flynn's brief

"Literary Importance of the *Western Messenger*" (Master's thesis, Wagner College, 1969) is limited by the scope of its coverage and by the superficiality of its assumptions about Transcendentalism.

Serious attention to the *Messenger* began with chapters in two books that appeared almost simultaneously and shaped our view of the magazine for decades: Frank Luther Mott, *A History of American Magazines 1741–1850* (New York and London: D. Appleton, 1930) and Clarence L. F. Gohdes, *The Periodicals of American Transcendentalism* (Durham, N.C.: Duke University Press, 1931). The first, part of Mott's definitive five-volume study of American magazines through 1930, accurately identifies the magazine's publishers and editors, though it follows closely the critical judgments of Rusk. Gohdes's book, prefaced by the questionable notion that "the [Transcendental] movement had little to do with *belles-lettres*," is still the best brief discussion of the *Messenger*'s relationship to other periodicals conducted by the New England group, and his chapter on the *Messenger*'s influence upon the *Dial* established the terms of discussion that have persisted for half a century. Criticized for his incomplete treatment of the *Dial*, Gohdes distorts the importance of the *Messenger* as well, by finding in the "striking sameness in the contents of the two magazines" evidence that the earlier one was primarily "a graft on Eastern stock." Nevertheless, by virtue of his careful reading of the magazines, Gohdes's study remains the starting point for anyone investigating the periodical literature of the Transcendental movement.

Most published scholarship on the *Messenger* since the appearance of Mott's and Gohdes's work has been sketchy and derivative. One recent study, however, deserves mention for its ambition if not, finally, for its compelling argument. Elizabeth R. McKinsey's *The Western Experiment: New England Transcendentalists in the Ohio Valley* (Cambridge: Harvard University Press, 1973) is less a study of the magazine than an examination of some of the men who directed it: Clarke, Channing, and Cranch. Working almost exclusively from published sources, McKinsey develops the thesis that all three men suffered Eriksonian identity crises in the West and returned to the

East "chastened [and] subdued." Provocative in its use of biographical data, the book is compromised by a tendency to bend fact to thesis: Clarke's marriage to Anna Huidekoper of Meadville, a village on the far western frontier of Pennsylvania, becomes evidence of his desire to wed only an "eastern girl" and thus confirms his need for the stability of New England society. McKinsey's psychological focus leads her to treat the *Messenger*'s failure as merely a consequence, rather than a cause, of the editors' departure from the West.

Probably the most adequately covered aspect of the *Messenger* is its writers' interest in foreign literature. For the connection with German literature and philosophy, the standard sources are Henry A. Pochmann, *German Culture in America: Philosophical and Literary Influences, 1600–1900* (Madison: University of Wisconsin Press, 1957) and Stanley M. Vogel, *German Literary Influences on the American Transcendentalists* (New Haven: Yale University Press, 1955). John Wesley Thomas discusses Clarke's important role in the transmission of German ideas in *James Freeman Clarke: Apostle of German Culture to America* (Boston: Luce, 1949); the relevant material for the *Messenger* is summarized in *"The Western Messenger* and German Culture," *American-German Review* 11 (1944): 17–18. For the *Messenger*'s attention to other foreign cultures, see Roger Chester Mueller, "The Orient in American Transcendental Periodicals (1835–1886)" (Ph.D. dissertation, University of Minnesota, 1968) and Georges Jules Joyaux, "French Thought in American Magazines: 1800–1848" (Ph.D. dissertation, Michigan State College, 1951).

III

Of the editors and major contributors to the *Messenger,* only Clarke, Cranch, and Eliot have received serious biographical study in this century; for the others, we must rely on obituaries, memorial biographies, and other contemporary accounts that often suffer from the twin faults of sentimentality and factual inaccuracy. For some of these writers, and for many of the minor contributors, the material in the *Messenger* offers important evidence of both the details of their lives and the cast of their minds. But those contributions present problems of their own: often pseudonymous, anonymous, or merely initialed, they are of biographical value only insofar as they can be attributed with some certainty. I have attempted to remedy the bibliographic and the biographical vagaries in "An Annotated List of Contributions to the *Western Messenger*," *Studies in the American Renaissance 1984,* ed. Joel Myerson (Charlottesville: University Press of Virginia, 1984), which also includes brief biographies for the known contributors to the magazine.

For literary figures in the Ohio Valley, useful biographical information can be found in a number of sources: William Coyle, ed., *Ohio Authors and Their Books* (Cleveland: World, 1962); Emerson Venable, ed., *Poets of Ohio* (Cincinnati: Robert Clark, 1909); and—to a lesser extent—Willard R. Jillson, *Early Kentucky Literature* (Frankfort: Kentucky State Historical Society, 1931). William H. Venable's *Beginnings of Literary Culture* is often the source for later biographical accounts of Ohio writers. Valuable contemporary anthologies that contain some necessarily incomplete biographical information for Western writers are *Selections from the Poetical Literature of the West,* ed. William D. Gallagher (Cincinnati: U. P. James, 1841) and William T. Coggeshall, *The Poets and Poetry of the West* (Cincinnati: Follett, Foster, 1860).

For New England Unitarians and Transcendentalists, the record is somewhat more complete. *Heralds* includes detailed biographies of many of the Unitarian ministers important to the history of the *Messenger,* as does volume 8 of William B. Sprague's *Annals of the American Pulpit,* 9 vols. (New York: Robert Carter and Brothers, 1859–69). *DivCat* is an accurate register of the students who attended Harvard's Divinity School—their birth and death dates, educational records, and parishes (or occupations if not ordained). Less useful is *HarCat,* which provides class year, degree, academic affiliation (if any), and year of death. The superb collections of class books, educational records, and biographical folders at the Harvard University Archives help to fill in the gaps. Fully annotated brief lives of many of the Transcendentalists, particularly the more "minor" ones, appear in Joel Myerson's valuable *New England*

Transcendentalists and the "Dial" (Rutherford, N.J.: Fairleigh Dickinson University Press, 1980). Of the members of the Transcendentalist group connected with the *Messenger,* Alcott, Bartol, Brooks, Brownson, William Henry Channing, Clarke, Cranch, Dwight, Emerson, Fuller, Hedge, Parker, Elizabeth Peabody, Ripley, and Very are given full bibliographical essays in *The Transcendentalists: A Review of Research and Criticism*—the best source for locating material on the movement, its participants, and its times.

The prime mover of the *Messenger,* James Freeman Clarke, is fortunately the figure who has gotten the most biographical attention. The standard biography is Arthur S. Bolster, Jr., *James Freeman Clarke: Disciple to Advancing Truth* (Boston: Beacon, 1954), which lacks the annotations of Bolster's massive "Life of James Freeman Clarke" (Ph.D. dissertation, Harvard University, 1953). Bolster's dissertation also includes the fullest bibliography of Clarke's published writing. Derek K. Colville considers Clarke's writing other than his *Messenger* work in "James Freeman Clarke: A Practical Transcendentalist and his Writings" (Ph.D. dissertation, Washington University, 1953). Parts of Clarke's voluminous correspondence, as well as his autobiography through 1840, are printed in *JFCAuto. Letters of JFC* prints some of the correspondence with Margaret Fuller, but the book is poorly annotated, and its textual accuracy suspect. I have edited "James Freeman Clarke's 1833 Letter-journal for Margaret Fuller," *ESQ: A Journal of the American Renaissance* 27 (1981): 47–56. The best guide to the many shorter works about Clarke, and to his major publications, is Neufeldt, "James Freeman Clarke: Notes toward a Comprehensive Bibliography." For Clarke family information, William W. Johnson, *Clarke–Clark Genealogy* (North Greenfield, Wis.: Privately printed, 1884) is useful.

A readable but sketchy biography of Ephraim Peabody is Robert S. Peabody and Francis G. Peabody, *A New England Romance: The Story of Ephraim and Mary Jane Peabody* (Boston: Houghton, Mifflin, 1920). Supplementary material appears in the memoir by Samuel A. Eliot in Ephraim Peabody, *Sermons* (Boston: Crosby, Nichols, 1857), expanded (with a brief bibliography) in *Heralds,* 3:297–303. John Hopkins Morison's preface to Peabody's *Christian Days and Thoughts,* 2d edition (Boston: Crosby, Nichols, 1858) is a reminiscence by a close friend and associate minister. Henry Wilder Foote assesses Peabody's later career in *Annals of King's Chapel,* 2 vols. (Boston: Little, Brown, 1881–96), 2:490–546.

The scarcity of information on James Handasyd Perkins illustrates one consequence of his suicide. Only his cousin William Channing was fully able to appreciate his frustrations in Cincinnati. *MemJHP* is thus the only full-length account of Perkins's life and works, though not without its flaws; not even Channing could deal with the suicide directly. Volume 1 contains the memoir and a selection of Perkins's poems and tales; volume 2 is a collection of his historical writings. More comprehensive information on the Perkins family appears in Edith Perkins Cunningham, *Owl's Nest* (Cambridge, Mass.: Privately printed, 1907), a "tribute" to Perkins's wife, Sarah Elliott Perkins. For a brief account of Perkins's death, see the obituary notice in the *New-York Tribune,* 17 December 1849, reprinted in the *Christian Register,* 22 December 1849.

Eliot's daughter-in-law Charlotte has written the only biography of him, *William Greenleaf Eliot: Minister, Educator, Philanthropist* (Cambridge, Mass.: Houghton, Mifflin, 1904). A sympathetic picture of a tireless minister and public servant, the book is weak on his early years in St. Louis, during which he was actively contributing to the *Messenger.* Many of Eliot's letters to Clarke, reprinted in part, are misdated entirely or identified only by year. (The manuscripts are in the Washington University Archives.) For family information, James E. Greenleaf, *Genealogy of the Greenleaf Family* (Boston: Frank Wood, 1896) and *The Family of William Greenleaf Eliot and Abby Adams Eliot of St. Louis, Missouri 1811–1921* (n.p., n.d.) are helpful.

For Harm Jan Huidekoper we are fortunate to have a comprehensive and reliable biography, *HJH.* Fully indexed, with a detailed genealogy, the book benefits from family reminiscences without being dominated by them. *HJH* is especially full on Huidekoper's work for the *Messenger.* Earl Morse Wilbur discusses Huidekoper's evangelical activity throughout *A Historical Sketch of the Independent Congregational Church, Meadville, Pennsylvania 1825–1900* (Meadville, Pa.: n.p., 1902), and

Bruce M. Stephens provides information about both Harm and his son Frederic in "Liberals in the Wilderness: The Meadville Theological School 1844–1856," *Pennsylvania History* 42 (1975): 291–302.

Of all the *Messenger*'s editors, Samuel Osgood has most escaped the notice of biographers. The most complete accounts of his life remain the memorial essays by James Osborne Wright in *NEHGR* 36 (1882): 113–122 and by Jacob B. Moore in *Magazine of American History* 5 (1880): 399–400. The brief entry in *Heralds,* 3:87 is a eulogistic portrait that hints nevertheless at the personal difficulties that led Osgood to abandon his Unitarian pulpit for ordination in the Protestant Episcopal Church. Octavius Brooks Frothingham, in *Recollections and Impressions* (New York: Putnam's, 1891), is refreshingly direct, if uncharacteristically caustic: Osgood, contends Frothingham, "had too much self-esteem to forget himself, and too little courage to assert himself"; his lack of popularity as minister of the Church of the Messiah, along with his need for "sympathy and fellowship and large scholarship," made the split from Unitarianism almost inevitable (pp. 94–99).

For Christopher Pearse Cranch, the biographical material most approaches completeness. Poet, translator, painter, and writer of children's books, Cranch numbered among his close friends Margaret Fuller, Emerson, the sculptor William Wetmore Story, and the poets Robert and Elizabeth Barrett Browning, and his name appears throughout their letters and biographies. Cranch himself has been the subject of two full-length biographies. Leonora Cranch Scott, his daughter, provides a detailed account in *The Life and Letters of Christopher Pearse Cranch* (Boston: Houghton, Mifflin, 1917). More comprehensive is F. DeWolfe Miller's "CPC," which includes a nearly complete bibliography of Cranch's poems and periodical contributions. Unfortunately, most of the manuscripts used and excerpted in "CPC" are now lost. Yet there is something of a renaissance in Cranch studies underway, with renewed interest in his published poems and the complexity of his life. Francis B. Dedmond argues for Cranch's continuing attraction to the new school in "Christopher Pearse Cranch: Emerson's Self-appointed Defender Against the Philistines," *Concord Saunterer*

15 (1980): 6–19. Dedmond has also edited Cranch's "Journal. 1839," *Studies in the American Renaissance 1983,* ed. Joel Myerson (Charlottesville: University Press of Virginia, 1983), pp. 129–49. David Robinson uses the poems to examine Cranch's personal relationships in "Christopher Pearse Cranch, Robert Browning, and the Problem of 'Transcendental' Friendship," *Studies in the American Renaissance 1977,* ed. Joel Myerson (Boston: Twayne, 1977), pp. 145–53. Robinson has also written two solid evaluations of Cranch's career and the scholarship about it: "The Career and Reputation of Christopher Pearse Cranch: An Essay in Biography and Bibliography," *Studies in the American Renaissance 1978,* ed. Joel Myerson (Boston: Twayne, 1978), pp. 453–72, and the bibliographic essay in *The Transcendentalists: A Review of Research and Criticism.* Cranch's verse has been reprinted, edited by Joseph M. De Falco, as *Collected Poems* (Gainesville, Fla.: Scholars' Facsimiles and Reprints, 1971).

For William Henry Channing, one of the most enigmatic of the Transcendental group, the only full-length biography is *MemWHC.* In O. B. Frothingham, Channing had an able biographer, a close friend, and a skilled writer with an unrivalled grasp of the Unitarian and Transcendentalist roots of Channing's life and thought. But *MemWHC* is limited nonetheless; Frothingham devotes only a few pages to the important Western years, glosses over Channing's long separation from his wife, and is suspect—if not wrong—about the "Deism" that caused Channing's breakdown in 1840. Because most of Channing's manuscripts have been lost since the writing of *MemWHC,* scholars have paid little attention to him in this century. A notable exception is David Robinson, "The Political Odyssey of William Henry Channing," *American Quarterly* 34 (1982): 165–84.

IV

To study a "living mirror of the times" is necessarily to study the times themselves, and the complexity of the American 1830s and 1840s makes any list of sources a very selective one. A useful starting place for the political and social history of the

Ohio Valley is Francis P. Weisenburger, *The Passing of the Frontier 1825–1850*, volume 3 of *The History of the State of Ohio* (Columbus: Ohio State Archaeological and Historical Society, 1941). R. Carlyle Buley's *The Old Northwest. Pioneer Period: 1815–1840*, 2 vols. (Bloomington: Indiana University Press, 1950) is informative about the religious conditions of the region; Louis B. Wright's *Culture on the Moving Frontier* (Bloomington: Indiana University Press, 1955) is stronger on literary and educational matters.

Nineteenth-century studies of the region, while colored by their lack of distance from the events, are important indicators of social values, as well as valuable sources of biographical information. A jingoistic account—and revealing precisely for that reason—is Caleb Atwater, *A History of the State of Ohio, Natural and Civil* (Cincinnati: Glezen & Shepard, 1838). Charles Cist includes biographical data unavailable elsewhere in *Cincinnati in 1841: Its Early Annals and Future Prospects* (Cincinnati: Privately printed, 1841). For information about Cincinnati's civic and cultural history, a good source is Henry A. Ford and Kate B. Ford, *History of Cincinnati, Ohio, with Illustrations and Biographical Sketches* (Cleveland: L. A. Williams, 1881); a similar early study of Louisville is *Memorial History of Louisville*, ed. Josiah Stoddard Johnston (Chicago and New York: American Biographical Publishing Co., [1896]).

Despite their age, Venable's and Rusk's studies remain the best general surveys of literary culture in the Ohio Valley. David D. Anderson, in "The Queen City and a New Literature," *Midamerica* 4 (1977): 7–17, discusses the work of William D. Gallagher and several other Western writers connected with the *Messenger*. For the important literary and social club frequented by Clarke, Perkins, Osgood, Cranch, and Channing, Louis L. Tucker's "The Semi-Colon Club of Cincinnati," *Ohio History* 73 (1964): 13–26 is the standard account; Frank R. Shivers misdates meetings and misidentifies participants in his often-cited "Western Chapter in the History of American Transcendentalism," *Bulletin of the Historical and Philosophical Society of Ohio* 15 (1957): 117–30. Samuel C. Gant's "Belletristic Literature in Kentucky and Tennessee Newspapers and Periodicals, 1820–1840" (Ph.D. dissertation, George Peabody College for

Teachers, Nashville, Tenn., 1977) devotes some space to the *Messenger,* but overall the literary judgments are so superficial, the categorization so elementary (poems about "religious encouragement" or "the weather," for instance), and the factual information so frequently inaccurate or undocumented that its important subject is poorly served.

First among the many good surveys of religion in America is Sydney E. Ahlstrom, *A Religious History of the American People* (New Haven: Yale University Press, 1972), a scholarly and reliable synthesis with bibliographic notes. William Warren Sweet's *Religion in the Development of American Culture 1765–1840* (New York: Scribners, 1952) is a useful starting point for the study of religion in the West, supplemented by Sweet's four-volume sourcebook, *Religion on the American Frontier: The Baptists* (New York: Henry Holt, 1931), *The Presbyterians* (New York: Harper and Brothers, 1936), *The Congregationalists* (Chicago: University of Chicago Press, 1939), and *The Methodists* (Chicago: University of Chicago Press, 1946).

Background studies of American Unitarianism are abundant. Joseph Henry Allen, *Our Liberal Movement in Theology* (Boston: Roberts Brothers, 1882) and idem, *Sequel to "Our Liberal Movement"* (Boston: Roberts Brothers, 1897) are topical and biographical accounts. Octavius Brooks Frothingham's *Boston Unitarianism 1820–1850* (New York: Putnam's, 1890) concentrates on the more conservative wing of the denomination represented by the author's father, Nathaniel Langdon Frothingham. George Willis Cooke, *Unitarianism in America* (Boston: American Unitarian Association, 1902) and Earl Morse Wilbur's scholarly *History of Unitarianism,* 2 vols. (Cambridge: Harvard University Press, 1946–52) are the commissioned denominational histories. A well-researched and authoritative brief study by leading Unitarian scholars is *A Stream of Light: A Short History of American Unitarianism,* ed. Conrad Wright (Boston: Unitarian Universalist Association, 1975). Daniel Walker Howe provides a superb analysis of the literary and ethical precepts that influenced young Unitarian ministers of the time in *The Unitarian Conscience: Harvard Moral Philosophy, 1805–1861* (Cambridge: Harvard University Press, 1970). Helpful church histories—written as anniversary tributes and therefore not to be wholly trusted for factual completeness—are George A. Thayer, *The First Congregational Church of Cincinnati (Unitarian): A History* (Cincinnati: n.p., 1917) and Edith Fosdick Bodley and Gustave Breaux, *An Historical Sketch of the First Unitarian Church of Louisville* (Louisville, Ky.: n.p., 1930). Charles H. Lyttle traces the later fortunes of Unitarianism in the West in *Freedom Moves West: A History of the Western Unitarian Conference* (Boston: Beacon, 1952).

Of the great amount of literature on American Transcendentalism, few studies deal with the *Messenger* in more than a cursory way. Octavius Brooks Frothingham's *Transcendentalism in New England* (New York: Putnam's, 1876) is a brilliant history by a later participant. William R. Hutchison mentions the magazine only in passing, but his *Transcendentalist Ministers: Church Reform in the New England Renaissance* (New Haven: Yale University Press, 1959) is a lucid and thorough discussion of the pressures within Unitarianism during the magazine's existence. On the aesthetic achievements of the Transcendental movement, Lawrence Buell's *Literary Transcendentalism: Style and Vision in the American Renaissance* (Ithaca, N.Y.: Cornell University Press, 1973) is the standard study, and promises to remain so. Anne C. Rose explores the social vision of the Transcendentalists in *Transcendentalism as a Social Movement, 1830–1850* (New Haven: Yale University Press, 1981), a well-researched but often unconvincing study. Primary documents relating to the Transcendental controversy are collected in Miller, *The Transcendentalists*. Lawrence Buell provides an extensive bibliogaphic guide to the movement in *The Transcendentalists: A Review of Research and Criticism.*

Index

DATE DUE